SOMERSET COUNTY

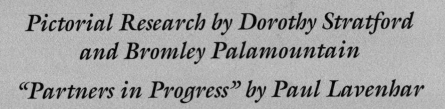

*Pictorial Research by Dorothy Stratford
and Bromley Palamountain*

"Partners in Progress" by Paul Lavenhar

*Produced in cooperation with
the Greater Somerset County Chamber of Commerce*

*Windsor Publications, Inc.
Chatsworth, California*

SOMERSET COUNTY

THREE CENTURIES OF PROGRESS

An Illustrated History by Jessie Lynes Havens

Windsor Publications, Inc.—History Book Division
Managing Editor: Karen Story
Design Director: Alexander D'Anca
Photo Director: Susan L. Wells
Executive Editor: Pamela Schroeder

Staff for *Somerset County: Three Centuries of Progress*
Manuscript Editor: Michael Nalick
Photo Editor: Robin Mastrogeorge Sterling
Senior Editor, Corporate Biographies: Judith L. Hunter
Editor, Corporate Biographies: Melissa Wells
Production Editor, Corporate Biographies:
    Doreen Nakakihara
Proofreaders: Mary Jo Scharf, Michael Moore
Customer Service Manager: Phyllis Feldman-Schroeder
Editorial Assistants: Dominique Jones, Kim Kievman,
    Michael Nugwynne, Kathy B. Peyser, Theresa J. Solis
Publisher's Representative, Corporate Biographies:
    Diane Murphy
Layout Artist, Corporate Biographies: Trish Meyer
Designer: Ellen Ifrah

Windsor Publications, Inc.
Elliot Martin, Chairman of the Board
James L. Fish III, Chief Operating Officer
Michele Sylvestro, Vice President/Sales-Marketing
Mac Buhler, Vice President/Sponsor Acquisitions

Library of Congress Cataloging-in-Publication Data:
Havens, Jessie Lynes, 1928-
Somerset County : three centuries of progress : an illustrat-
ed history / by Jessie Lynes Havens.
p. 200 cm. 23 X 31
Includes bibliographical references and index.
ISBN 0-89781-364-2
1. Somerset County (N.J.)—History. 2. Somerset County
(N.J.)—Description and travel—Views. 3. Somerset Coun-
ty (N.J.)—Industries. I. Title.
F142.S6H38 1990
974.9'44—dc20 90-12719
CIP

*FRONTISPIECE: A traditional rural atmo-
sphere still pervades today's Somerset County. Open
spaces abound, and scenes such as this one near
South Branch are a daily delight. Photo by Mary
Ann Brockman*

*RIGHT: Majestic Christmas trees and hand-
made wreaths were festively displayed along Main
Street in Somerville around the turn of the century. Courtesy, Somerset Messenger-Gazette*

CONTENTS

To Julia Mason,
a super librarian.
Without her,
this book would not
have been written.

ACKNOWLEDGMENTS

A history of Somerset County proved more difficult to write than I had imagined, not because of any lack of information, but, to the contrary, because there is so much to tell and only limited space between the covers of one book.

Somerset County is rich in historical resources. The county library's New Jersey collection is exceptionally good. Local libraries are mines of valuable material also. We have available to us, as well, the Special Collections at Rutgers University Library and the state library in Trenton. Librarians, both staff and volunteer, who manage these collections are endlessly helpful. I cannot thank them enough.

The record of Somerset County is preserved at length also in microfilmed back issues of newspapers—more than 150 years of the *Somerset Messenger-Gazette* and its predecessors, as well as good long runs of the *Bound Brook Chronicle,* the *Bernardsville News,* and the *Courier News.* And we have the official record kept for us in deeds and wills and minute books and great masses of information assembled by the county planning board.

With sources so plentiful there nevertheless remain elusive bits of information, tantalizingly difficult to discover. Many public officials and private citizens have gone out of their way to try to supply answers to questions which doubtless seemed to them strange and unnecessary.

Gathering knowledge is one thing, transmitting it is another. Friends and family, most especially a husband and a typist, have patiently given encouragement and support to this undertaking. In sum, although only one name appears on the cover of this book, the combined efforts of many, many more have produced it.

Autumn leaves add beauty to the
Millstone River near Rocky Hill.
Photo by Mary Ann Brockman

PREFACE

To write a history of Somerset County is to confront the old truism: the more things change, the more they stay the same. In 300 years the cast of characters has changed many times, so has the technology. The plot has many variations, but the theme is ever the same.

Developers in 1990, no less than explorers sailing up the Raritan in 1650, are looking for profitable opportunities with little regard for the comfort and welfare of people who are already occupying the land. Overwhelmed by the powers outsiders possess, those who are present accept what is offered to them by way of payment and relinquish control. They are too disorganized and too confused by what is happening to effectively do otherwise. If they were able to resist, it would serve little purpose, for a new social order is about to work its will on this landscape. What has been will no longer be. Only vestiges will survive, giving later generations clues to a world they never saw and scarcely can understand.

Outside forces are always at work: kings and their thrones, entrepreneurs and their balance sheets, generals and their armies, politicians and their power struggles. The sum of their impact shapes history. The people who live it make the story unique by virtue of who they are, where they live, and what has gone before. So, no matter how many times history repeats itself, the story is never twice the same.

There has been no attempt to chronicle the overall history of Somerset County in more than a hundred years, not since James P. Snell in 1881 produced the compendium of data which serves as a standby reference to this day. The account which follows, unlike Snell's, touches only on the highlights. Its function is to stimulate interest and curiosity as much as to inform. Hopefully, it will also give greater substance to Somerset County's identity and a little better understanding of this amalgamation of 21

municipalities forming the "Blue Chip" in the middle of the mosaic known as New Jersey.

First and foremost, Somerset County is a political entity. It was in the beginning: the product of 50 years of adjusting differences among diverse peoples. The ebb and flow of commerce traveling up rivers, over turnpikes, along canals, railroads, highways, and freeways has tugged and pulled the social and economic fabric of Somerset this way and that; but the glue of a political jurisdiction has kept it one, with the exception of two limited grab-backs.

Counties came into existence in colonial New Jersey as a venue for small courts, and having once been established they served also as administrative units for electing representatives, mustering militia, and collecting taxes. The courthouse was the symbol and the synonym for county and all a county stood for. No more. Traditional county functions have been taken away and assigned to a welter of specially drawn districts. At the same time, counties have increasingly been given responsibility for delivering services and are coming to be also agencies for directing growth and development. Thus, the county of the past has been superceded by one which is very different. Yet, geographically, counties remain apparently the same.

Somerset County's proud traditions overlay a rich heritage of hills and valleys and rivers. The past explains the present. It can inform the future if the profit-takers come to see more than financial opportunity.

THE HANDSOMEST, PLEASANTEST COUNTRY

FERTILE AND INVITING, SOMERSET ENCOMPASSES THE CURVING SOUTHERN RIM OF NEW
Jersey's hilly upland region and the gently rolling plains of red soil piedmont to the south.
Across its narrow waist and down its eastern boundary flows the Raritan River, fed from the
south by the Millstone River and from the north by the Green Brook, the Middle Brook,
and two major tributaries—the North Branch and South Branch, whose confluence lies near
Somerset's western border.

Cornelius van Tienhoven, secretary of New Netherland, who explored the Raritan
Valley in 1650, set down descriptions of a forested wilderness well watered by good
streams. He found that some lands along the waterways were clear of trees and that, on
these lands, Indian inhabitants grew abundant crops of maize, beans, and pumpkins. Van
Tienhoven had no doubt the territory was well suited for farming and cattle-raising; he rated
it "the handsomest and pleasantest country man can behold."

The Dutch West India Co. found these observations by van Tienhoven of little interest. They wanted to trade, not plant settlements. What pleased them was his report of various Indian tribes who regularly passed through the valley on their way north or east. Their
trails—the Assanpink, the Tuckaraming, and a branch of the Minisink—would become
principal routes to the interior, across Somerset County, after New Netherland ceased block-
ing the way.

The English, rivals of the Dutch for supremacy of the seas, already had successful
colonies planted all along the Atlantic Coast to the north and south and were eager to gain
total control from Maine to the Carolinas. Only the Dutch foothold at the Hudson River

The William Baird house and its
Dutch-style barn were typical of the
architectural design used by early
Dutch settlers of the Millstone Valley.
The Baird farm was located on
Millstone River Road and is shown
here in the 1890s. Courtesy, Van
Harlingen Historical Society

kept England from colonizing the Middle Atlantic region as well. In 1664, after his brother
Charles II had granted him all the land between the Connecticut and Delaware rivers,
James, duke of York, dispatched four ships under Colonel Richard Nicolls to drive out the
competition; Governor Peter Stuyvesant of New Netherland capitulated without firing a
shot, on assurance that all who were established there would be safe in their persons and
their property. With that, Nicolls renamed the place New York and invited settlers from
Connecticut and Rhode Island to come and choose land for themselves.

Several groups readily accepted the terms Nicolls offered and began to occupy the
rim of the great New York Bay. After settlement had begun, a ship arrived from England
bringing an expedition to found a colony to be called New Jersey. York had decided to
grant all the lands between the Hudson and Delaware rivers to two old, loyal friends of his
father, Charles I. Lord John Berkeley and Sir George Carteret were pleased with the
opportunity to found a colony; the two had drawn up "Concessions and Agreements" calculated to attract people and recruited a company of settlers headed by Carteret's cousin,
Philip. These new arrivals also planted themselves on the bay, naming their settlement Elizabethtown in honor of Lady Carteret.

Unfortunately the terms laid down by Berkeley and Carteret clashed with agreements
Nicolls had made. Philip Carteret, inexperienced in colonial affairs and unsure what to do,
did nothing, and disagreements festered until his adversaries had him arrested and forcibly
removed.

Contentions grew worse after Carteret and Berkeley's interests in the colony were liquidated. The group of 12 investors who purchased the eastern half of Jersey from Carteret's widow in 1682 was headed by William Penn. He, at the time, was busy with other colonial undertakings, so he turned this one over to his friend Robert Barclay, the noted Quaker apologist from Scotland. More men were brought into the enterprise by dividing each of the twelve shares in two. Six of the buyers were Scots, and they became the dominant faction of these 24 East Jersey Proprietors who were to set policy and govern the colony's affairs. The Proprietors appointed Barclay governor for life, but he remained at home, and deputy governors were sent overseas to handle day-to-day administration.

Barclay and his associates saw in East Jersey a chance for Scots to reap the same sorts of benefits that the English were realizing in their New World adventures. Theirs, however, was to be a Scottish colony, patterned on Scottish systems of land tenure and social order. Instead of following the English custom of dividing the countryside into small freehold farms, they would parcel out huge tracts of land as manors for lairds who would employ servants or lease to tenant farmers. "Fundamental Concessions" were drawn up as the basis for carrying their policies into effect.

Scots considered the terms they offered progressive and generous, but those who had already settled in East Jersey were not of the same mind. Their disagreements were long and bitter.

The most violent discord was over land titles. As frustrations mounted over conflicting claims of ownership, riots, disorders, arrests, and jailbreaks ensued. Fights over who owned what were still going on at the time of the Revolution, but, by that time, in the form of highly complicated legal battles waged in the courts.

At the root of these disputes was the East Jersey Proprietors' understanding that all lands unoccupied when they took over were theirs to dispose of as they saw fit. Earlier arrivals had a different view; the Elizabethtown Associates, for example, interpreted their grant as conferring title from the coastline all the way inland to the western bounds of the province. This interpretation entitled Elizabethtown to sell lots in what became Bernards and Bedminster townships, 30 miles away. Elizabethtown's sales infringed on the Basking Ridge estate of James Alexander and the Peapack patent of John Johnstone and George Willocks. For these men who held proprietary title to their lands, trying to evict settlers occupying so-called clinker lots was vexatious at best, and nigh impossible at times.

Scots, to avoid potential conflict with prior arrivals, deliberately selected areas well apart from the settlements along the coast. One of the prime prospects for Scottish settlement was the Upper Raritan Valley. A further safeguard to peaceable settlement was a stipulation by Proprietors that no land be occupied until after a purchase treaty had been concluded with the Indians.

Neither the Dutch, the English, nor the Scots evinced much concern for the welfare of the Indians, or even much curiosity about them. Their manuscripts record little concerning Native Americans other than trade and land sales, and consequently not a great deal is known about the various Lenni Lenape tribes who inhabited this region. It is estimated that only 8,000 to 12,000 were living in all of what is now the state of New Jersey, and some of the interior and mountain regions were scarcely inhabited at all. Most numerous in the area which became Somerset County were the Raritans, and there may have been as many as 18 different politically independent groups within this one tribe. West of the Raritan confluence were the Neshanocks, along the Millstone River the Mattawang. All cultivated crops of corn, beans, and squash, so they were not fully dependent on hunting, fishing, and wild plants. They moved their villages whenever the supply of game and firewood became depleted, probably every 15 or 20 years.

Lenni Lenape were not a warlike people, and they readily accepted trade goods from the white men in exchange for giving up hunting rights to sections of land and moving elsewhere. They thought of the land as belonging to everyone; only the use of it was being traded away. Sometimes several tribes demanded payment for the same territory. As fast as negotiations with the Indians were finalized, East Jersey surveyors mapped out lots.

The Raritan Lots were huge slices of real estate—500, 1,000, 3,000 acres. Almost all had river frontage, if only a little, because waterways were the primary route of access. As a result the lots were narrow and very deep, some as much as a mile or more.

Both East Jersey and West Jersey coveted the lands along the Upper Raritan. Daniel Coxe, governor of West Jersey, described the valley as "some of the most rich, beautiful and pleasant tracts of land in either Jersies." He contended West Jersey owned land as far east as the Millstone River.

East Jersey Proprietors conceded nothing of the sort. Without waiting for the issue to

The original copy of this land deed now hangs in Cooperstown, New York, and is perhaps one of the last remaining documents of its kind around today. It conveys Indian property to the state's early white settlers in the region of the County of Middlesex and the province of East New Jersey in what appears to be the year 1700. Note the marks of the seven tribal leaders on the right, which were used in lieu of signatures. Courtesy, Somerville Free Public Library

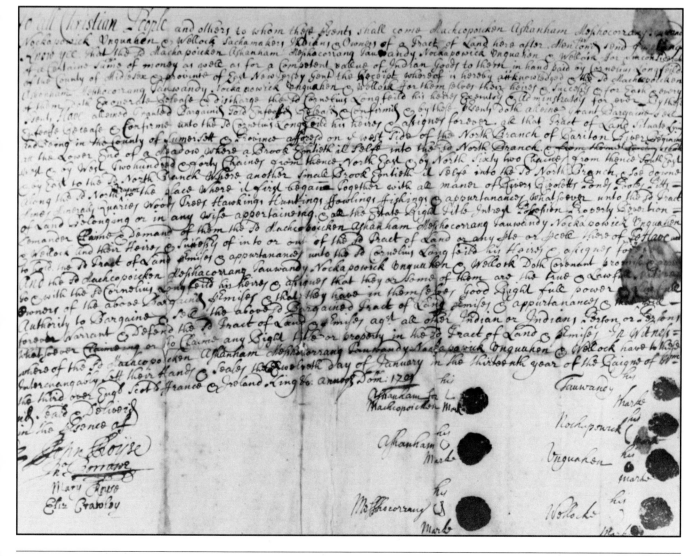

ABOVE: This cannon serves as a reminder of the Middlebrook Encampment in Bridgewater in 1778-1779. Washington twice stationed his troops in the vicinity of Middlebrook during the course of the American Revolution. Photo by Christopher Lauber

TOP: Historic "Rockingham" was headquarters for General George Washington and his aides from August to November in 1783, while Congress was meeting in nearby Princeton. It was during this stay that he wrote his "Farewell Orders Issued to the Armies of the United States of America." Located close to Rocky Hill in southern Somerset County, this farmhouse is an exceptional treasure and is open for the viewing pleasure of the public. Photo by Mary Ann Brockman

The Jockey Hollow section of the Morristown National Historic Park, situated in Bernardsville and neighboring Morris County, features outstanding replicas of the barracks in which the Pennsylvania Brigade encamped during the winter of 1779-1780, during the Revolutionary War. Photo by Mary Ann Brockman

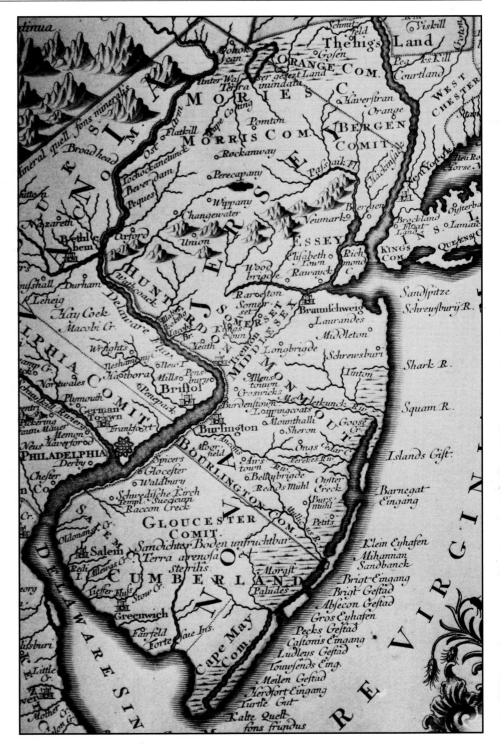

Printed in Europe in the mid-1700s, this early map of New Jersey depicts county boundaries as well as towns and villages when Somerset Court House (now Millstone) was the county seat. It is interesting to note the name spellings of the area's older settlements. Courtesy, Special Collections/Alexander Library/Rutgers University

be resolved, they allowed John Campbell and John Dobie to select tracts for themselves on the South Branch.

In hopes of arriving at an amicable solution, a conference was called at Henry Greenland's on the Millstone River. There it was agreed the boundary should be surveyed to put a stop to arguments and further agreed no one already settled would be dispossessed. Without this escape clause, if the line had been run precisely along the compass course agreed to by Berkeley and Carteret, a number of Scots along the Raritan, including Lord Neil Campbell, deputy governor of East Jersey, would have found themselves on the wrong side. As things turned out, they were spared.

The job of surveying the boundary was entrusted in 1685 to George Keith, surveyor-general of East Jersey. He was a brilliant mathematician; nevertheless, the line he ran, starting from Little Egg Harbor, was a trifle off course. His slight departure from the specified compass reading was just enough so that proceeding northward in a perfectly straight line he came out at John Dobie's plantation, the westernmost in East Jersey.

To West Jersey the boundary Keith had surveyed was wholly unacceptable, and discussion of the matter proved fruitless. Keith quit surveying, went to Philadelphia, and became headmaster of a school. East Jersey arrested a West Jersey agent for infringing on its territory. The dispute might have degenerated into still worse episodes if Coxe and Barclay had not met in London and hammered out a compromise. They decided on a new boundary that incorporated Keith's line as far as it went, then skirted along the west of East Jersey's Raritan Lots to the Lamington River, and, to compensate West Jersey for lost territory, continued northward along a zigzag series of water courses to the New York border.

This line, dividing East from West, was to become Somerset County's western boundary; but when it was proposed in 1688 to create a fifth county in East Jersey, boundaries got only cursory attention. With surveying still not completed, indefinite descriptions such as "northwest into the hills" had to suffice. Governor Hamilton and his council spelled out their reasons for setting off the interior of Middlesex County to be a new county called Somerset, but their preamble leaves much to be understood. The act states:

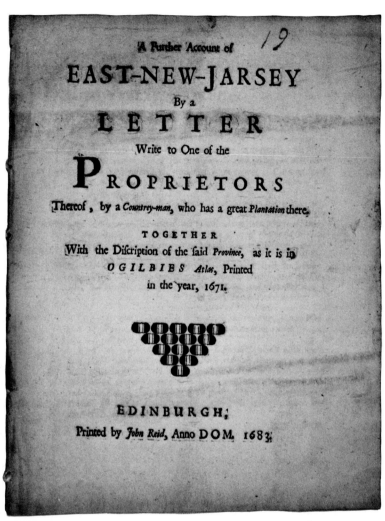

This rare promotional pamphlet, touting the benefits of settlement in New Jersey, was published in Edinburgh, Scotland, in 1683 just five years before Somerset County was established. A number of these publications were circulated throughout Great Britain and Europe to induce settlement of the then sparsely settled lands. Most were purported to be letters from people who had traveled to this wonderful new world and who wrote home to extol the advantages of the region. Courtesy, Special Collections/Alexander Library/ Rutgers University

FORASMUCH as the uppermost Part of Rariton River, is settled by Persons whom in their Husbandry and manuring their Land, forced upon quite different ways and methods from the other Farmers and Inhabitants of the County of Middlesex, because of the frequent Floods that carry away their Fences on their Meadows, the only arable Land they have, and so by Consequence their Interest is divided from the other Inhabitants of the said County. BE IT THEREFORE ENACTED by the Governor, Council and Deputies now met in General Assembly, and by the Authority of the same, that the said uppermost Part of the Rariton, beginning at the mouth of the Bound Brook, where it empties itself into the Rariton River, and to run up the said Brook, to the meeting of the said Brook with the Green Brook, and from the said meeting to run upon a North West line into the hills, and upon the South West side of Rariton, to begin at a small Brook, where it empties itself into the Rariton, about Seventy Chains below the Bound Brook, and from thence to run upon a South West Line to the uttermost Line of the Province, be divided from the said County of Middlesex, and hereafter to be deem'd, taken, and be a County of this Province; and that the same County be called the County of Somerset; any Statute, Law or Usage, to the Contrary hereof in any Ways notwithstanding.

ABOVE: Scottish-born Robert Hunter held the position of British colonial governor of New York and the Jerseys from 1709 until 1719. Considered to have been a generally popular and effective public official, despite being hampered by disputing Proprietors, Hunter owned some 500 acres of land along the Raritan in Somerset County during his tenure as governor. Courtesy, Special Collections/Alexander Library/Rutgers University

RIGHT: The Franklin Inn in East Millstone (at one time known as Johnsville) was built in 1734, a time when most villages consisted of little more than a small cluster of homes around a mill or forge with the possible addition of a general store or roadside inn. Located on Amwell Road, the Franklin Inn served as a stopping place for stagecoach passengers and for the heavily laden freight wagons, which made their way from the Millstone Valley to Raritan Landing prior to the construction of the Delaware and Raritan Canal. Pictured here in the early 1900s, the inn has since suffered periods of neglect and is now in poor repair. Courtesy, Special Collections/ Alexander Library/Rutgers University

Later surveys would show that no portion of the hill country lay within the northern Middlesex boundary; Somerset as described proved to be merely a triangular wedge of the plains at the base of the Blue Hills (Watchung Mountains). It encompassed little more than the Upper Raritan Lots laid out by the East Jersey Proprietors; along the Bound Brook, Somerset included the lands of Thomas Rudyard and Thomas Codrington; along the South Branch, it extended past the home of Lord Neil Campbell to include the properties of John Campbell, Andrew Hamilton, and John Dobie.

Within the territory assigned to Somerset in 1688, a mixed population had already begun to settle. Of the Scots, Campbell had made the most substantial effort to develop a manor along the lines envisioned by the Proprietors. He named his vast plantation "Rariton River," and he brought over 56 servants to work on it. Campbell's big interest in this undertaking was no accident: both his father and his brother had been beheaded for leading uprisings against English kings, and he, himself, was under an edict of banishment. But Campbell did not continue in personal charge very long. In December 1687 he returned to Scotland on urgent business affairs, leaving Andrew Hamilton to carry on as deputy governor. Hamilton, a canny Scot, held the office intermittently from then until 1702, when East and West Jersey were united as a royal colony, and the Proprietors ceased to govern.

The shift in political climate, which influenced Campbell to return home, substantial-

ly altered the whole Scottish plan for colonization. After 1690 Scottish emigration all but ceased. Although it resumed again three decades later, by then the character of the colony had been set in a different pattern, and Scots were not able to replicate their social order here. Never more than a numerous minority, Scots were nevertheless highly influential, far more so than their numbers would seem to warrant.

It has been estimated that as many as 700 or 800 Scots came to East Jersey in that first wave of immigration. Not all chose the Raritan Valley; small clusters of Scots were dispersed in widely separated locations.

By creating a separate county for those whose methods of husbandry were based on large manors or estates rather than small farms, Hamilton and his council were, in effect, acknowledging that East Jersey was not going to be patterned after Scotland as the Proprietors had intended. There would be just one county where Scots' ways could prevail; here the courts that decided local disputes would have juries made up of men whose understanding of property rights had been molded by Scottish law and custom. But they acted too late to forestall others from moving into this promising territory.

The first to arrive, Thomas Codrington, had taken up land in 1683 and built his house at what later became Bound Brook. By 1688 there were people here and there all along the river. Some of the names which can be pieced together from old records are Peter Van Neste, from whom Peter's Brook in Somerville takes its name, John White, James Gyles, Aaron Jacobs, Vincent Rungimone, and John Rudyard. Across the river was John Royce who claimed to own 20,000 acres by deed of purchase from the Indians. The Proprietors thought it a dubious title but to be rid of the argument granted him 6,000 acres. Instead of solving the problem, that only made matters worse; Royce sold off land on the basis of both deeds, causing trouble galore. The rascal is immortalized by Royce Brook in Hillsborough and by Peace Brook in Millstone, used to form a demarcation line in ironing out disputes he had caused.

The new Somerset County's net effect on Raritan Valley settlement was nil. Before 1688 was over, an edict of King James II suspended all local government. He had decided to make East Jersey, along with West Jersey and New York, part of a Dominion of New England in America, with a strongly centralized administration headquartered in Boston. It was an abortive, but disruptive scheme. James was driven from the throne very soon after, leaving colonial affairs in chaos.

East Jersey did not succeed in putting its internal affairs in good order for several years. One of the reorganizing efforts after Hamilton had been restored to the governor's office was an act in 1693 dividing counties into townships. But only four counties were divided; little Somerset was not. It was accorded the status of a township with the consolation that when "any county shall hereafter come to be better settled and inhabited, this shall not hinder other subdivisions to be made." It was a meaningless concession given the very limited territory Somerset had been assigned.

Nothing was done about Somerset County's anomalous status by the next three governors, but changes were in order during Richard Ingoldsby's brief tenure. Among the reforms he effected was a substantial redrawing of county boundaries in 1709. As part of the package, a giant slice of Middlesex was annexed to Somerset on the south. Their common boundary was moved eight miles down the Raritan River to the mouth of Lawrence Brook. The new line ran southwestward along that stream and Cranbury Road, then jogged northwestward along the Assanpink Creek.

At last Somerset was on more equal footing with other counties in terms of territory, population, and access to tidewater. These new

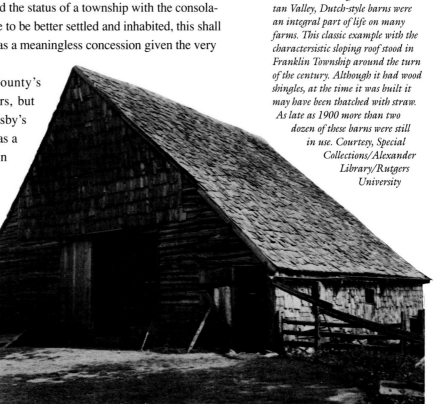

Once a common sight in the Raritan Valley, Dutch-style barns were an integral part of life on many farms. This classic example with the characteristic sloping roof stood in Franklin Township around the turn of the century. Although it had wood shingles, at the time it was built it may have been thatched with straw. As late as 1900 more than two dozen of these barns were still in use. Courtesy, Special Collections/Alexander Library/Rutgers University

advantages were followed up with a notice to build a courthouse and jail so that normal county functions could be conducted. The site chosen was at Six Mile Run (Franklin Park), about midway between the Raritan River and Somerset's western boundary, on the road from the Raritan ferry (New Brunswick) to the falls of the Delaware (Trenton)—NJ Route 27.

Astride the central corridor of the colony, spanning a prime route between New York and Philadelphia, Somerset had indeed become advantageously situated. It was too good to last. Middlesex began agitating for relief from the injustice done to her and in 1714 succeeded in having the boundary pushed back several miles. It could not be moved back any farther than the road without taking Somerset's courthouse, so there it was run and has continued to be.

As a result of this road (NJ Route 27) becoming the boundary, both New Brunswick and Princeton grew up half in Somerset and half in Middlesex. Throughout the colonial and federal period these towns were Somerset's principal population centers. The commerce flowing through New Brunswick at the head of navigation on the Raritan and the intellectual stimulus flowing from the College of New Jersey at Princeton were notably influential in Somerset's affairs.

The grab-back by Middlesex still left Somerset triple the territory it had had before. Somerset now extended from the hills southward the full breadth of the piedmont plain and the full width of the Millstone Valley. When its courthouse accidentally burned in 1737, a more central location was chosen for its replacement—where the road leading west from New Brunswick crossed the Millstone River, whose valley was a corridor for travel north and south.

Religion played a leading role in the lives of the early Dutch settlers in Somerset County. Among the treasured family possessions of these people, who had made the long journey from their homes to the new world were the magnificent "Great Dutch Bibles." Printed in Holland in 1702, this bible is encased in tooled leather with heavy brass ornamentation and is part of the Wallace House collection in Somerville. Courtesy, James Kurzenberger

The Somerset plains, only two days' journey from New York, offered a promising area for settlement, and after 1700 increasing numbers of Dutch from Brooklyn, Long Island, Staten Island, and Gowanus bought land throughout the Raritan Valley and began clearing forests and building homes. Eventually the concentration of Dutch in this central part of New Jersey became so great, the most-traveled road from New Brunswick to Princeton came to be known as the Old Dutch Road.

For the most part these Dutch settlers were second and third generation Americans, knowledgeable about the climate and suitable crops and livestock. What drew them here was cheap land. A man could sell his farm on Long Island and, with the proceeds, buy a fine spread in New Jersey for each of his sons. Such was Cornelius Wyckoff who, with seven other Dutchmen, in 1701, purchased 10,000 acres east of the Millstone from John Harrison. Wyckoff's share was 1,200 acres, stretching the full width of what became Franklin Township; four of his sons—Simon, Jacob, Peter, and John—each received 300 acres to clear and cultivate.

Methods used for taming the forested wilderness were expedient and effective; settlers killed trees by girdling their trunks and planted crops among the standing skeletons, leaving the heavy work of cutting down trees and grubbing out stumps to be done when time and labor were available.

There was a chronic shortage of manpower even though the Dutch were renowned for their large broods of children who made up the family work force. Christian and Altje Van Doren of Middlebush outdid all their neighbors in this respect, producing a family of 17 sons and daughters, of whom only one died during childhood. The rest married and had children and grandchildren. When Altje died at 96, she had no fewer than 352 descendants.

A more immediate way to gain manpower was to buy African slaves. Dutch were by no means the only ones in Somerset who used them, but the incidence of slaveholding was noticeably greater among the Dutch population. Few owned more than one or two slaves. Even so, the use of slaves was so prevalent, Somerset came to have the second-highest black population in New Jersey, exceeded only by Bergen, the state's other Dutch county.

In place of slaves, others made use of indentured servants. A great many of these were Irish, and their status while the term of service lasted was little better than that of a slave. But indentured servants could look forward to freedom at the end of a specified

Dinah Van Bergh (1725-1807) came to Somerset County as the bride of the Reverend John Frelinghuysen when he assumed the pastorate of the Dutch Reformed Church of Raritan. Frelinghuysen died three years later and Van Bergh subsequently married one of his students, the Reverend Jacob R. Hardenbergh. The Hardenberghs resided in the Dutch Parsonage in Somerville while he too served as pastor of the Raritan church. Hardenbergh later became the first president of Queens College (Rutgers University). This elaborate gown, which was part of Van Bergh's wardrobe, is embroidered with flowers, trimmed in lace, and features a Watteau-style train. Two centuries later, this gown is preserved in excellent condition. Courtesy, Special Collections/Alexander Library/Rutgers University

number of years. They also had a decided advantage if they tried to run away, blending quite easily into the general population. So common were runaways and so hard to recover, use of the system was limited.

When Irish bond servants did attain the status of free men, they were still denied one liberty: freedom to worship as Catholics. East Jersey guaranteed religious toleration, but only to Protestants. The Scots of Somerset County and the Dutch were both staunch adherents of the teachings of Calvin, but different languages necessitated separate worship. Their respective Presbyterian and Reformed churches are the most lasting imprint left on the landscape indicating the geographic distribution and relative numbers of these two ethnic groups.

At Bound Brook a Presbyterian church founded by the Scots in 1688 claims the dis-

Local craftsman and skilled clock-maker Isaac Brokaw (1746-1826) is believed to have learned his trade as an apprentice of Aaron Miller of Elizabethtown. Brokaw married Miller's daughter and was residing in Bridgewater Township in 1770 when a local justice ordered his effects sold to settle outstanding debts. Brokaw was permitted to keep 30 pounds of lead for counterweights to continue his trade and proceeded to create many fine pieces, some of which are still around today. Made of cherry and poplar wood, this circa 1765 Chippendale Tall-Case clock is one of Brokaw's earliest works and is inscribed with a Hillsborough Township identification. Courtesy, Fred Sisser III

tinction of being the county's oldest congregation. Basking Ridge Presbyterian was established about 1720, Kingston Presbyterian in 1732, and Lamington Presbyterian was formally organized in 1740.

Earliest record of a Dutch Reformed congregation on the Raritan is at Finderne in 1699. A second Dutch congregation was worshipping at Three Mile Run by 1703, another located at Six Mile Run about 1710, and a fourth was established on the other side of the North Branch, near the Raritan confluence, in 1719. By the end of the colonial period, four more had been added in Harlingen, Neshanic, Millstone, and Bedminster. The nineteenth century would see a dozen more established.

Organizing a church was one thing, securing a pastor quite another. The first to come from Holland to the Dutch congregations in the Raritan Valley was Theodorus Jacobus Frelinghuysen, who did not arrive until 1720. He took charge of the four churches then existing and made the rounds of his far-flung flock for 27 years. Frelinghuysen died about 1747 and was succeeded by his son John, whose descendants for generations to come would earn high esteem for the name Frelinghuysen in the public life of county, state, and nation.

Because few trained clergy were willing to cross the Atlantic to serve congregations which were being formed, and young men who were tutored by established pastors were being obliged to travel across the ocean to undergo examination and be ordained, both Dutch Reformed and Presbyterians were impelled to found colleges of their own in the New World. The Presbyterian College of New Jersey, founded in Elizabethtown in 1746, was moved from the distracting influences of town life to the rural serenity of Princeton 10 years later. Although this made excellent classical education readily available, the Dutch preferred to have their young men taught in their own language and, to this end, secured a charter to establish Queens College (Rutgers) in Somerset County at New Brunswick in 1766. Two of the leaders largely responsible for accomplishing this were Hendrick Fisher, who as a very young man had been a protégé of the first Frelinghuysen, and the Reverend Jacob Hardenbergh, who had studied under his son, John Frelinghuysen. Hardenbergh became the school's first president.

The population supporting these educational endeavors was, of course, not just Somerset. In 1737 the county had a population of only 4,500 out of a New Jersey population nearing 50,000. Ten years later the colony topped 60,000. Settlement frontiers were being pushed northward decade by decade as the eighteenth century advanced.

Infilling of the hill country which was to become part of Somerset flowed from many different directions. Quakers of New England origin came very early by way of Woodbridge to the valley of Green Brook. Later, Baptists from Piscataway worked their way up over the hill to the valley beyond; they planted a meetinghouse at Mt. Bethel in 1767.

Palatine Germans from among the thousands of refugees who arrived in New York and Philadelphia in the early eighteenth century found their way here by various routes. Some came overland from the Delaware Valley, others came up the Raritan Valley and the Peapack Road, and still others traveled from the Hudson Valley by way of the Passaic River. They settled east, west, and north of Pluckemin and established a Lutheran congregation before 1724. A hundred years later the Pluckemin church was abandoned; its people had dispersed. A number attached themselves to the Lutheran church at New Germantown (Oldwick); most of the others joined the Bedminster Dutch Reformed.

Dutch who filtered northward kept on the west side of the hills, for the most part. Scots, Scotch-Irish, English, and French Huguenots settled throughout the promising hill country north of the Raritan Valley.

By mid-century the population of the colony's interior had grown sufficiently to warrant breaking up some of the original counties to form new ones. In 1744 the western Essex territories were annexed to the northern part of Somerset, thus creating a county whose north and south were as dissimilar in population as they were in terrain.

Before long the enlarged county was subdivided into three voting districts—the Northern Precinct being everything north of the Raritan River, and the Eastern and Western precincts lying on either side of the Millstone River. Five years later, in 1749, Bridgewater and Bedminster were chartered as townships; the remaining eastern portion of the Northern Precinct became Bernards Township in approximately 1760. South County remained unchanged until 1771 when Hillsborough Township was formed from the northern portion of the Western Precinct. The remainder subsequently assumed the identity of Montgomery Township, and the Eastern Precinct was renamed Franklin Township.

Somerset's population by the end of its first century was about 10,000, the majority living on small farms which grew crops of wheat, rye, oats, maize, barley, peas, beans, and some flax. They raised cattle, sheep, and hogs and had extensive orchards and plentiful vegetable gardens. Most of what they produced was for home consumption, but they did ship wheat, beef, pork, hides, and timber to market. The Raritan River was their artery of commerce, with shipping wharfs at Raritan Landing and New Brunswick.

During the colonial period Somerset had no interior towns of significant size. The only substantial villages were Bound Brook, Pluckemin, and Somerset Court House (Millstone). There were, however, numerous crossroad hamlets consisting of clusters of houses around a mill and a forge, with perhaps an inn or a store.

In less than 100 years a forested wilderness had been transformed into a prosperous agricultural region of substantially self-sufficient farmers. English was the language of commerce, but not of the majority of people, and only a well educated minority concerned themselves with politics and public affairs. The general populace looked to New York and to Philadelphia for trade and information. England and its king were remote from their concern. East Jersey had a strong tradition of internal self-government, and they asked nothing more than to be left in peace to look after their own affairs. Few had any idea they might be called upon to fight in defense of their way of life.

William Griffith was born in the Middlebrook section of Somerset County in 1766, the son of Dr. William Griffith, one of the area's early settlers. Griffith became an attorney with a flourishing practice in nearby Burlington and authored a number of books on legal matters. He also served as mayor of Burlington and was married to Ann Maria Howell, daughter of Andrew and Mary Hardenbergh, on January 5, 1797, in Somerville. Courtesy, Special Collections/Alexander Library/Rutgers University

THE FIGHT
FOR FREEDOM

MERICA'S STRUGGLE FOR INDEPENDENCE (1776-1783) CONFERRED ON SOMERSET COUNTY TWO
unique distinctions: it was the only New Jersey county with two signers of the Declaration
of Independence—John Witherspoon and Richard Stockton—and is the only county where
two George Washington headquarters are preserved and maintained as historic museums—
the Wallace House in Somerville and Rockingham in Franklin Township.

For Somerset County an even more significant legacy of the Revolution was a new
courthouse at a new location. The courthouse on the Millstone that had been built in 1738
was burned in a daring British raid.

Military strategies focusing on New York and Philadelphia made it inevitable for
Somerset, situated between the two, to become a theater of operations. Advancing and
retreating, George Washington led his armies across Somerset; maneuvering and encamp-
ing, he used the Somerset Hills to strategic advantage. And when at last he bid farewell to
his army, it was in Somerset that his parting address was delivered. Washington also penned
a special valedictory to the Somerset County Militia:

*With a heart deeply impressed by the happy issue of a long and painful contest I most cor-
dially participate with you in the general Joy and earnestly join my wishes with yours for
the future prosperity and happiness of our Country. The repeated proofs of unabated valour
and perseverance which I have been witness to in the Officers and Militia of the County of
Somerset demand from me the acknowledgements which, for the last time, I have now the
honor of making you, and as your Zeal in the field and in the services of your Country*

cannot fail to endear you to your fellow Citizens It is with much pleasure that in taking my final leave of you I can with the purest sincerity add this last testimony in your favor. I now bid you Gentlemen a long farewell in the fullest confidence that Men who have so bravely defended their Country, will likewise in their peaceable retirements contribute their best endeavors to confirm and perpetuate that happy Union of the States and its Citizens which under Providence has so visibly been the means of our deliverance and Independence.

Kind words, but small compensation for losses exacted by prolonged warfare: not only a courthouse burned down, but bridges torn up; farmhouses torched; cattle, forage, and timber confiscated; sons called up for duty never to return.

Mustering militia and forming select companies of minutemen began in Somerset 10 days after word of Lexington and Concord reached Princeton on April 24, 1775. The spirit of resistance was by then well advanced. It had been fed by the teachings of John Witherspoon, president of the College of New Jersey at Princeton, and by the reports that Somerset's delegate, Hendrick Fisher, brought back from meetings of the general assembly.

Fisher is credited with summoning New Jersey's Committee of Correspondence and Inquiry to New Brunswick to consider how to respond to the closing of the port of Boston. Out of that meeting came a call for a Provincial Congress on May 23, 1775; 87 delegates attended, those from Somerset included Fisher, John Roy, Peter Schenck, Abraham Van Nest, Enos Kelsey, Jonathan D. Sergeant, Frederick Frelinghuysen, and William Paterson. Fisher was chosen to preside. Paterson and Frelinghuysen were assistant secretaries. Vigor-

The signing of the Constitution of the United States on September 17, 1787, was a triumphant moment in the history of our country. Captured by artist Howard Chandler Christy, this historic gathering was the culmination of America's battle for independence in which the people and places of Somerset County played a significant role. Courtesy, National Park Service

ous preparation for armed resistance was the chief order of business.

Military preparedness took on increasing importance after the people of Somerset saw Washington pass by en route to taking command in Boston in June 1775. New Jersey recruited two battalions for the Continental Army and gave command of the eastern division to William Alexander, also known as Lord Stirling of Basking Ridge. In addition the Provincial Congress formed two companies of artillery for defense of the colony and commissioned Frederick Frelinghuysen as captain. In the course of the war Stirling became one of Washington's most trusted generals. Frelinghuysen, on the other hand, relinquished his military command in 1778 to serve in the Continental Congress.

New Jersey elected delegates to a new Provincial Congress in May 1776. Somerset sent Witherspoon; three graduates of his college, Paterson, Frelinghuysen, and James Linn; and Jacob R. Hardenbergh, president of Queen's College. This congress in turn appointed delegates to Philadelphia, empowering them to approve a declaration of independence. Two of New Jersey's five were from Somerset: John Witherspoon and Richard Stockton, the prominent Princeton lawyer who had personally persuaded Witherspoon to leave Scotland to become president of a colonial college.

Inaugurated as the first president of the United States in 1789, General George Washington crisscrossed Somerset County with the Continental Army as he led them to victory during the American Revolution. This famous portrait of Washington was painted by well-known artist Charles Willson Peale. Courtesy, National Park Service

The NJ Congress, still in session after drafting a new state constitution, immediately ratified the Declaration of Independence on July 17 and set about the business of self-government. Paterson was named the state's first attorney general. The young lawyer found it an arduous assignment because he was constantly called upon to travel from county to county to prosecute persons accused of being loyalists. All who were convicted had their property confiscated and sold. Paterson spared no one, not even the brother of his beloved wife.

Even harsher consequences of war were visited on Somerset starting in December 1776. Down the road from New Brunswick to Princeton went Washington and his tattered army in wretched retreat. Hard behind them came marching thousands of well-fed, well-equipped Redcoats and Hessians. New York had fallen. Philadelphia would be next.

The British commander, William Howe, published a proclamation to the people of New Jersey offering them amnesty if they would take oaths of loyalty to the king. Many prudently complied. Howe backed up his magnanimity with military might just in case any holdouts became rambunctious. He stationed garrisons of troops at New Brunswick and Princeton and elsewhere in the Jerseys then returned to New York for the winter, leaving General Charles Cornwallis in charge.

Washington, at bay on the Pennsylvania side of the Delaware, sent an urgent call for reinforcements to his second in command, General Charles Lee, stationed in the Hudson Valley. On learning of Lee's advance into Jersey, the British grew nervous, fearful lest he strike. Scouting parties were dispatched, and a small company of dragoons probing northward into the Somerset Hills discovered its quarry nearby. Lee and his aides had spent the night at Widow White's tavern in Basking Ridge while his army encamped two miles away at Vealtown (Bernardsville). Seizing their opportunity, the dragoons charged furiously up to the tavern, creating such a commotion that Lee's guard panicked, and Lee was taken prisoner.

Capturing Lee was such a formidable coup, the British expected it to hasten the end of the war. It actually proved of little effect. General John Sullivan lost no time in marching Lee's forces by way of Pluckemin to join Washington and arrived in time to provide additional men needed for a Christmas night crossing of the Delaware and attack on Trenton—a masterstroke which, according to Somerset traditions, was planned on the strength of information Washington received from John Honeyman of Griggstown, who had acted as a double agent.

Victory followed victory. Three weeks after watching Sullivan and his soldiers march through, the people of Pluckemin saw them return, and with them came the rest of Washington's army and hundreds of prisoners of war, besides. It caused a great celebration. Not only had the Continentals achieved signal success at Trenton, they had outflanked their enemy, descended at dawn on Princeton, overcome the Redcoats there, and escaped largely unscathed. With his men too exhausted to press their advantage further, Washington had withdrawn down the Millstone Valley. They slept in the frozen fields at Somerset Court House (Millstone) then pressed on northward to the shelter of the Somerset Hills. For two nights they rested at Pluckemin with rocks as their pillows, filling their empty bellies with provisions brought to them by people of the countryside. Then they moved on through Vealtown to Morristown, where Washington made his headquarters for the rest of that winter.

War in their midst brought the local militia into action. They took delight in harrying the enemy. Cornwallis, after suffering defeat at Princeton, decided to call in all his scattered garrisons and concentrate his forces in New Brunswick, where they spent a miserable winter in badly overcrowded quarters, short of food and firewood.

Whenever foraging parties were sent out to gather supplies they found themselves sniped at or waylaid. Washington stationed companies of his men at strategic outposts

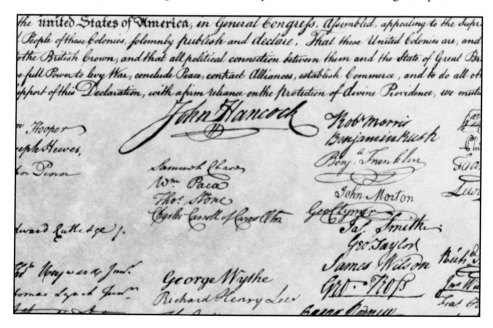

ABOVE:
William Alexander, also known as Lord Stirling of Basking Ridge, was the son of New Jersey's colonial Surveyor General. He lived in northern Somerset County, in a baronial style on land-holdings largely inherited from his father, and was a prominent officer in the patriot army during the American Revolution. A portion of his estate is now part of the Somerset County Park System. Courtesy, Special Collections/Alexander Library/Rutgers University

LEFT: Expressing the high ideals of the American Revolution and the hopes of the people for a better society and a government created by the people for the people, the Declaration of Independence was sanctioned on July 4, 1776, creating the new and independent United States of America. Two of the original signers, Richard Stockton and John Witherspoon, were from Somerset County. Courtesy, National Park Service

throughout the surrounding countryside so any movement by the enemy would bring on an encounter. Even more troublesome to Cornwallis were the militia; he fumed about the impossibility of distinguishing these citizen soldiers from peaceable farmers until they started shooting.

Stronger and stronger guards were assigned to British foraging parties. On January 20, 1777, more than 400 armed men and three fieldpieces were sent on a sweep through Middlebush to Van Nest's Mill (Weston). Frelinghuysen in Millstone dispatched a slave on horseback to alert General Philemon Dickinson, who was posted a few miles away on the Raritan. His men marched on the double, forded the Millstone River, and surprised and routed the enemy—capturing horses, cattle, sheep, flour, and prisoners.

The representative for New Jersey in both the First and Second Continental congresses in 1774 and 1775, respectively, William Livingston served as the state's first governor during the chaotic days of the Revolutionary War and up until the time of his death in 1790. Courtesy, Special Collections/Alexander Library/Rutgers University

Cornwallis nursed a grievance against the deliverers of this ignominious blow for weeks, finally retaliating on April 13 with a massive strike against the little Continental outpost at Queens Bridge in Bound Brook. More than 4,000 men marched by night over several routes on both sides of the Raritan to converge at dawn on the bridge. Their charge sent General Benjamin Lincoln dashing to safety in the hills without his breeches. Most of his men were taken prisoner.

Tradition says when the smoke of battle cleared, General Cornwallis breakfasted with his old friend, retired Colonel Philip Van Horne, at nearby Middlebrook (American Cyanamid), while his soldiers looted the village. After Cornwallis and his troops returned to Brunswick, Lincoln slipped back into town and supped with Van Horne, who throughout the war extended impartial hospitality to officers on both sides. He did so with good reason: he had four marriageable daughters.

Spring in eighteenth-century warfare signaled the resumption of campaigns. Howe's obvious objective was to secure Philadelphia, but his strategy was a puzzle. Washington, in June 1777, brought most of his army to encamp along the Middle Brook behind the first ridge of the Blue Hills (Watchung Mountains), from whose heights he could observe troop movements around Brunswick, nine miles away.

From that secure vantage point Washington saw his expectations confirmed. On June 13, the British army, 14,000 strong, began a march westward across Somerset County. That afternoon they fortified positions at Middlebush and Somerset Court House and settled in for the night. Except for skirmishing near the courthouse, all was quiet. It stayed quiet the next night and the next. For a full week both sides stayed put, until Howe finally abandoned hope of luring Washington into attacking his superior forces and marched his army back to Brunswick, setting fire to every farm he passed.

Three days later British evacuation of Brunswick began. Men and supplies were moved to Perth Amboy, where transport ships were waiting off Staten Island. Washington shifted most of his forces eastward, hugging the hills. Sure enough, Howe turned and launched another strike; but after a day of sharp fighting, he gave it up, embarked his army, and sailed away to strike at Philadelphia, from the head of the Chesapeake.

The New Jersey campaign was over. Washington decamped from Middlebrook, and a year elapsed before he appeared in Somerset County again. In June 1778 he passed through on a march eastward from Valley Forge, shadowing the route of Howe's army as it crossed New Jersey from Philadelphia to New York. Washington crossed the Delaware at Coryell's Ferry (Lambertville) and took the road through Hopewell, Rocky Hill, and Kingston (Co. Route 518) to Monmouth Court House.

In December 1778 the Continental Army returned to Somerset. Washington had decided to base his winter encampment in Middlebrook and have Mrs. Washington join him at his headquarters, a home on the Raritan he leased from John Wallace of Philadelphia. The Virginia, Maryland, and Delaware brigades built their winter huts on the south face of the Blue Hills where they could benefit from the warmth of the sun. Pennsylvania, arriving last, was assigned a position across the Raritan, just west of the Millstone River

This structure was known as the Battery House because General Benjamin Lincoln quartered his garrison guarding Queens Bridge in Bound Brook here in 1777. However, time was not kind to the old building. Here in a state of evident neglect, it was being used as a marble yard by Essex Yawger. Bolmer Brothers razed the building early in the twentieth century to make way for its auto dealership. Courtesy, Somerset County Historical Society

RIGHT, TOP AND BOTTOM:
On the eve of the Revolutionary
War, the wealthy Philadelphia mer-
chant John Wallace was building a
summer retreat on a large tract of
land along the Raritan River in
Bridgewater Township. It was nearly completed when General George
Washington made it his headquarters during the Middlebrook
encampment of 1778-1779. These
two portraits of Wallace and his
wife, Mary Maddox, are part of the
current Wallace House furnishings
in Somerville. Courtesy, James
Kurzenberger

(Manville). General Nathanael Green was quartered near them at the home of Michael Van Veghten (Somerset County Historical Society Headquarters, Finderne), with some of the Pennsylvania brigades occupying Van Veght-en's land.

The artillery under General Henry Knox were stationed in Pluckemin, where the general and his wife were housed by Jacobus Van der Veer. Instead of log huts, like those built by other brigades, artillerymen undertook a more ambitious project, erecting a long, low building around three sides of a square in the center of which was a big assembly hall. This hall was so large it served in February as the grand ballroom for a huge celebration of the French Alliance. All the officers brought their ladies, and entertainment included 13 elegant illuminations prepared by Charles Wilson Peale and a spectacular pyrotechnic display, courtesy of the artillerymen.

The winter at Middlebrook was fairly mild and was made even more agreeable by receipt of a large shipment of uniforms from France. Provisioning an army as numerous as the entire county population (about 10,000) was difficult, but no one starved, although many of the horses did. Under these relatively favorable conditions Baron Frederick von Steuben, who quartered with Abraham Staats just south of Bound Brook, had a good opportunity to train Washington's soldiers in military drill and put them on more equal footing with their adversaries.

Lord Stirling that winter was assigned to develop a chain of hilltop beacons to be used for calling out the militia in case of an enemy advance into New Jersey. But military activity was largely directed elsewhere in the ensuing months, except for intermittent raiding. The beacons did not prove their worth until the Battle of Springfield in 1780.

British raids into New Jersey from the New York stronghold continued throughout the war. Perhaps the most daring was a sweep into Somerset County by the loyalist Queen's Rangers under Colonel John Simcoe on October 27, 1779. Ferried across from Staten Island by night, they rode inland, across Piscataway to Bound Brook and Middlebrook, where they paid a surprise call on Colonel Van Horne. Several American officers found tarrying there were made prisoners but released on parole, and Simcoe's corps advanced to Van Veghten's bridge (Finderne) where they were expecting to destroy a fleet of flatboats that Washington supposedly was readying for an attack on New York. That report proved to have little foundation, but Simcoe did find a cache of supplies in the nearby Dutch church, so he set that building on fire before proceeding south to Somerset Court House where he released prisoners from the jail and torched the county building.

By then word had spread through the countryside that a raid was in progress. Even so, Simcoe might have made his getaway to a rendezvous at the South River if the landmark for his turning in Middlebush had not been a farmhouse burned down by the British in '77. Mistakenly he continued eastward and fell into an ambush laid for him on the outskirts of Brunswick (Battle Place, Franklin Township). Simcoe was captured; a

This rendering of the encampment site at Pluckemin was drawn by Captain John Lillie of the Third Regiment of the Continental Army. General Henry Knox and his artillery were stationed here during the winter of 1778-1779. Built on a site carved from the forest, the structures were raised in about three months and served as a military stores depot and a training academy for artillery officers. Several archaeological excavations have been conducted on this site. The final dig was completed in the 1980s prior to subdivision development. Courtesy, Somerset County Historical Society

few of his men escaped.

That was the last military engagement in Somerset County, but not the last of soldiers on the move. In August 1781 General Jean Baptiste Rochambeau and his splendid French army marched from Connecticut to Yorktown, taking a route across Somerset—from Morristown through Basking Ridge to Bullion's Tavern (Liberty Corner), over Steel Gap and Van Veghten Bridge to Somerset Court House, and on down the Millstone Valley through Griggstown and Rocky Hill to Princeton. They returned victorious over the same route a year later.

Cornwallis' surrender at Yorktown on October 19, 1781, virtually ended the war but did not end Washington's visits to Somerset County. He returned, one more time, in 1783 to wait on Congress, which had moved its meetings from Philadelphia to Princeton. Finding suitable accommodations in that village already taken, Washington and his lady established themselves at Rockingham, the Berrien homestead in Franklin Township, near Rocky Hill. It was during his 10 weeks at Rockingham that Washington gave his formal farewells.

War's end left Somerset County beset with disagreements over where to build a new courthouse and jail to replace what Simcoe had destroyed. Some wanted to rebuild on the same spot, while others wanted to choose a new location more conveniently central to the county as it had been redrawn in 1743. Unable to agree, they requested the NJ General Assembly to authorize a special vote by the inhabitants. South County lost.

The majority decision to relocate the courthouse to a place on Raritan Road where

The famous Middlebrook Hotel (sometimes known as Fisher's Hotel) occupied a prominent site on the Old York Road for many years and was believed to have been built as early as 1735. It served as a popular stagecoach stop and was the site of the first Masonic Lodge meetings in Somerset County. Attending lodge members included General George Washington during the Middlebrook winter encampment. It was visited by Colonel John Simcoe's Queen's Rangers in 1779. Pictured here on a sleepy afternoon in 1895, the hotel lost its trade during the years of Prohibition and was demolished shortly after being sold at a sheriff's auction in 1925. Courtesy, Somerset County Historical Society

the only settlement was Cornelius Tunison's tavern produced only more delay. Somerset was still without a jail and courthouse in 1781 when Peter D. Vroom became sheriff, so he began lodging protests with the county board of freeholders and justices over the great inconvenience of not having a lockup for prisoners. In addition to formal protests, he helped put together a package of proposals which freeholders could hardly refuse.

The first break in the impasse was an offer by Tunison to donate 40 feet of the land next to his tavern for a courthouse and, in conjunction, to sell 20 perches of land a little way down the hill to be used for the jail. Separating courthouse and jail was important to phase two of the plan. Vroom and Tunison, both members of the Dutch church that Simcoe had burned, persuaded their consistory, as a temporary measure, to offer to share with the county the cost of putting up a building for joint use. On those terms a bargain was struck. In 1783 a jail was built, and, soon after, a second building was constructed; it served as courthouse and church for two years, after which the congregation built their own house of worship nearby and left the county in sole possession of the original structure.

A more spacious and gracious brick courthouse, with a jail in the basement, was built next to the new church in 1799; by this time the county seat had become the nucleus of a village which would soon be known as Somerville.

Vroom and Tunison and others reaped profits from appreciated land values around the courthouse, but not as quickly as they doubtless wished. The town growth they rightly anticipated was slow to start. It needed the additional stimulus which nineteenth-century enterprise supplied.

THE AGE OF ENTERPRISE

THE INDUSTRIAL AGE CAME TO SOMERSET COUNTY VIA TURNPIKE, CANAL, AND RAILROAD. Somerset's hills and valleys shaped their routes, and the flow of commerce shaped the county's future. Vigor and enthusiasm mounted as the nineteenth century advanced and prosperity increased. The spirit of this age was in sharp contrast to that which preceded it.

New Jersey, in the wake of the Revolution, had gone through long years of deep depression. Seven years of war left the state economically and emotionally exhausted. Worthless currency brought business almost to a standstill. Agriculture was suffering: a century of exploitative farming had depleted the fertility of the land. With little prospect of better days ahead, a great many sons of Somerset removed west to the virgin soils of Ohio, Kentucky, and upstate New York. The exodus was so massive, Somerset's population of 12,296 in the first federal census increased very little over the next 10 years. It stood at 12,815 in 1800.

Difficult as times were, one section of the state did thrive, the central corridor connecting New York and Philadelphia. A visitor to America in 1791 observed that within this strip were located "the principal towns, the more passable roads and the only stage lines, most of the academies, the more attractive church buildings, all of the post offices, newspaper establishments and colleges."

Small wonder a successful lawyer like William Paterson decided to move from rural stagnation in the upper Raritan Valley to bustling New Brunswick. It was from there he went to serve in the Constitutional Convention of 1787 and, by his astute arguments, initiate the compromise which gave small states like New Jersey equal representation in the

U.S. Senate. Fittingly, he served as one of the first senators. In 1790 Paterson assumed the governorship, and from 1793 until his death in 1805, he was a U.S. Supreme Court justice.

Other Somerset men from that central corridor who served in the U.S. Senate included Frederick Frelinghuysen, 1793-96, and Richard Stockton, son of the signer of the Declaration of Independence, 1796-99. These Princeton graduates did not, however, play as telling a role in shaping our nation as another from that school, James Linn of Bernards Township. Linn was elected to a single term in Congress and took office just as the House of Representatives was called upon to break an Electoral College tie between Thomas Jefferson and Aaron Burr for the presidency. Linn's was the deciding vote giving New Jersey's ballot to Jefferson, and he was identified as one of three members who, by holding out and refusing to change their vote, kept Congress deadlocked for 35 ballots. A confirmed Jeffersonian, Linn refused to alter his vote and put New Jersey behind Burr. His stubbornness was rewarded, not only by seeing his man win, but also with an appointment to be supervisor of revenue of New Jersey after his term in Washington ended.

The virtual monopoly on travel between New York and Philadelphia, from which the central corridor benefitted, began to erode after the turn of the century, and the Upper Raritan Valley gained fresh stimulus for growth as more and more traffic began to funnel between the Watchung Mountains and the Raritan River at Bound Brook. The first new transportation link to come this way was the Swift Sure stage line, which began in 1799 to offer through overland service between New York and Philadelphia. Instead of obliging travelers to transfer from ship to stage at New Brunswick, the Swift Sure ran over-

Opened in 1834, the Delaware and Raritan Canal helped to establish a new era of business and commerce for the towns situated along its routes. Residents were quick to respond to the need for wharves and other commercial structures along the waterway, including stable facilities for the mules used to pull the barges. After World War I, traffic on the canal was limited to pleasure boats and a few coal barges, similar to the one shown here being towed by a steamboat in the 1920s. Courtesy, Special Collections/ Alexander Library/Rutgers University

land from a Hudson River crossing at Powles Hook (Jersey City) by way of Newark, Springfield, Scotch Plains, Bound Brook, Somerville, Centerville, Flemington, and Lambertville, all the way to Philadelphia. This journey over what came to be called the Old York Road took four hours longer, two days instead of a day and a half. The fare was the same: five dollars for a seat in a 12-passenger wagon. Even so, the option appealed to enough travelers to give serious competition to stage operators and inn keepers in the New Brunswick-Princeton corridor, and the rivalry became more intense after the Swift Sure began Sunday service in 1808.

Stages carried not only passengers but letters, newspapers, parcels, and a limited amount of freight, as well. They served as an important tie to the major cities at either end and stimulated development of short-haul lines to connect them with various towns along their routes. Anticipating similar benefits for other areas if improved roads opened them up to travel, the NJ Legislature chartered 51 turnpike companies between 1801 and 1829. Many of the proposed roads were never built, and very few were financially successful. One that did prove profitable for a time was the New Jersey Turnpike Co., which connected New Brunswick, the head of navigation on the Raritan River, with Easton, gateway to Pennsylvania's Lehigh Valley, an important route to the West that proved to be even more important as a source of coal. Easton Avenue was the turnpike's route from New Brunswick to Bound Brook, and county maps still bear the Easton Turnpike designation on the Bridgewater section, although common usage has adopted NJ Route 28.

Chartered in 1806 and completed three years later, this turnpike was a valuable artery of commerce until it was superceded by the railroad. Over it farmers from the North Branch Valley drove their cattle, flocks of sheep, and wagons laden with grain to be sold at New Brunswick markets. A tollgate keeper in Middlebrook reported collecting 500 fares in one day during a busy season. The volume of agricultural shipments was all the greater because this toll road happened to tap the region of Somerset County where German farmers who were wise in the ways of applying lime to sweeten the soil were making good use of deposits they had found conveniently available. A local crossroads settlement grew to be the village of Peapack as a result of this lime-mining activity.

A second toll road was constructed across Somerset County after 1820. Georgetown-Franklin Turnpike, for most of its length, was an improvement of existing roads across Franklin and Montgomery townships leading to Hopewell and Lambertville (County Route 518), as was its extension from Ten Mile Run to New Brunswick (NJ Route 27). Less ambitious than the Easton Turnpike,

These 1804 Travelers Directory map details show the location of inns and mills along the route to Philadelphia, which crossed Somerset County through portions of Franklin and Montgomery townships. Note the location of Devils Feather Bed, Jugtown, and Wheat Sheaf. Courtesy, Special Collections/Alexander Library/Rutgers University

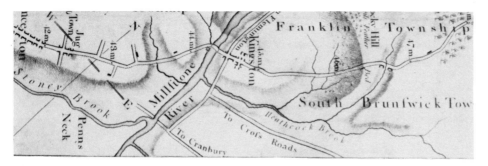

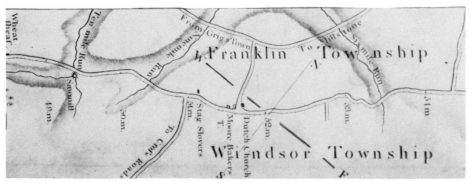

King George Inn has served the local and traveling public as a stagecoach stop and community center since the early 1800s. Located on a road that followed an early Indian trail between Perth Amboy and Morristown, the inn accommodated about 30 guests and included a spacious ballroom on the second floor. After suffering through fluctuating periods of prosperity and decline, it stands today as a proud and well-kept landmark in Warren Township. Courtesy, Special Collections/Alexander Library/Rutgers University

it was also far less successful.

Those who chose not to pay a toll to journey from Lambertville to New Brunswick had the option of going to the north of the Sourland Mountain along the heavily traveled Amwell Road, by way of Clover Hill, Neshanic, Woods Tavern, Millstone, and Middlebush. Unlike turnpikes, which were improved and maintained at the expense of chartered companies, public roads such as Amwell were as good or bad as the local population saw fit to make them. Farmers, when not busy in their fields, would spend some time doing road work in lieu of paying taxes; they were given extra credit for using a wagon and team. But no amount of ditching and filling of dirt roads could eliminate the frozen ruts of winter or the bottomless quagmires of spring when red New Jersey mud totally immobilized teams of horses and swallowed whole wagon loads of broken stone without a trace.

To extricate themselves from mud, men of the nineteenth century dreamed of railroads and canals. The feasibility of a waterway crossing central New Jersey was obvious. William Penn had discussed it, so had George Washington. William Paterson was a leading member of a company chartered in 1804 to build one, but they had insufficient capital. After successful completion of the Erie Canal in 1825, the idea of utilizing the beds of various streams to create a canal linking the Delaware and Raritan rivers attracted a fresh following. Again a company was formed, and again the venture failed. By the time a third attempt got under way, a new and formidable obstacle had materialized—competition from railroad interests.

The New Jersey Turnpike was a connecting link between the Raritan Valley and the developing West for post-Revolutionary War New Jersey. Vast quantities of food, produce, and supplies went over it across the state. Somerset County profited greatly from this new roadway that ran from New Brunswick to Easton, Pennsylvania. The turnpike was chartered in 1806, and shares of stock were sold to the public to finance its construction. This certificate was issued in 1819 to a member of the Morris family of Somerville. Courtesy, Special Collections/Alexander Library/Rutgers University

The NJ Legislature found itself besieged by backers of both enterprises. Unable to decide which to charter, the sages of Trenton wavered and delayed until, in desperation, canal and railroad men found their own way out of the dilemma by combining forces and becoming a joint company. With that, charters were given to build both.

Raising one million dollars to construct the Delaware & Raritan (D&R) Canal was still no easy matter. The goal was finally reached after Robert F. Stockton of Princeton (grandson of the signer of the Declaration of Independence) and his father-in-law, John Potter, purchased half the stock, prompting scoffers to refer to

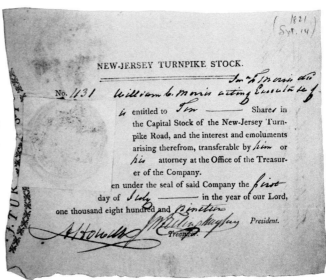

the project as "Stockton's Folly."

Excavation of a ditch, 75 feet wide and up to nine feet deep, began near the future canal's midpoint in Kingston in 1830. Gangs of Irish laborers were recruited to dig with pick and shovel and horse-drawn scoop. Paid a pittance and housed abominably, laborers suffered a tragic plight when Asiatic cholera broke out among them in 1832. Hundreds died and were buried in unmarked graves along the canal.

In spite of adversities, digging continued, and four years after it was begun, the canal was completed. Governor Peter D. Vroom and a bargeload of notables made the inaugural two-day trip on June 24 and 25, 1834. Their progress was cheered by crowds that gathered at every one of the locks and bridges, and a 25-gun salute welcomed the governor and his party to New Brunswick.

Looping through Somerset County for almost half its length, the D&R Canal passed through seven locks as it followed the Millstone and Raritan rivers from Princeton to New Brunswick. All the crossings were equipped with swing bridges to allow masted vessels passage, and houses for the bridge-keepers and lock-tenders put them and their families continuously at the service of canal traffic, except for a few hours each night. They caught up on their rest during the winter months when the canal shut down for repairs and maintenance. The D&R was one of the longest, most efficient, and busiest canals built in the United States. During its 40-year heyday it carried more tonnage than the celebrated Erie. But a fatal flaw had been introduced at its inception: ties to the railroad.

At first the jointly owned, but separately managed, routes coexisted successfully, but when the Pennsylvania Railroad leased the properties in 1871, it began diverting traffic and allowed the canal to die a slow death. Significant tonnage still went through the canal during the remainder of the nineteenth century, but usage dwindled away to nothing after World War I, and in 1933 the canal ceased to operate. Taken over by the State of New Jersey, the D&R was saved from destruction by its value as a source of water supply. It was made a state park in 1974 and has been listed on the National Register of Historic Places.

Coal, a commodity of minor importance when the canal was conceived, proved to be its chief source of revenue. Millions of tons of Pennsylvania coal were barged down feeder canals to the D&R, across New Jersey through New Brunswick, and on down the Raritan to New York Harbor.

The canal took away New Brunswick's importance as head of navigation on the Raritan River and brought new prosperity to the towns along its route. Princeton experienced a minor boom as the canal's main toll station. Barge basins at Rocky Hill, Millstone, and Bound Brook were ports on the canal and magnets for hotels, coal yards, lumber yards, grain dealers, and small factories. At Millstone and Bound Brook the surge of business development crossed the river to the canal side, giving rise to entire new towns. East Millstone called itself Johnstown for a time, and South Bound Brook styled itself Bloomington; but in the long run local usage prevailed over those assumed names.

The D&R Canal benefitted not only towns along its route but the entire countryside, as well. It allowed farmers to market their grain closer to home and gave them ready access to deliveries of lime, fertilizer, and machinery, which were of steadily increasing importance.

Advantages brought to South County by the canal came to the Upper Raritan Valley a decade later by rail. Construction of the Elizabeth-Town & Somerville Rail-Road (E&S)

began in 1834, the same year the D&R was completed. Meetings were held in towns all along the projected route to promote sales of stock. Although the enterprise survived the financial panic of 1837, it suffered continually from shaky finances. Nevertheless, mile by mile and town by town, it progressed westward, reaching Bound Brook in 1841 and, by dint of the principals, themselves, joining the workforce, managed to get to Somerville a year later.

Construction was pushed on a few miles beyond Somerville to a railhead which could serve any industries that might be attracted to facilities being developed by Somerville Water Power Co. on the Raritan River. This group of local investors, which included the perspicacious Joshua Doughty, had only the year before reorganized efforts to exploit the waterpower potential of falls in the Raritan. It was a promising location and had been considered by the Society for Establishing Useful Manufactures (SUM) before they fixed on the falls of the Passaic in 1792. Raritan Water Power Co., chartered in 1820, undertook development but, after building a dam, a three-mile canal, and reservoirs to har-

The tranquil reflection of this lock house on the Delaware and Raritan Canal at Griggstown is all that remains of the once busy scene of boats, mules, and barges that were here in the 1800s when the canal was at its peak. A boom to Somerset County for transportation of freight, the canal carried a wealth of supplies and produce over its waters to and from nearby city markets. Courtesy, Special Collections/ Alexander Library/Rutgers University

ness the water, they ran out of money. Now with local businessmen taking charge, there was renewed expectation of success; the realization was still in the future, however, delayed by protracted litigation over water rights. Unfortunately when the railroad arrived in Raritan, there was no significant industry to serve: the nascent town boasted only two flour mills, a machine shop, a manufacturer of wooden screws, and one or two other small struggling concerns.

Another disappointment for promoters of E&S was a failed copper mine at Chimney Rock. There had been earlier attempts to exploit rich veins of copper in the region, chiefly at New Brunswick (Mine Street) in 1750 and Griggstown (Copper Mine Road) 1753-64. There had also been sporadic attempts to probe deposits along the face of the Watchung.

Augustus Cammann, a German investor who settled in Somerville, turned his attention in this direction, reopening diggings at Chimney Rock in 1821. Work continued for several years. A smelting works was built, and skilled men were brought from Germany to operate it. But financial diffi-

culties stopped operations. Cammann's son, Albert, still convinced there were profits to be made, teamed up with Dr. Peter I. Stryker of Somerville in 1835 to try again. Their Washington Mining Co. opened a fresh drift and arranged to ship ore to Boston for smelting; but even though their trimmed ore was 75 percent copper, the end profit was not worth their time and effort. Various subsequent copper mining attempts at this and other locations proved equally fruitless.

Even if copper mines and factories had been in place, the feebly financed railroad would probably have folded. Although it was cheaper to travel to New York on the E&S than it had been to go by stage to New Brunswick and take the train from there, as Somerville and Bound Brook people had been doing since 1839, and although travel time was down from four and five hours to three, almost half of this being the ferry ride from Elizabethport, there just was not enough business to make this railroad a profitable venture.

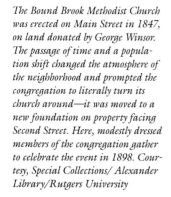

The Bound Brook Methodist Church was erected on Main Street in 1847, on land donated by George Winsor. The passage of time and a population shift changed the atmosphere of the neighborhood and prompted the congregation to literally turn its church around—it was moved to a new foundation on property facing Second Street. Here, modestly dressed members of the congregation gather to celebrate the event in 1898. Courtesy, Special Collections/ Alexander Library/Rutgers University

It went bankrupt in 1846.

Ruin turned to good fortune when control of this railroad passed to John Taylor Johnston, a young, gifted promoter with a flair for novel ideas. To get more passengers, he bought up land and initiated development schemes that created new towns along the right-of-way. He upgraded operations with clever innovations like uniformed train crews, attractive stations, and separate accommodations for women. At the same time he stressed efficiency. Most important of all, he extended the road both east and west. The eastern terminus was moved to Jersey City by filling in a swamp with New York City garbage, and to the west, track was extended through North Branch to Phillipsburg, on the Delaware River. This link, completed in 1852, made it possible for the railroad to pick up a valuable share of coal shipments. The sum of Johnston's many strategies transformed a failure into a high-quality, highly profitable operation, which he renamed the Central Railroad of New Jersey.

Railroad and canal infused renewed prosperity into Somerset County's agricultural economy. Proximity to New York markets was a decided competitive edge, and farmers increasingly emphasized growing cash crops and enhancing profits. Apples went to market as hard cider, applejack, and vinegar. Corn fattened cattle and hogs, especially huge Jersey reds. Raising horses was a good-paying sideline; so was poultry. But wheat and other small grains were staple, and yields improved with the introduction of lime, land plaster, and marl. There were also new varieties to grow and new tools to use: the iron plow, the rectangular harrow, the hay rake, and the threshing machine.

Mechanized farming was becoming more and more essential because of chronic labor shortages, brought on in part by New Jersey's gradual emancipation of slaves that began to take effect in 1825. Few who had been slaves chose to continue as hired hands. Some acquired small holdings of their own and stayed on the land, but most looked to town for opportunities. Settlements of former slaves developed in Somerville and South Bound Brook and in Montgomery, at the foot of Sourland Mountain. Many more newly freed men went off to the big city.

Immigrants were the labor pool farmers drew upon to replace the emancipated slaves. Irish by the thousands were flooding into America, and hundreds found their way inland via canal and railroad work gangs. Not all returned whence they had come once those projects were completed. Although the Irish were despised as ignorant, quarrelsome, shiftless, and overly fond of alcohol, they were nevertheless willing to work. Many of them took jobs as farmhands; their womenfolk hired on as domestics. In time their shantytown at the Raritan railhead gave way to a little factory village. Small foundries and machine shops were established, as were cotton and woolen mills, a rope and bagging plant, and a shingle manufacturing business.

In staunchly Protestant Somerset County there was no place for these Irish Catholics to worship, so priests came periodically to Raritan to minister to the community's spiritual needs. A few German immigrants from the surrounding area were served as well. Ground was purchased for a Roman Catholic church in 1847, but the endeavor was abandoned a few years later, and Raritan continued to be a mission station until St. Bernard's was established in 1853. By this time the Dutch Reformed had also organized a church to serve the growing village of Raritan.

The early nineteenth century was a mighty season of church planting for the Dutch Reformed and for Methodists, as well. Religious work among the Dutch was greatly strengthened by the founding of New Brunswick Theological Seminary on the outskirts of that town in Somerset County. It was, in 1810, the first theological school in America. Great revivals followed, and one of these gave rise to a new church at North Branch in 1825. Harlingen congregation divided in 1830 to form another at Blawenberg. Three new churches were added in 1834: Clover Hill, Middlebush, and Second Reformed in Somerville. The Griggstown church was established in 1842, and in 1848 three more churches sprouted in the growing communities of Raritan, South Bound Brook, and Peapack.

Methodist inroads into Somerset County were the work of itinerant preachers who conducted joyous, hymn-filled services, often in out-of-the-way places back in the hills. Methodist churches had taken root at Union Village by 1822, Mt. Horeb by 1824, and at Rock Mills, atop the Sourland, about 1830. Circuit-riding preachers also sought converts in

Somerset County supplied the 1844 candidate for vice president of the United States in the person of Theodore Frelinghuysen. Born in Franklin County in 1787, he grew up in Millstone, attended the Basking Ridge academy, and became a successful lawyer. Frelinghuysen served as mayor of Newark for two terms and was elected U.S. senator in 1829. In Washington he became known as the "Christian Statesman," and was nominated as the running mate for presidential candidate Henry Clay. This Currier lithograph was done from an original daguerreotype during that campaign. Courtesy, Special Collections/Alexander Library/Rutgers University

growing towns and villages. In 1831 Methodists began a church in Pluckemin, but it was short-lived. In 1832 they started a very successful church in Somerville. Their Peapack church was formed in 1834 and a Bernardsville church grew out of meetings begun in 1840.

Baptists, too, gained a foothold in Somerville. Two local men, Pethuel Mason and Samuel B. Tunison, arranged for meetings and preaching to begin in 1843, and a congregation was soon established.

Presbyterians did not participate in this season of church expansion. Their denomination was preoccupied with internal disagreement between "old" and "new" doctrines, and their one new congregation, Liberty Corner (1837), grew out of this dissension. Instead of churches, the Presbyterians' legacy to the county was famous men. Andrew Kirkpatrick, NJ Supreme Court chief justice from 1799 to 1824, got his start under the tutelage of the Reverend Samuel Kennedy in Basking Ridge. The Reverend Robert Finley, who next assumed the Basking Ridge pastorate, achieved even more noteworthy results. In his first class were Theodore Frelinghuysen, a U.S. senator (1829-35) and candidate for vice president on the ticket with Henry Clay in 1844, and Samuel L. Southard, a U.S. senator (1821-33 and again from 1833-42—during which time he authored the Missouri Compromise), NJ governor (1832-33), Secretary of the Navy (1823-29), and, also, a NJ Supreme Court justice. A later graduate was William L. Dayton, a U.S. senator (1842-1851) and Republican candidate for vice president on the John C. Freemont ticket in 1856.

Many prominent figures in the ministry and law were schooled in Reverend Robert Finley's "Brick Academy," and he, himself, was a man of public affairs, best known as founder of the American Colonization Society. Its purpose was "to transport free people of color, with their consent, back to Africa, or elsewhere as may be thought most advisable," and it managed, with the support of Henry Clay, Andrew Jackson, and James Monroe, to found the nation of Liberia on Africa's east coast before its goals were denounced and its work abandoned.

Presbyterian emphasis on education also was evident in a classical school conducted by the Reverend William Boyd in Lamington and in a Bound Brook academy that was funded by a generous bequest from a leading parishioner.

Educational advancement was a concern of the Dutch, as well. In 1818 the Reverend Charles Hardenbergh began a classical school in Pluckemin, and Reverend John Cornell conducted one in Millstone from 1828 to 1835. A school designed to prepare boys for admission to Rutgers College had begun in New Brunswick prior to 1771 and has the distinction of being the oldest school in the county, although the Rutgers Preparatory School campus in Franklin is not its original location; it was moved in 1963. None of these schools gained the reputation of the Somerville Academy, however, because among its first graduates was Peter D. Vroom, who capped a distinguished legal career with four years as governor, beginning in 1829.

Governor Vroom's father had used his influence to secure an academy for Somerville, much as he had done to get the courthouse located there. The onetime sheriff, having advanced to clerk of the county Board of Chosen Freeholders in 1802, persuaded other local men with promising sons to form a stock company to finance a suitable school that would be conveniently close to home. After the academy had proved a success, towns-

people organized stock companies to finance other local improvements. Somerville Aqueduct Co., formed in 1807, attempted to bring a supply of pure water to the village from a spring up on the mountain, but this venture failed because the wooden pipe that was laid could not handle the water pressure. A public library established about the same time managed to struggle along for a while, but it too failed. Somerville's eagerness for such improvements was premature.

The town around the courthouse grew slowly at first, gaining momentum after turnpike and railroad came through. A post office was established in 1822. The county's first successful newspaper, the *Somerset Messenger,* began publication in 1823. A volunteer fire company was organized in 1835.

Several men invested largely and profitably in Somerville real estate. Most prominent was Joshua Doughty, who came to town with his brother Eugene and opened a store on Main Street in 1838. Seizing upon national prosperity of the 1840s and local optimism generated by reorganization of the railroad, Doughty persuaded fellow townsmen to raise $100,000 in capital and establish Somerset County's first bank. It was chartered in 1848, and he was its president for 30 years.

No sooner had Doughty begun Somerset County Bank than he started to champion demands for a larger county courthouse. At first the architect's plans for adding a second story and a stylish portico were rejected as too costly, but proponents eventually won out. Doughty, himself, had charge of planting trees and installing an iron fence—additions intended to endow this symbol of Somerset with the impressive dignity befitting a thriving county with a population of almost 20,000. But building a courthouse was one thing, and building county unity was quite another.

Reverend Robert Finley assumed the duties of the Basking Ridge Presbyterian Church pastorate in 1787 after the death of Reverend Samuel Kennedy and continued his predecessor's educational work. Finley's classical academy, for which this building was erected in 1809, turned out many prominent figures in the fields of the ministry and the law. In later years this brick structure housed a public school. It is now the home of the Somerset Hills Historical Society. Courtesy, Special Collections/Alexander Library/ Rutgers University

RIVALRIES WITHOUT AND WITHIN

SOMERSET, DURING AMERICA'S CIVIL WAR, WAS A COUNTY DIVIDED. IN THE HILL COUNTRY of North County were numerous Peace Democrats, while sentiments in South County were ardently Unionist. The factions eyed each other with unconcealed distrust and seized opportunities to provoke each other with shows of partisanship.

Somerville was home turf to both, and its two newspapers, *The Somerset Unionist* and *Somerset Messenger* kept citizens well aware of their disagreements. The rival papers carped at each other incessantly. Townspeople, too, found ample opportunity to display petty prejudice. When the school board appointed a Democrat as headmaster, some Unionist parents kept their children home. When the school subsequently came under Republican control, that side did not hesitate to flaunt their own sentiments by running up the school flag in celebration each time Union armies scored a victory.

Proud old Somerset was no more. In its place was emerging a county of quite a different complexion. The Dutch language had disappeared with the passing of generations, yet the Dutch remained closely knit, held firmly together by ties to their beloved church. They were industrious farmers and most were content to prosper on their land, letting others chase the lure of business opportunities. But they were never loath to take part in government and politics. Sheer numbers assured them of winning a goodly share of elective offices, and they might have totally dominated county affairs had it not been that each township was entitled to elect two men to sit on the Board of Chosen Freeholders.

There were three townships north of the Raritan and three to the south, but astute political minds in 1806 ensured that in the future the balance would fall in North County's

favor by creating a seventh township out of the Baptist portions of Bridgewater and Bernards. It was named Warren after the patriot who died in the Battle of Bunker Hill.

In 1845 an eighth township was added by a further division of Bridgewater. The action was dictated by a new state constitution making it mandatory for elections to be carried out in a single day. Prior to this, elections had lasted several days, with ballot boxes taken from place to place—one day here, another there—until all parts of a township had had a chance to vote. Since smaller units made more sense if only one day was allowed, territory embraced in the curving arms of the North Branch and the South Branch of the Raritan River was set off and called, appropriately, Branchburg Township.

Other, less welcome changes to Somerset were dictated by Trenton's ongoing political tug-of-war. Railroad interests, industrialists, and rising cities crowded with immigrants were making demands and winning recognition. The influence of rural counties was on the wane.

Taking Princeton away from Somerset in 1838 demonstrated just how little status this county had left in statewide politics. The Princeton grab was a purely partisan action engineered by the Whigs, who had only recently been able to regain power with the help of Somerset votes. Once in, the Whigs were bent on perpetuating their hold on the statehouse by creating a new county around industrial Trenton, from which they anticipated gaining more safe seats. To this end they revived a 1781 proposal to divide Hunterdon County. Leading men of Princeton expanded on that idea, helping to draw the new county's boundaries so as to encompass portions of neighboring Middlesex and Somerset. Walter Kirkpatrick, Somerset's representative in the upper house, tried to organize support for a

On May 2, 1898, these men of Somerset County were ready to leave for the Spanish-American War. Somerset's soldiers had shown themselves to be patriotic and brave, fighting with George Washington during the American Revolution and nearly saving the day in the 1863 Battle at Chancellorsville during the Civil War. They were equally proud and determined in 1898. Courtesy, Somerville Free Public Library

ABOVE: Little did the residents of bucolic Far Hills know as they went about their daily lives in the late 1800s that this quiet thoroughfare would one day become the site of today's U.S. Route 202. Courtesy, Somerville Free Public Library

RIGHT: Country stores like this one located at North Branch in the late 1880s dispensed all the necessities that the average farm family might need, making trips to nearby towns such as Somerville somewhat of a luxury. Courtesy, Special Collections/Alexander Library/Rutgers University

counterproposal which would have created a new county, entirely east of the old Province Line, out of portions of Middlesex and Somerset, but to no avail. Minds were made up.

Seeing the loss of Princeton as inevitable, Somerset moved in the assembly to have it named Mercer, after the general who was killed in the Battle of Princeton, instead of Delaware as had been proposed. Somerset also fought off attempts to have the new county's boundary drawn as far north as the Georgetown Franklin Turnpike (County Route 518). Still not satisfied when Mercer was put to a vote in the assembly, Somerset voted No. The bill failed, but the Whigs were not to be denied. They amended the measure, deleting the Somerset portion of Mercer, and called again for a vote. This time Somerset added its three votes in favor and Mercer County was approved. However, the Whigs were not done: they went back to the upper house, brought forth a bill adding Somerset territories to newly formed Mercer, and easily rammed this through the assembly with the help of the opposition party. Somerset had been duped.

Having lost the Mercer battle, Somerset scarcely bothered to put up a fuss when, in 1850, it was proposed to redraw the Middlesex boundary so that New Brunswick would lie wholly within one county. In retrospect it is a wonder this restructuring had not taken place earlier. The legislature in 1784 had granted New Brunswick a charter to govern itself as a city, and in 1792 Middlesex had chosen it to be their county seat. Yet the city remained divided between two counties, and Somerset's tax receipts were enhanced by the assessments it was able to levy on its half of a city steadily gaining importance as a manufacturing center. When the cutoff came, the loss of New Brunswick ratables occasioned a good deal of grumbling, the more so because Somerset had gone into debt only two years before to finance improvements to the courthouse in Somerville. Nor were losses purely monetary; Somerset was also deprived of a seat in the NJ Assembly. Where before the county had been entitled to three representatives, henceforth, because of reduced population, it had only two.

In the presidential election of 1844, an anti-Whig cartoonist illustrated the dilemma of the oddly matched running mates, Henry Clay, an inveterate politician, and Theodore Frelinghuysen, then-chancellor of New York University. Frelinghuysen, a United States senator from 1829 to 1835, was known for his integrity and support of social reform. Courtesy, Somerset County Historical Society

The new Middlesex-Somerset boundary was laid along Mile Run, lopping off the eastern tip of Franklin Township to give New Brunswick ample room to expand. Thus reduced, Somerset County had at last attained—almost 162 years after its inception—a configuration which was to remain essentially unchanged. A few minor adjustments have been made since then, but none significantly altered the Somerset County outline.

Amputating New Brunswick and Princeton rendered Raritan, Somerville, and the sister towns of Bound Brook and South Bound Brook of far greater importance within the county framework. But avenues of trade were already too well established to transform those towns into the county's commercial hub. New Brunswick continued to be the focus of much of Franklin. Montgomery and the south end of Franklin did business with Princeton. Basking Ridge and Bernardsville were oriented to Elizabethtown and Morristown, and Warren increasingly was drawn into the sphere of growing Plainfield.

The political fabric of Somerset overlay a diversity of people and markets. The population was mostly rural. Farm families only occasionally went to town; their more immediate needs were met by a crossroads general store which accepted eggs and butter in trade as well as cash and extended credit to regular customers by simply jotting amounts in a ledger book. Some crossroads stores doubled as post offices. Nearby might be a tavern, a mill, or a blacksmith's workshop. Such crossroads settlements were found over every second hill and round every other bend in the road. Now, a hundred years later, they are gone; only their names remain, a litany of long-ago memories: Larger Crossroads, Stone House, White

Established as the Old Stone Hotel in 1849, this striking three-story structure has stood in Bernardsville for nearly 150 years. The building is now home to "Freddy's"—a popular local gathering place. Courtesy, Bernardsville Public Library

Bridge, Hickory Corners, Mount Airy, Pleasant Plains, Gatesville, Kline's Mill, Stoutsburg, Weston.

Scattered randomly among the crossroads settlements were one-room country schoolhouses whose seemingly haphazard locations were often dictated by where a district school board could find someone to donate a lot or sell one cheap. Each self-governing school district spent as much or as little as its people thought fit to supplement the money apportioned to them (on a per pupil basis) from the state school fund. Most charged tuition to make up the difference; wood for the stove, board and lodging for the teacher, or repairs to the roof were acceptable substitutes. Children whose parents were unable to pay were allowed by law to attend school free, but most families kept their children home rather than ask for charity.

In theory there was education for all, but in practice both the poor and the blacks were denied. New Jersey had dictated that slaveholders must provide basic education, but the state did not mandate as much for children of freed men and women.

Civil War propaganda brought home the message of injustice in education, and on April 9, 1864, some Somerville women started a "colored school," whose pupils, teachers proudly declared, learned as readily as any children. When the novelty of playing teacher wore thin, they held fund-raisers to finance their school's continuance. Eventually it became tax-supported.

Also during the Civil War era, much more radical innovations began to interest

Shown here on Doughty Avenue in Somerville around 1870, John Wagoner's hearse provided service to the community, with driver Howell King at the reins in the stylish attire of top hat and cutaway coat. Courtesy, Somerset County Historical Society

Somerville. The village around the courthouse had grown into a pretty little town of 2,000 with tree-shaded streets, comfortable homes, and busy shops. But those streets were unpaved, those homes unsewered. Outhouses, public pumps, and intermittent lengths of sidewalk left a lot to be desired.

Bridgewater Township Committee begrudged expenditures for Somerville improvements. Tired of asking and being ignored, townspeople in 1863 directed their petitioning elsewhere and secured from the NJ Legislature a charter allowing limited self-government by an elected commission. Although still a part of Bridgewater, they were empowered to tax themselves separately to improve their streets and local drainage and to provide fire protection.

While Somerville's wish to indulge itself in extra niceties had provoked scorn in Bridgewater in the past, grasping at semi-independence elicited downright antagonism. The township committee delayed and obstructed any transfer of funds as long as it possibly could, but change in the power structure had been inexorably imposed. Visible effects of the new order were slow in taking form, however, because the new town commission operated on a pay-as-you-go basis. Needed improvements were still decades away.

A more immediate result of Somerville's partial breakaway from Bridgewater was to encourage other towns to cut loose also. Raritan made a similar move in 1868, and Bound Brook followed in 1869; South Bound Brook became semi-independent from Franklin Township that same year. In the eastern arm of the county, a severing of ties was accomplished by dividing Warren Township in two, the more populous southern half taking the name of North Plainfield Township.

Challenge to the existing order took other forms as well. Local businessmen who thought Joshua Doughty's Somerset County Bank had had things all to itself long enough found the way open to provide some competition under new laws for the chartering of national banks. Envisioning substantial profits from underwriting bond issues that townships were floating to finance payment of army volunteers' bounties, in 1864 businessmen raised the capital to found First National Bank of Somerville (later Somerset Trust Co.).

Those enlistment bounties grew to be substantial, increasing year by year as the War Between the States dragged on and the glory of soldiering lost its appeal. Even with generous cash inducements to sign up, it became very doubtful New Jersey could continue to fill its army quotas, so a draft law was passed with the understanding it would not be invoked if enough men were forthcoming. And if a draft were instituted, there was almost sure to be trouble. Opposition was widespread and bitter. By 1863 tensions were building, and the mood was becoming ominous.

Education and the establishment of proper school facilities were high priorities in developing Somerset County communities. The woman pictured here on the far left, second row, is believed to be Elizabeth Vanderbeek who taught in Somerville from 1876-1922. Courtesy, Somerset Messenger-Gazette

A district provost marshall opened a draft office in Somerville that June and began a county-wide canvass to prepare lists of eligible young men. Stern warnings of stiff penalties for resisting the draft were issued. Many people were apprehensive. Draft officers making their rounds were received gruffly and answered evasively. Often they found no one home. But they went right ahead compiling their lists, using indirect sources of information. By the end of June it was reported that the tally was almost complete.

From up in Bedminster came reports of Copperhead (Peace Democrat) meetings. A mass rally of Democrats was announced, to be held at the courthouse on July 2. The draft riots in New York that resulted in more than 1,000 casualties were still a week away, otherwise townspeople would have been far more seriously alarmed when banner-decked wagons began rolling into town that morning. As it was, they were worried and more than a little curious about the outcome.

Hundreds ringed the courthouse steps when former Governor Peter D. Vroom stood up to speak. The little, old, silver-haired man had come a long journey on a hot day to deliver a personal message to his friends and former neighbors. "It is the duty of all citizens to submit to and obey all laws," he said. "Though they be unwise or unconstitutional laws and the enforcement attained through a stretch of constitutional authority, yet until they are decided illegal they are bound to obey them." Vroom counseled his fellow Democrats as their trusted friend. He assured them repeatedly that if their rights were invaded, they could

ABOVE: Peter D. Vroom (1791-1873) was born in Hillsborough Township and served as governor of New Jersey from 1829 to 1832 and again from 1833 to 1836. Educated at the Somerville Academy and graduated from Columbia College, he read law in Somerville and practiced in Sussex and Hunterdon counties as well as Somerset County. Vroom became governor of New Jersey when Garret D. Wall refused his elected position. After a six-year term, Vroom resumed law practice in Somerville only to leave again in 1838 to serve in Congress. After that he resided in Trenton and played a major role in revising the New Jersey Constitution. Courtesy, Special Collections/ Alexander Library/Rutgers University

RIGHT: William Hush, shown here draped in the American flag, was the child of former slaves. Longtime residents of Franklin Township, his family most likely took their name from the Hushes, who were early settlers of the Sand Hills section of South Brunswick Township in adjoining Middlesex County. Courtesy, Special Collections/Alexander Library/Rutgers University

come to him, and he would take care of and defend their interests in court.

The crowd grew restless as Vroom talked on; this was not the message they had come to hear. "Speak of our great debt and the enormous taxes we will have to pay," urged a redoubtable Democrat at his elbow. "Yes," said Vroom. "Yes, we will have a large debt and our taxes will be high and it becomes us to look seriously into this matter." Then he took up his theme once more. When he had done, he was answered by a chorus of huzzahs; many who cheered were Unionists who had mingled in the throng.

Ultimately, Somerset County avoided conscription. Townships met their quotas by floating bonds so they could pay each man who enlisted a bounty of $300. This was in addition to a state bounty and other inducements which raised the total each man was paid to a tempting $725.

Money flowed freely in that wartime economy. The cavalry needed horses, and the army needed bread. Woolen mills in Raritan turned out blankets. And prospects for profitable enterprise were even brighter after peace had been achieved. The victors were anxious for the good life, and markets seemed insatiable. For Somerset farmers these were halcyon days indeed, halcyon and fleeting.

While the good times lasted, people happily borrowed money to build new homes, improve their farms, even to invest in stocks and bonds. Who could have dreamed that the railroads that were making everyone rich were soon going to make them poor. But that is what happened. Those steel rails reaching across the Western plains brought millions of bushels of grain to Eastern markets. New Jersey farmers' products could not begin to compete with wheat produced on cheaper land and bigger farms. The absence of a distinction between short-haul and long-haul rates on the railroad worsened the disadvantage still further. Somerset's agricultural economy was never again the same.

The slump slipped into serious depression when the national economy took a precipitous dive in 1873. Where everything had been spruce and tidy, buildings were allowed to grow dingy for want of a coat of paint. Weeds grew in Somerville's dusty streets, and nobody seemed to do anything but wait for times to get better.

This late nineteenth-century bird's-eye view of Bernardsville was taken from "the Slope" and depicts the growth and development of that time. Claremont Road is visible in the foreground with the town's railroad station pictured on the right. Courtesy, Bernardsville Public Library

NEW MARKETS AND NEW FACES

AS THE NINETEENTH CENTURY RAN ITS COURSE, SOMERSET COUNTY PROSPERED ONCE MORE: A land of peaches and cream for those who farmed, a Mecca of daily pilgrimage for successful New York businessmen, an Elysian playland for millionaires.

Railroads, railroads, and more railroads were the route to these good times. Of the eight major roads serving New Jersey after 1875, five operated in Somerset County: Central Railroad of New Jersey, Lehigh, Reading, Pennsylvania, and Delaware, Lackawanna & Western (DL&W). Wherever rails ran, fresh growth took hold; where they did not, local people dreamed and schemed and agitated in hopes a railroad would soon be built. Some had a long, long wait: Peapack and Plainfield Railroad was incorporated in 1855, but no engine came puffing into Peapack until 1890.

Before the Civil War, railroads were interested in building spur lines. Pennsylvania Railroad completed its Millstone and New Brunswick line in 1855; trains stopped at Voorhees Station, Clyde, and Middlebush en route to East Millstone. The Rocky Hill Railroad, another Pennsylvania spur, opened in 1864; it connected to Monmouth Junction by way of Kingston. New Jersey Central opened the South Branch Railroad from Somerville to Flemington by way of Roycefield, New Center, Flagtown, and Neshanic Station in 1864. But postwar years saw railroad builders concentrating on bigger objectives and bolder plans. They raced one another to build routes to the West and waged political wars in Trenton to break up the New York-Philadelphia monopoly that New Jersey had granted to the United Canal and Railroad Companies in 1834.

New railroads between New York and Philadelphia excited great expectations. As

soon as New Jersey passed the General Railroad Law in 1873, a race developed between two of the major railroad companies, and Somerset County was astride both routes. Delaware and Bound Brook Railroad (Philadelphia & Reading) laid track from Jenkintown, Pa., to Bound Brook, where it connected with the Jersey Central. The Pennsylvania Railroad, in an effort to eclipse this competition, built the Mercer and Somerset Railroad to extend its East Millstone spur to Trenton. Rivalry was so bitter, at one point the National Guard was called out to keep peace. Although both roads were completed, only the Reading, with stations at Stoutsburg, Skillman, Harlingen, Belle Mead, Hamilton, and Weston, was a success. The Pennsylvania, having failed to thwart its rival, gave up Mercer and Somerset operations after only a few years.

Railroads were a boon, but not for all. Villages like Neshanic that were bypassed in favor of easy grades and stream crossings lost out. A station was opened just a mile away to serve Neshanic but it became the nucleus for a new town which eclipsed its namesake. Grain and coal dealers, hotel owners, and hay press operators preferred to be near the depot.

Not every station attracted enough business to give rise to as sizeable a settlement as Neshanic Station, however. Flagtown, for example, doubtless expected impressive development. A small factory did settle in, but what really put it on the map was a little enterprise of a very different sort undertaken by a man named Emanuel Ninger. Neighbors supposed that the bearded German who lived with his family in modest comfort on the edge of the village was receiving a pension for serving in the Franco-Prussian War, while, actually, the sometime sign-painter was quietly engaged in hand drawing $50 bank notes,

The advent of the railroad introduced a new era of prosperity to Somerset County in the late 1800s. Here, an unidentified man and child patiently wait for the next train to roll into the sleepy Finderne depot around the turn of the century. This station also housed an office of the United States Express Company. Courtesy, Somerville Free Public Library

which he put into circulation by taking the Friday morning train into New York. So artful were Ninger's painstaking forgeries, and so small his output, he escaped detection and supported his household in this fashion for 14 years. Finally apprehended in 1896 he received a prison sentence and enduring fame as a counterfeiter without equal before or since.

Despite remaining small, Flagtown fared better than the city envisioned by William Van Aken of New York. He lost a fortune buying up farms in Hillsborough and Montgomery and laying out a town which never materialized. U.S. Senator John R. McPherson, a powerful Hudson County Democrat, acquired Van Aken's landholdings in 1879, built himself a 20-room summer home in Belle Mead, and transformed the 800-plus acres into a model dairy farm for which he assembled a herd of choice purebred Holsteins. Among his purchases was a prize herd of 34 head from Holland. Local farmers had never before seen such cows, and they eyed these black-and-white giants with considerable interest. Access to railroads and the proximity of New York, Trenton, and Philadelphia had made it possible for milk to replace small grains as Somerset County's most important cash crop.

Farming was undergoing all sorts of transformations during the second half of the nineteenth century. Knowledge handed down from father to son was no longer enough. Scientific study was unlocking nature's secrets, finding ways to boost production and lower costs. A land grant provided for the establishment of an agricultural experiment station at Rutgers College in New Brunswick, and men like McPherson who put the station's discoveries into practice were stimulating their neighbors to try new ideas. Disc harrows and manure spreaders appeared, as did side delivery rakes and hay loaders. Inventive talent and a small machine shop put Andrew Dietz and J.P. Dunham of Raritan into business with a reaper; later, as Dunham and Dietz, they made thrashers as well. John Smalley of Bound

Brook manufactured cultivators.

Newfangled machinery was only a part of the changing farm picture. Purebred cattle were being introduced, as were milk marketing cooperatives. Tall round silos punctuated the landscape. Moonlit nights found farmers driving to meetings of their agricultural societies and granges. At these meetings they exchanged tips with one another and listened to guest speakers explain the dollars and sense of introducing a few Jerseys or Guernseys into a herd to boost butterfat content.

Farmers were also discovering a new golden opportunity in peaches. This fragile fruit could not stand up to shipping over bumpy roads in hot weather, but when it could glide on rails in the cool night hours to a major city, there seemed to be no limit to how much of this delectable delicacy people would gobble up. During good years peach growers found themselves harvesting spectacular profits. More orchards were planted; basket factories sprang up; railroads ran special peach trains. Some thought there was need for still better train service, so a new railroad was plannd to run right through the heart of Hunterdon-Somerset peach country. Many of the investors were peach growers themselves.

Construction of Rockaway Valley Railroad began in 1888 from White House, at a junction with Jersey Central. Finances were shaky, and the roadbed hardly more stable. Tracklaying proceeded northward over farm fields to New Germantown, Pottersville, and Peapack. As each town was reached, backers reincorporated and refinanced, and by 1892 they had 25 miles of track and a Morristown terminus. Dubbed the Rock-A-Bye Baby, this line became a local joke. Its equipment was sometimes makeshift; its operations erratic. Even cows did not take it seriously and would refuse to get off the tracks. But for a few years the Rock-A-Bye did make money, and the little village of Pottersville sprouted a hotel that catered to tourists brought by excursion trains to the picturesque glen at Black River Falls.

Good years were few, however. Markets were becoming glutted with peaches, and in 1895 word came that New Jersey orchards were infected with San Jose scale. This blight, for which there was no remedy, spread rapidly and within a few years destroyed the peach indus-

In the late 1800s and early 1900s, peach orchards proved to be extremely profitable in the Somerset County region. Many basket factories, like this one pictured here in Pottersville, sprang up to meet the shipping needs of this delicious crop. Courtesy, Somerset County Historical Society

try. The Rock-A-Bye railroad still ran, serving farmers, mills, and small factories; but it was a loser over time. It did not even enjoy a monopoly on the territory it had chosen to serve because the Passaic & Western (DL&W) had pushed through from Bernardsville to Peapack in 1890. The village that had waited so long for a railroad found itself with two, but not for long. Rockaway Valley Railroad struggled along for only 25 years before it died.

The Peapack branch of the DL&W fulfilled the dreams of men long dead—men like Lord Stirling, who in the eighteenth century had used both his money and his powers of persuasion to promote better roads so the potential of this area could be realized.

Unfortunately the very terrain that furnished abundant waterpower and made the Somerset Hills such a promising area was an obstacle to improved transportation. Although railroads were chartered, they were not built.

Railroad or no railroad, the hills were humming by mid-nineteenth century. There were numerous grist mills and saw mills and wood-turning mills. Basking Ridge, with daily stages to Morristown and twice-weekly stages to Plainfield, was the hub of a lively flow of commerce that was attracting enterprising businessmen. Job opportunities drew immigrant workers, and the population influx was such that it warranted three new Basking Ridge churches: Episcopal, 1850; Methodist, 1853; and Catholic, 1855.

St. Mark's Episcopal started as a mission of the Morristown church with only four families, yet just two years later they built a church. More people were served by the Catholic mission outreach, but they were less affluent. Many were Irish farmhands who, with their meager resources, purchased an old carpenter shop and converted it into St. James Church, but not without opposition. Both Catholics and Methodists had to hide behind go-betweens in order to buy property in the village.

Local people deeply distrusted the religious beliefs of foreigners. And Methodists

The rural hamlet of Pottersville took on new importance with the advent of the Rockaway Valley Railroad, which began service in 1888. It brought tourists by excursion trains to nearby Black River Falls and encouraged development of local industries. Pictured here around that time is the staff of the town's Sovereign mill, with owner Henry M. Sovereign shown on the far right. Courtesy, Bernardsville Public Library

The Gernert Brothers general store featured tobacco, stationery, books, toys, hardware, and even a Peerless Croquet set around the turn of the century. The staff is arranged here in order of growing importance from left to right: the stockkeeper, the clerk, and the owner. Courtesy, Somerville Free Public Library

were resented for taking attendance away from the Presbyterians. Only the personal involvement of Bishop Edmund S. Janes, who summered with his family in nearby Bernardsville, persuaded the small band of Basking Ridge Methodists to set out on faith and build a chapel.

The bishop's choice of summer residence was typical of the times. City people had taken to seeking out country places for their health and relaxation. At the foot of the Watchungs in North Plainfield was Brookside, a noted sanitarium where patients benefitted from healthful air in the "Colorado of the East."

A Delaware, Lackawanna & Western (DL&W) train crosses over the railroad bridge at Millington. Courtesy, Bernardsville Public Library

Hotels and resorts catered to many different tastes and pocketbooks as summering in Somerset grew increasingly popular. Atop the Watchung ridge above Plainfield was the Washington House commanding a spectacular view. Between Bound Brook and Somerville was the tall, many-towered Finderne Hotel. It had 88 rooms, and close at hand for guests to enjoy was Chimney Rock gorge, where the Middle Brook plunged and leaped over Buttermilk Falls. Less elaborate, but quite fashionable, was the Kenilworth in Pluckemin. None, however, rivaled George Seney's Somerset Inn, on the Mendham Road outside of Bernardsville. The inn was a long, low, frame building with shady verandas and it catered to a wealthy elite with elegant tastes.

Somerset Inn during the summer season entertained as many as 500 guests once the railroad had reached Bernardsville, a feat accomplished at last only by the intervention of Asa Packer, president of Lehigh Valley Railroad. Laying track for the West Line Railroad from Summit into the Somerset Hills had gone so slowly that six years into the project, pick and shovel crews were still inching their way round the bend and over the grade from Basking Ridge to Bernardsville. At that stage, promoters ran out of money. Packer saw a possibility of extending the line west to the Delaware and put the resources of the Lehigh company behind the West Line. In eight months the job was completed, and the first train chugged from Bernardsville to Summit in January 1872. No sooner was the line operating than Packer found another route west and withdrew Lehigh support, leaving the 14-mile West Line floundering in debt.

Delaware, Lackawanna & Western was the parent company of Passaic & Delaware Railroad Co., which undertook to reorganize and upgrade the troubled West Line. They made a success of it, and no railroad ever had more a dramatic impact on the territory it served. Millionaires who vacationed at Somerset Inn saw in the quiet countryside a perfect place to establish country estates. They began buying up farms on which to build imposing manor houses—houses designed to rival the stately homes of Britain. Cost was no object, and the results were magnificent.

From Jockey Hollow and Hardscrabble roads west to Peapack and south to Burnt Mills, the hills were rapidly transformed into a world of palatial residences robed in rich green lawns and luxurious landscapes. Each estate had its stables and dairy, gardens and greenhouses. Families who owned them spent winters in the city and vacationed elsewhere in summer, but during spring, fall, and Christmastime, life on "Millionaires' Mountain" consisted of elaborate rituals: riding to the hunt, golfing at the country club, playing polo, and holding race meets, agricultural fairs, horse shows, and dog shows. While it lasted, Bernardsville was reputed to be the second wealthiest town in the United States.

William Haelig purchased the Chimney Rock hotel in Bound Brook soon after he emigrated from Germany with his new bride around 1886. A popular resort prior to World War I, the Haelig Hotel included picnic grounds and a bowling alley for its guests. Courtesy, John Haelig

Although this wealthy enclave lived a life apart from the people of the countryside around them, money flowed down the mountain to tradesmen and merchants, and those wanting to work hard had ample opportunity to take jobs as grooms and gardeners, upstairs maids, parlor maids, and kitchen maids. Specialists of every description were required to support a gilded lifestyle, and local people could not begin to satisfy all their requirements. Estate owners imported Irish horse-trainers, English kennel-masters, Italian stonemasons, Hungarians, Slovaks; nationality did not matter so long as they had skills, and Bernardsville in consequence acquired a substantial foreign-born population.

By 1890 the mountain colony was pushing westward into Bedminster, and Grant B. Schley spearheaded a move to extend the railroad through Far Hills to Peapack. Hundreds of Italian laborers were recruited, and the new railhead was established in just a few months. With that, Peapack began to anticipate its own rise to importance. But with a name like Peapack, who would take the town seriously? Some folks felt that a more dignified name was needed, a name resonant with honor and distinction. They suggested that the village be renamed after England's prime minister, William Gladstone, but the chorus of objections was vehement and unyielding; a name of Indian origin was a treasured Ameri-

ABOVE: The local railroad depot was a beehive of activity during the late 1800s and an integral part of daily life. This 1896 overview of the station at Bernardsville shows Engine #108, driven by Henry Dalrymple, pulling into the station where townspeople have gathered to greet arriving passengers. George T. Bunn is visible in the foreground in his shirtsleeves coming to collect the day's mail, and the carriage to the right awaits the luggage for arriving guests of the Somerset Inn. Courtesy, Bernardsville Public Library

LEFT: One of the busiest craftsman in the nineteenth-century Somerset village was the blacksmith, who remained so until the newfangled automobile replaced the ever-dependable horse. This smith plied his trade at Six Mile Run in Franklin Township in the late 1800s. Courtesy, Special Collections/Alexander Library/ Rutgers University

The chapel at Chimney Rock had a romantic air about it, very different from other houses of worship in Somerset County. It was eradicated long ago by quarrying operations, but in the late 1800s, services and Sunday School classes held here by various Bound Brook churches were well attended by families in surrounding Bridgewater. Courtesy, Somerset County Historical Society

can tradition. So what could the U.S. government do when assailed by two factions—each with significant political clout—but cut it down the middle and give the tiny town two post offices. Peapack remained, and a mile away Gladstone was added in 1886. The DL&W likewise established two stations: Peapack at the south end of the village, Gladstone at the north. With the Gladstone branch line completed, all of Somerset County had direct, convenient access to New York.

Each of the rail lines fanning out from the city had a markedly different effect on the area it served. The coal-carrying Jersey Central attracted factories, and towns along it grew accordingly. There were paper mills and a big carriage-maker at the eastern tip of the county in North Plainfield. In Bound Brook lubricating oils, paint, heating apparatus, hose, and pumps were manufactured. Somerville had a brickyard and a meat-packing plant. The factory town of Raritan boasted foundries, forges, machine shops, and paint works. But the industry with by far the biggest work force was textiles.

By 1880 Raritan Woolen Mills employed 600 hands, the adjoining Somerset Manufacturing Co. employed 350, and Bound Brook Woolen Mills, 300. Somerville Woolen Mill started in Pluckemin in 1873, outgrew its plant there, and moved in 1889 to Somerville, where, in addition to 100 mill hands, it employed 500 operatives who made men's suits and overcoats. The mill building at Pluckemin was taken over by Superior Thread and Yarn Co. Silk mills were established in North Plainfield in 1900.

All these factory jobs were magnets to foreign-born workers: Germans, Irish, Italians, Poles, Hungarians, Slovaks. Commercial banks had little interest in doing business with them because their pay packets were too slim. But other businessmen who believed large numbers made up for small amounts founded Raritan Savings Bank in 1869 and Somerville Dime Savings in 1871. Working people helped themselves as well by joining forces to organize building and loan associations. The people of East Millstone started one in 1871. In Somerville, People's Building and Loan was begun in 1887. Bound Brook Savings and Loan was organized in 1890, as was Somerville's second one, Citizens Savings and Loan. Savings accumulated in these institutions enabled hundreds to build homes of their own.

Long before building their own homes though, immigrant laborers built community churches. Germans attracted to the Plainfield area built St. Mary of Stony Hill in Watchung in 1847. In the decades that followed, other German-speaking congregations built German

Reformed and German Lutheran churches in North Plainfield and an Evangelical Lutheran church over the mountain in Coontown. A German Reformed opened its doors in Somerville in 1874.

Italians settling in Bound Brook overflowed the little frame church Roman Catholics had built there in 1865, so St. Joseph's built a handsome stone sanctuary in 1890 and used the old building for their parochial school. St. Bernard's parish in Raritan also built anew. Then it divided: Italians formed St. Ann's Church in 1903, and Slovaks founded St. Joseph's in 1912. Lutheran worship services begun by Slovaks in Raritan in 1882 led to the 1894 establishment of St. Paul's. And Poles in Bound Brook organized their own Catholic church, St. Mary's, in 1914.

However, newly arrived immigrants were not the only ones involved in church planting and building. In 1876 an African Methodist Episcopal (AME) congregation bought a building on South Middlebush Road in Franklin. St Luke's AME in South Bound Brook incorporated in 1878. Mt. Zion AME moved from its little chapel on Sourland Mountain to a new building on Hollow Road in 1890, and St. Thomas AME in Somerville built a fine new church in 1891 to replace the little building it had used since 1861.

Older Protestant denominations also were building and expanding. Their new churches were symbols of affluence as well as Christian faith, testifying to profound changes taking place in the Raritan Valley. Indeed, growth and development in the valley exceeded the most optimistic expectations of well-heeled and well-edu-

BELOW: Sitting with straight backs and hands tightly folded, this Somerville grade school class brings to mind the old rhyme, ". . . all in our places, with bright shiny faces . . ." as they pose for their school portrait in the early 1900s. Courtesy, Somerset Messenger-Gazette

LEFT: Johannes Moelich purchased land in Bedminster Township in 1751, erected a stone farmhouse, and raised a large family. His descendant Andrew Melick tells the story of Moelich's life in his book The Story of An Old Farm, *which has become a classic of Somerset County history. Members of the Camp Middlebrook Chapter of the Daughters of the American Revolution (D.A.R.) posed for this 1898 photograph while visiting this historic farm site during one of their monthly meetings. Courtesy, Somerset County Historical Society*

After attending Vassar College and graduating from Philadelphia Medical School, Mary Gaston (1856-1956) became the first female physician to practice in Somerset County. She founded an emergency hospital, which functioned for two years in a building on Maple Street in Somerville, and then helped to establish Somerset Hospital. Pictured here in her later years, Gaston in her retirement was active in community affairs and is credited with founding the Somerville Civic League. Courtesy, Somerset County Medical Society Archives

cated individuals (with an eye for good investments) who had established country residences along the Jersey Central right after the Civil War. Such was George LaMonte, a manufacturer of specialty papers, whose broad acres north of Bound Brook were known as Piedmont Farm. Such, too, were Samuel Blackwell and his wife, the Reverend Antoinette Louise Brown, the first woman in America to be ordained. They bought a home on the east edge of Somerville in 1868, and over the next 20 years Blackwell laid out streets and sold off lots while his wife wrote articles for literary journals and raised five daughters. Both were active in good works for the town's betterment, helping found a public library and a literary club.

The Blackwells' real estate dabblings also gave Somerville a claim to fame as the hometown of Ruth St. Denis, the originator of modern dance. Her parents leased Pin Oak Farm, near Adamsville, from the Blackwells and supported the family by taking in summer boarders.

It is reasonable to surmise that Mrs. Blackwell may have served as a role model for other Somerville women: Miss Mary Gaston became one of New Jersey's first woman physicians in 1889, and Miss Mary Steele became in 1897 the second woman to pass the New Jersey bar exam and become an attorney. These departures from tradition are not recorded to have set off any local shock waves. Their hometown, like others along the Jersey Central, had become markedly more cosmopolitan as the nineteenth century unwound. These were backwards country towns no longer; they were suburbs of New York.

A home in the country came to be something successful businessmen thought they owed themselves because the city was increasingly grimy with soot, crowded with immigrants, and choked with traffic. Wall Street men found it easier to escape across the Hudson than to fight their way uptown through streets clogged with vehicles and pedestrians. It took as long for a carriage to make its way up to Central Park as it did for a commuter to cross the river and ride the train to Plainfield. Hundreds crossed the river daily, then thousands and, ultimately, tens of thousands.

After the Civil War Plainfield, just one hour from Manhattan, became the "Queen City" where wealthy bankers and businessmen rivaled one another in building homes of breathtaking elegance. Washington Park in North Plainfield, its 300 acres laced with winding streets, its exclusiveness guaranteed by restrictive deed covenants, defined the height of Gilded Age residential perfection. (It is now on the National Register as a historic district.) Men with even more expensive tastes built grand estates a short drive out of town.

John Taylor Johnston, president of the Central Railroad, chose this premier location for his own imposing country place and purchased extensive landholdings all the way up to the crest of the

ABOVE: Somerville's Central Hook & Ladder Fire Company boasted this fine fire engine in 1906. Developing technology had introduced the steam pump after years of fighting fires with hand-drawn and hand-pumped equipment. Pulled by a team of handsome horses, this fire truck was the pride of the town well into the twentieth century and in 1912 was driven all the way to East Millstone to put out a disastrous fire. Courtesy, Somerville Free Public Library

LEFT: Somerset Hospital opened its doors to serve the health-care needs of the county on February 15, 1901, in what had been the home of the Lord family on East Main Street in Somerville. That first hospital had 10 physicians, 12 beds, and three wards. A school of nursing was established in conjunction with the hospital in 1911. A growing population led to the erection of a new hospital facility on Rehill Avenue in 1925, which has since been repeatedly expanded to keep pace with the medical needs of the community. Courtesy, Special Collections/ Alexander Library/Rutgers University

Watchung ridge, where in 1877 he laid out a scenic roadway. Johnston Drive, nine feet wide, three-and-a-half miles long, and macadamized its entire length, was the first hard surface road of this extent in central New Jersey. On fine days hundreds would drive out to marvel at it and at the sweeping panorama spread out below.

Farther out on the Jersey Central, Bound Brook and Somerville were a little less convenient for commuters, a little less fashionable, and a little less expensive. Nonetheless they were attractive places of residence that enjoyed building booms which left them architecturally enriched and economically transformed. Their Main Streets were tied as firmly to New York as to local farms and factories.

Although commuters fancied a home in the country, they had no patience with rustic inconveniences. They wanted sidewalks and streetlights and public water supply so their big homes could have indoor plumbing. All that water in turn generated a need for sewer systems to carry it away. Commuters' votes supported demands by fledgling fire companies for equipment, firehouses, and uniforms. Commuters gladly subscribed to emerging electric and telephone services and were benevolent supporters of worthwhile charities such as Somerset Hospital, which Dr. Mary Gaston helped organize in 1899.

Well-to-do commuters made up a new class of customer that attracted Jewish mer-

This gathering of townsmen was photographed in front of the majestic Somerset County Courthouse sometime after World War I. Designed by architect James Reily Gordon, the courthouse was constructed in 1907, and that date was inscribed in Roman numerals above the building's main entrance. Courtesy, Somerset Messenger-Gazette

chants to the Raritan Valley. German Jews came first; later, others came from Eastern Europe. Not to be outdone by this competition, local storekeepers vied with the newcomers in putting up ornately stylish new storefronts. Main Streets were further enhanced by impressive bank buildings. A burgeoning business climate gave rise to two new banks: First National of Bound Brook, chartered in 1888, and Second National Bank of Somerville, chartered in 1894. (The two merged in 1969 to become the First National Bank of Somerset County.)

When the Jersey Central opened a new train station in Somerville, every bit as grand as civic pride demanded, the town went wild with delight. Only one more improvement

According to early records the landmark Washington House in North Plainfield, situated at the top of the gap in the Watchung Mountains, had been a tavern and hotel since it was first constructed in 1773. A favorite stop on the stage route from Trenton to Morristown, the hostelry was also a local gathering place. The first meeting to discuss the formation of Warren Township was held here in 1806. The Demler family leased the structure in 1848 and purchased it in 1868, so it was widely known as the Demler Hotel. A spectacular fire in 1963 destroyed it completely. Courtesy, Margaret Demler

was needed to make the county seat truly outstanding: a new courthouse.

Some traditionalists protested against razing a cherished landmark; their voices were scarcely heard. County freeholders who objected to the unwarranted expense were not reelected. Alvah A. Clark, a prominent attorney, expressed the mood of the day when he said, "I think new county buildings would attract more rich people to settle here."

Nothing but the best would do for the county Somerset was becoming. They commissioned Fifth Avenue architect James Reily Gordon, a specialist in public buildings who had on his impressive list of credentials the Mississippi State Capitol and the Statehouse of Arizona. For Somerset he designed a white marble edifice capped with a colonnaded dome. Sited discreetly behind it was an escape-proof jail that echoed the classical theme and proportions, but was modestly executed in brick. The Masonic Order of New Jersey laid the cornerstone in November 1907 with great pomp and ceremony. A bond issue of $280,000, floated at four percent, paid for it all.

The new courthouse also brought all county offices—the sheriff, surrogate, and county clerk—under one roof, plus it provided a meeting room for freeholders. Efficient as well as beautiful, it was a fitting centerpiece for a county of 36,000. It stood, moreover, as triumphant reaffirmation of the integrity of Somerset County and the importance of Somerville as county seat. But Somerville's practical politicians knew in their hearts that no matter how much they played up the town's "marble dignity," the power of the ballot box had shifted. By 1905 Bound Brook and Raritan populations were overtaking Somerville's. The Borough of North Plainfield had more people than Somerville by 1900, and the voting power it represented demanded special consideration; for while the borough remained a part of Somerset, to a large extent its interests were apart from those of the county as a whole.

For a time there had been serious doubt which way North Plainfield would go. The town began to distance itself from the rest of the county in 1885 by declaring independence from North Plainfield Township and becoming a separately governed borough. Thereafter Plainfield and North Plainfield were distinguished from one another as the "City" and the "Borough," respectively. Geographically and economically they were very nearly one. Some thought the political division should be eliminated. Put to a vote in 1897, the proposal did not generate much interest and was defeated. Instead of settling the question, however, that attempt alerted politicians in Trenton to the possibility of annexing North Plainfield to Union County. In 1902 a bill slid through the legislature so fast, Somerset County leaders barely had time to protest. Governor Franklin Murphy signed it, saying a suburb whose men went to the city each day was out of harmony with a county governed by farmers' points of view. The final decision was left to North Plainfield voters, and a spirited campaign was waged. Tactics became fiercely imaginative

This photograph of Main Street in Bound Brook was taken the day after a destructive hurricane and catastrophic fire struck the town on February 6, 1896. The lower part of town had always been prone to flooding, but this blow was devastating because storm damage touched off a fire, which destroyed much of the community's business section. Courtesy, Somerset County Historical Society

North Plainfield Borough voted itself independence from North Plainfield Township in 1885, establishing itself as a separate municipality. These two communities were for years distinguished from one another as "the City" and "the Borough." Shown here in the 1890s is the section of North Plainfield along Somerset Street known as the "Notch." The Demler Hotel is on the right in this view, looking north toward the Watchung Mountains. Courtesy, Margaret Demler

and stirred up the citizenry so completely that 1,024 of 1,300 registered voters went to the polls. Annexation lost by 161 votes.

Governor Murphy was right though, about townspeople and farmers having divided interests. Those who had no need for curbs, gutters, water mains, and drains were not about to pay taxes so others could have them. Separating town from township allowed them to go separate ways and gave Somerset County three additional political units along the Delaware and Raritan Canal and five along the Jersey Central.

East Millstone loosened ties to Franklin Township in 1873 by adopting a town commission with limited powers. Rocky Hill voted to cut itself entirely free from Montgomery in 1889 and become an independent borough. Both East Millstone and Rocky Hill were thriving little commercial centers with hotels and shops and neat blocks of frame dwellings. East Millstone, population 400, had a distillery, which had grown into a sizeable industry, and had sprouted Reformed, Methodist, and Catholic churches. Rocky Hill, population 350, had a quarry and a brickyard and had also added three churches: Reformed, Methodist, and Episcopal.

Millstone followed suit in 1894. It had a population of 200, no significant industry, and its one church antedated the Revolution. But it had shops and stores, a hotel, a proud history as Somerset Court House, and a fine brick schoolhouse, far and away superior to any other in Hillsborough Township. Faced with the prospect of the state abolishing independent school districts and its school coming under direction of a township board of education, Millstone chose instead to preserve local control by becoming a borough.

Bound Brook moved to full independence from Bridgewater in 1891. The town had nearly tripled in size in two decades; population was nearing 1,500. Somerville still held back. Its population exceeded that of the rest of Bridgewater, so it enjoyed the upper hand. But after South Bound Brook, population 950, separated from Franklin Township to become an autonomous borough in 1905, Somerville was persuaded to do likewise. With a population just short of 5,000, it became a borough in 1909, leaving Raritan, still semi-

St. Bernard's School celebrated
Columbus Day in grand style
around the turn of the century.
Feathered caps, costumes, and ban-
ners helped to create an atmosphere
of pageantry and festivity. Courtesy,
Somerset Messenger-Gazette

independent under a town commission, as seat of the township government.

Whatever might divide the people of Somerset County, there remained two interests which drew them together: old-time gospel religion and fast horses. Presbyterians, Dutch Reformed, and Baptists united in the work of the Somerset County Bible Society to distribute Bibles and Testaments to the poor. Annual meetings, rotated around the county, were always largely attended, and the society's works were generously supported. Likewise, Somerset County Sunday School Association, organized in 1860, was an interdenominational effort to provide religious instruction to all children. Classes were held in churches, schoolhouses, and public halls. By 1880 the organization boasted 93 schools meeting regularly, for a total average weekly attendance of 5,000, more than 18 percent of the county's population. Not all were children; adults too frequented these Sunday afternoon classes.

Many young men nurtured in this religious climate entered the ministry and acquitted themselves with distinction, and one became the foremost preacher of the age. The Reverend T. DeWitt Talmage, whose folksy style drew generously on childhood memories, preached to as many as 4,000 on Sunday in his Brooklyn tabernacle, and some 3,500 newspapers across the nation printed his sermons as a regular weekly feature; yet he never withdrew his membership from Bound Brook Reformed Church where he had made his profession of faith at age 18.

Sunday churchgoing did not fill men's minds with religion exclusively, however. It was also a day to take the road horse out of the barn and give her a run. Sunday rides provided an opportunity to look over other men's horses, too; for this was indeed horse country. Somerville was known as a town where men talked about little else besides horses. In fact all through the county were notable breeders' and trainers' facilities: John Shaw's Riverside Farm in Finderne, the Belle Mead Stock Farm of William C. Hendrickson, and the Ardmaer Farm, west of Raritan, owned by William Bradley. Bradley was long remembered for paying the then-unheard-of price of $30,000 for "Todd," only to have the horse die a few days after arriving at Ardmaer.

A pervasive sporting spirit no doubt encouraged Diamond Jim Brady to set up a little country place for himself on the South Branch. Here he could enjoy good black-bass fishing. There was good shooting, too; Bound Brook was especially noted for plover and duck.

But Somerset's sport of sports was definitely horses. The big race meet was in October at the Somerset County Fair; informal racing went on at other times, as well. In winter the place for sleigh races was Somerville's High Street.

A favorite training ground for local horses was Duke's Park. Tobacco king James B.

While the men discussed the burning political issues of the day on a languid summer afternoon, the women retired to the comfort and shade of the veranda in turn-of-the-century Somerset County. Courtesy, Somerset Messenger-Gazette

Duke had laid out wonderful roads on his palatial estate just across the river from Somerville. Shunning the millionaires' colony in the Somerset Hills, Duke had bought up 2,300 acres of Hillsborough farms, carved out a landscape of lakes and wooded vistas, and studded it with statuary. The public was welcome to enjoy his drives for many years, but when he found visitors abusing the privilege, Duke closed his gates.

The privileged life which great wealth afforded was a passing show Somerset gloried in, while it lasted. A new generation in a new century would begin to define the good life differently, and people of wealth would give ground to others no less eager to grasp at the benefits of life in Somerset.

IMMIGRANTS AND INDUSTRIAL GIANTS

P ROGRESS, PROGRESS, AND MORE PROGRESS INVIGORATED SOMERSET COUNTY'S ADVANCE
into the twentieth century. Westward expansion of New York's metropolitan region was
making New Jersey the most urban state in the nation, and Somerset was within the city's
"Golden Zone."

Commuter towns expanded. Factories multiplied. New towns were added. The county
population doubled between 1900 and 1930, with gains concentrated in six major towns:
North Plainfield, Somerville, Bound Brook, Manville, Raritan, and Bernardsville. Somerset's state senator, Clarence E. Case, (later a NJ Supreme Court justice) lamented "the passing of the old country towns' tree-shaded business streets and quaint landmarks to a bald
thoroughfare with its pitiless heat and glaring pavements, all necessary to meet demands of
modern traffic and business."

With population approaching 65,000 in 1930, half of Somerset was still agricultural. But the countryside was changing. Barbed wire had taken the place of zigzagging
worm fences. Tractors chugged and snorted in the fields. Telephone poles marched single
file along country roads. And here and there deserted farms appeared. Somerset boasted
proudly of itself as "The Center of Health, Wealth, and Happiness," but agriculture was in
trouble.

The success of dairy farming was proving to be its own undoing. Too many farmers
were producing too much milk, and improved transportation allowed farmers as far away
as Pennsylvania and upper New York to sell in the same markets as Somerset. Glut de-
pressed prices and induced farmers to increase output in order to realize the same income

from lower profits. The smarter they farmed, the greater the oversupply and the tighter the price squeeze. Farmers formed cooperatives; the one at Belle Mead was most enduring. They mechanized, modernized, and struggled to survive.

A demonstration agent from Rutgers Cooperative Extension Service was assigned to Somerset County in 1917 to help farmers remain competitive. Know-how and necessity pushed per-acre yields of hay, small grains, and corn to new highs. Milk and eggs remained the chief cash crops. There were also orchards and truck farms, and a unique goldfish hatchery along the Raritan, near North Branch, annually marketed 4 million fancy goldfish.

Understandably many farmers were of a mind to sell out, and some got their chance because social agencies had adopted the idea of building their institutions on the margins of metropolitan regions. In 1898 New Jersey purchased 1,000 acres near Skillman to establish the State Village for Epileptics and remove these unfortunates from a society that did not accept them. In 1910 Dr. John J. Kindred bought up 300 acres in Belle Mead for a farm colony and sanitarium to treat nervous and mental diseases, the forerunner of today's Carrier Foundation. Near Liberty Corner the Episcopal church acquired in 1920 almost 400 acres for Bonnie Brae, a working farm where homeless boys could grow up in wholesome surroundings. And in 1928 the United States chose 700 acres at Lyons for the nation's second-largest facility to care for veterans suffering from neuropsychiatric disorders.

Rural settings also appealed to religious organizations. The Pillar of Fire had assembled 500 acres along the Delaware & Raritan Canal in Franklin by 1908 and named their settlement Zarephath; hundreds more acres were added in the years which followed.

Leading community citizens gathered to participate in the ground-breaking ceremony for a new Somerville school on Cliff Street in the early 1900s. The construction of proper educational facilities to meet the needs of a growing population was just one of the challenges facing Somerset County as it advanced into the twentieth century. Courtesy, Somerset Messenger-Gazette

Bands of itinerant gypsies were not an uncommon sight traveling the roads of Somerset County in the early years of this century. This family was photographed with their gaily painted wagon at their encampment along the Raritan River near Somerville around 1910. Courtesy, Special Collections/Alexander Library/Rutgers University

Ukrainian refugees from the Bolshevik Revolution acquired acreage near South Bound Brook in 1928 and subsequently added to their holdings to establish a national home for their branch of the Orthodox church. A Lutheran sisterhood, unhappy in Hitler's Germany, transplanted their work to Liberty Corner in 1933, acquiring properties for a religious training school, a Bible conference center, and a nursing home they named Liberty Deaconry.

Real estate speculators were also big buyers of farmland. New construction materials, such as cinder blocks and asphalt shingles, were making a home in the suburbs affordable to thousands more New York commuters. Middle management and white-collar workers filled up block after block with their comfortable new homes, and paper streets fringed every town in the expectation of still more to come.

Public water supply became imperative. It was the first order of business for Peapack-Gladstone after the borough separated from Bedminster Township in 1912. Trouble over sewers led to Far Hills dropping out of Bernards and assuming borough status in 1921, and a flurry of agitation over roads and police protection convinced Bernardsville to make the same move in 1924.

Somerset's growing communities had many of their needs met by enterprising businessmen who saw money to be made in local utility companies. Bound Brook Water Co. built reservoirs in Chimney Rock gorge. Somerville Water Co. announced such ambitious

plans for trunk mains that town fathers panicked and filed suit to halt the project. In Bernardsville the chief promoter of the electric, water, and ice companies was a benevolent millionaire, Samuel S. Childs.

As a young man Childs had left his father's nearby farm, started a restaurant in New York City, and built his venture into a successful nationwide chain. Having amassed a considerable fortune, Childs returned to his old home community and interested himself largely in public affairs. He served in the U.S. Senate, 1902-1905. Later he caught sight of the potential for an entirely new kind of restaurant, one catering to the motoring public, and his Old Mill Inn became a landmark on the picturesque road between Bernardsville and Morristown.

Towns gained a dual advantage from water mains: safe drinking water and improved fire protection. But public water supply also accelerated the emergence of a fresh problem: more and more people flushing more and more water down sewers was seriously polluting the Raritan River. In 1907 the state ordered Somerville and towns downstream to treat their

sewage, but none paid much heed. Local officials were far more concerned with satisfying the demands of their own electorates. Citizens were clamoring for improved streets, garbage collection, and better schools.

In the last quarter of the nineteenth century, elementary education in New Jersey was made compulsory. High school was made free to all, and enrollments were increasing. When a graduate of Somerville's "colored school" applied to enter high school, the board of education found itself obliged to integrate; it was either that or stand the expense of his transportation and tuition to another high school.

In its heyday Raritan Valley Farms produced some 4,000 quarts of milk per day and was by far the largest dairy farm in Somerset County. Joseph S. Frelinghuysen was president of the company, and Anton Schieferstein served as manager of dairy operations. This enterprise was so impressive that it undoubtedly helped Frelinghuysen gain the appointment as New Jersey's first secretary of agriculture in 1911. The Ethicon plant now occupies much of this farmland. Courtesy, Special Collections/Alexander Library/ Rutgers University

Somerville's change of policy influenced the Reverend William D. Robeson to accept the pastorate of St. Thomas AME Zion Church, and his son, in due course, became the high school's star pupil.

Paul Robeson was president of the Class of 1915 and valedictorian, a football hero, debating champ, and glee club soloist. Outstanding as he was, no one in town dreamed when he set off for Rutgers College that he would quickly achieve world renown as a singer, actor, and civil rights activist. Paul Robeson had won their friendship, and they simply wished him well.

However, more than schools, water, or sewers, the most eagerly demanded form of progress was improved transportation. In the 1890s it seemed electric trolley cars would soon be taking everybody everywhere. Promoters scrambled for interurban routes and talked of trolleys to Peapack, a trolley line through the Millstone Valley, and one from Plainfield to Washingtonville (Watchung). The latter was built as far as Johnston Drive, at the base of the hill. But the only through route established in Somerset County ran from Plainfield to Raritan, with connections at Bound Brook carbarns for New Brunswick.

Rivalry for this franchise was fierce. New York and Philadelphia Traction Co. (NY&P), pushing westward from Plainfield, and Brunswick Traction Co., coming up the Raritan Valley, both applied to Bridgewater for permission to proceed. Paralyzed by indecision the township committee delayed choosing for so long, NY&P wearied of waiting and decided in 1897 to build first and argue later.

Work began in the wee hours of a Saturday night, and the countryside roused from slumber. Township committeemen were summoned. They sent for the sheriff and he assembled a posse of deputies. Brunswick Traction urged wholesale arrests. But on whose authority? NY&P gangs went right on working. By Monday tracks were laid. By Tuesday wires were strung, a dynamo was in place, and cars began running. By Friday a court order halted operations.

It took more than a year of legal unraveling to start the cars running again. After that the line was taken over by Public Service of NJ, extended to Raritan, and for 30 years trolleys rumbled and screeched their way back and forth to Plainfield. At first, just about everyone rode. Trolleys were so much handier than the train and cheaper too. But trolleys began losing out to automobiles after World War I and ceased running by 1933. Henceforth roads not rails were to shape the future.

Rural Somerset had little clout in the political games which initially determined where state highways would run, but central location was reason enough to bring it two of the 15 routes in New Jersey's first intrastate highway system announced in 1917. Route No. 9, from Elizabeth to Phillipsburg, followed the old Swiftsure Stage road across Somerset (Route 28), and Route No. 13 followed the old stage route from New Brunswick to Princeton (Route 27). Good-roads advocates in Somerset wanted far more than this, how-

ever, so county and township governments came increasingly under pressure.

By state law, if property owners along a county road petitioned to have it improved and agreed to share the cost, it had to be done. Some used this form of persuasion in Somerset, but the resulting improvement was little more than a layer of broken stone laid over the old roadbed, and these stone roads left a lot to be desired. For one thing automobile traffic tore up the stone surface; for another, stone roads were bad for horses to run on, so drivers of fast road horses kept off to one side, creating, in effect, two roadways side by side. Twice as much road therefore had to be maintained. As far as the Somerset County Board of Chosen Freeholders could see, the only gains from road improvements were

ABOVE: Somerset County's developing communities experienced the need for expanded local services and utilities in the early years of the 1900s. Here, the fire fighters of the Far Hills Union Hook & Ladder Company No. 1 proudly pose for a group portrait in 1915. Courtesy, Anne O'Brien Collection, Clarence Dillon Public Library, Bedminster

LEFT: These young Warren Township students were photographed in the early 1900s as they made their way to class in this early horse-drawn school bus. Courtesy, Warren Township Historical Society

added headaches and added expense.

America's entry into World War I gave freeholders an excuse to do nothing about roads for a while. The war also brought to the county an encampment by Company M, First Infantry, on the outskirts of Somerville, and hundreds of horses awaiting shipment overseas put out to pasture on the Raritan meadows in Finderne. When the war was over and the county board still talked of filling potholes, patience came to an end. A big public meeting was called, at which freeholders were told in no uncertain terms that Somerset County had the worst roads in the state; so bad, they were a joke to everyone but those who had to use them. A north-south highway the length of the county was urged, and Wall Street men from Somerset Hills said they would personally handle a bond issue to pay for it so that there need be no worry about financing. Frugal freeholders saw things differently: The county was still paying off bonds for its 1907 courthouse; that was debt enough, they said.

After that meeting, good-roads agitators stopped arguing and started circulating petitions to change county government. Instead of each township electing a free-holder to represent them on the county board, reformers urged that a three-man board be elected at large and that these three be paid annual salaries instead of per diem stipends, to ensure that their time and attention would be devoted to running the county. Objectors decried centralized control, but a referendum passed handily. Riding the coattails of Warren G. Harding's 1920 landslide victory, Republicans filled every seat on the new, smaller board, thus beginning a political denomination that has endured with but one interruption for 70 years.

The son of a Methodist minister, Paul Robeson grew up in Somerville where his father was pastor of the St. Thomas AME Zion Church. Following graduation from Somerville High School, where he was named valedictorian and elected president of the class of 1915, Robeson attended Rutgers University, lettering in four varsity sports, and earning a Phi Beta Kappa Key. Robeson went on to earn a law degree from Columbia University and become a world-renowned singer, actor, and civil rights leader. He is pictured here (second row, center) with fellow teammates at Rutgers in 1915. Courtesy, Special Collections/Alexander Library/ Rutgers University

Two members on the new Somerset County board were carryovers from the big board; nevertheless, work on a north-south highway (Route 202-206) was begun the following year—not so much because freeholder attitudes had changed, as because astute lobbying in the statehouse had added a Trenton-Morristown highway to the state road network.

Counties were authorized to build roads according to state specifications. To undertake the project, Somerset engaged a new county engineer, Harry C. Van Emburgh. He was well versed in the latest methods of permanent road construction and built not only the state road, but county roads, as well, in conformance with newly set standards for portland cement. He also replaced obsolete bridges with new and larger ones. Van Emburgh was long remembered in Somerset as a man who built things to last.

In the 1920s road building by the state, counties, and townships was a big stimulus to quarry operations, and Somerset became the state's leading producer of traprock, a preemi-

ABOVE: The increasing popularity of automobiles created a need for new and improved state highways, and Somerset County's central location brought it two of the 15 intrastate highways planned in 1917. This new mode of transportation also prompted petroleum and oil companies to open filling stations; this early one in Somerset County promoted "That Good Gulf Gasoline." Courtesy, Somerville Free Public Library

LEFT: It took quite a while for Somerset County roads to improve enough to accomodate the automobile. Drivers who braved the hazards of these dirt roads sometimes lost wheels and went out of control, crashing through fences into the farmer's fields. Courtesy, Somerset Messenger-Gazette

Most of America celebrated the end of World War I during the summer of 1919, and Somerville's festivities included elaborate floats depicting themes in United States history. This display shows a soldier returning home to Lady Liberty. Courtesy, Somerset Messenger-Gazette

nence which has continued to 1990. Crushed stone surpassed the dwindling textile industry in economic importance by 1930. But this industry was in turn overshadowed by the emergence of major new manufacturing plants. Two new companies, H.W. Johns-Manville and Calco, employed more than a thousand workers each, while small local enterprises—mills, creameries, foundries, machine shops, and factories—ceased to be prime sources of employment.

One of Somerset's first major industries grew out of an earlier small one—South Bound Brook's Standard Paint Co., a manufacturer of roofing tar. In 1892 William Griscom, superintendent of the works, hit on the idea of coating roofing felt with Standard's asphalt tar and thereby produced a new material which made roofing a one-step operation. This product was selling well when it occurred to someone to cut the roll into shingle-size pieces and imbed stone chips in the tar surface. Sold under the trade name Rubberoid, these shingles were so successful, the company adopted the name of its product and was for decades an industry leader. Eventually it had plants in 15 states in addition to its home factory in South Bound Brook, which employed 300 workers. Under the stimulus of Rubberoid, South Bound Brook's population doubled between 1900 and 1930.

Rocky Hill similarly experienced a spurt of growth thanks to a successful industry. The old brickworks along the Delaware & Raritan Canal was taken over in 1907 by Excelsior Terra Cotta, and they quickly prospered from a vogue for this decorative building

In the presidential campaign of 1904, Democrats opposing Teddy Roosevelt set up this booth and held a rally in Olcott Square in Bernardsville. Courtesy, Bernardsville Public Library

material. Atlantic Terra Cotta stepped in and further expanded the operation until, in its heyday, the plant was employing about 400 workers, a great many of whom were Italian artisans skilled in the highly specialized processes of making pieces to customers' exact specifications. Two of Atlantic's most notable commissions were the red and blue tile roof of Philadelphia Art Museum and the gleaming white exterior of the Woolworth Building in New York.

Atlantic Terra Cotta flourished only so long as architectural style demanded its product. When the plant shut down in the 1930s, Rocky Hill experienced a significant drop in population.

Loss of a single key industry was even more devastating for East Millstone. There, the Fleischmann distillery had expanded upon an older operation, and its output of rye whiskey was aged in a bonded warehouse which at that time was the largest in the United States. Fleischmann also marketed yeast derived from its fermentation process and fattened cattle for New York markets on spent mash. The Fleischmanns profited nicely and built themselves big houses. They raised prize livestock, kept fine horses and polo ponies, and built a racetrack. The village basked in the lustre of the good life, and local merchants did a thriving business. But in 1910 the distillery was relocated to Poughkeepsie, NY; most of the 50 hands and their families went along. A rubber reclaimer took over the buildings, but his operation needed fewer workers and it supplied little stimulus to the local economy. East Millstone never fully recovered.

For a large commuter town like Somerville, loss of its biggest industry was not as severe a blow. When repeal of protective tariffs forced Somerville Woolen Mill out of busi-

The Chimney Rock stone quarry north of Bound Brook has supplied stone for roads, buildings, and seashore jetties for some 100 years. In 1905, around the time this photograph was taken, William Haelig, the quarry's first owner, was killed when he was pinned beneath a railcar filled with stone. Courtesy, John Haelig

ness, the loss was offset by new plants. Somerville Iron Works, a foundry making cast-iron soil pipe, and a sister concern, Somerville Stove Works, together, employed close to 400. The mill building itself was taken over in 1909 by Cott-a-Lapp, a manufacturer of floor and wall coverings, and Redfern Lace Works opened next door in 1914, providing another 150 steady jobs.

Other woolen mills in the Raritan Valley did not succumb to foreign competition so quickly as Somerville. Looms continued to clatter profitably in Raritan and Bound Brook during the twenties, keeping a thousand workers employed. A silk mill in North Plainfield had a payroll of 200, and there were numerous small sewing factories in the towns of the valley, as well.

Industrial diversity was spreading, however. And nowhere was this more evident than in Bound Brook. Its population tripled in 30 years, partly from an infusion of New York commuters, but more from an influx of Italian, Hungarian, and Polish immigrants attracted by a wealth of new jobs. Federal Creosoting, Graphite Lubricating, Bound Brook Oil-Less Bearing, Hemingway Chemicals, and Sherwin Williams—making pigments and acids—were all significant employers. Bigger still was Pathe Freres, a maker of film for the new motion pictures industry; it had a work force of 250. But Calco Chemical Co., just west of town, eclipsed them all.

Calco, Somerset County's biggest homegrown success story, was born of shortages induced by economic blockades during World War I. Overnight, German-made aniline oil, the basis for hundreds of widely used dyestuffs, became unobtainable. American scientists scrambled to unlock the secrets of its manufacture, and a rank amateur at Cott-a-Lapp in Somerville, guided by a chemistry textbook, stumbled onto the answer. Having succeeded in producing a small amount, he submitted a sample to a midwestern firm to see if they would find it acceptable and place an order. Indeed they would, for as much as Cott-a-Lapp

LEFT: When the Somerville Iron Works caught fire and exploded in the early 1900s, 250 men lost their jobs. Courtesy, Somerville Free Public Library

BELOW: The Johns-Manville Company was for half a century one of the biggest industries in Somerset County. The town of Manville developed around this successful enterprise, enticing new residents who were searching for steady work and a decent wage. Pictured here at the peak of productivity in 1948, the Johns-Manville facility employed more than 3,000 workers. Courtesy, Manville Public Library

ABOVE: The H.W. Johns-Manville Company purchased 300 acres of farmland in Hillsborough Township and began construction of an asbestos products plant in 1912. The lure of new jobs attracted a diverse ethnic work force and many new businesses were established to serve them. One such enterprise was the store of Bellomo and Saia, which featured a variety of canned goods, Gold Dust washing powder, and Cocomalt. Shown here in the early 1920s, the store was destroyed by fire not long after this photograph was taken. Courtesy, Alan Moore

RIGHT: Textbooks and puzzles were in order for the day's studies at this Manville school in the early 1900s. The varied nationalities of Manville's burgeoning population are apparent in the somber faces of these attentive schoolchildren. Courtesy, Somerset Messenger-Gazette

could supply. Output commenced with all possible speed, but then Somerville, perceiving there might well be noxious odors and other unpleasantness, objected to any expansion of chemical production in the Cott-a-Lapp plant. Operations were relocated to a suitably isolated 18-acre spread along the Raritan River.

A new company was formed to take over the oil production part of the business and was given the name Calco, an acronym for Cott-a-Lapp Co. Before long a small complex of buildings was operating at capacity. More land was purchased, and more buildings went up. Calco rapidly grew to be a chemical "city." It sprawled over 400 acres and was employing more than 1,000 people when it was taken over by American Cyanamid in 1929.

Two miles upstream an even bigger success story was unfolding at the same time. In 1911 H. W. Johns-Manville Co. of Brooklyn had decided to transfer its manufacturing operations to a rural location where it could grow as demand for its miracle fireproof asbestos products increased. Abundant water supply and three railroads made 200 acres of Hillsborough farmland at the confluence of the Millstone and Raritan rivers an ideal location for a modern, well-lit, fireproof factory.

When construction of the one-story factory started in 1912, the word was that the company would also build homes for 600 workers. But that was not Johns-Manville's style of operation. The company preferred to let hands look after themselves and only minimally accommodated workers' housing needs—by running trucks back and forth to Finderne, so men could catch the trolley to Bound Brook or Somerville.

Real estate speculators went into action almost as soon as Johns-Manville steam shovels did. They bought up nearby farms, converted the dwellings into boarding houses, and divided the land into 25-foot lots, which were peddled to immigrant families in Brooklyn, Bayonne, Jersey City, and the coal towns of Pennsylvania. Excursion trains brought prospective buyers to see this wonderful place in the country where they could purchase on the installment plan enough land for a house, a garden patch, a few fruit trees, and some chickens and still be within walking distance of a paying job; there was no shortage of buyers.

Soon horse-drawn scoops blazed roads across Manville's fields. Builders sketched floor plans on bits of paper and sealed the deal with a handshake. Hundreds of homes went up. Harmony Plains School overflowed, as did a bigger one which replaced it. A polyglot population of Poles, Ukrainians, Slavs, Carpathians, Germans, Hungarians, and Italians, fiercely proud of their American way of life, organized churches, fire companies, social clubs, a savings and loan, and a bank. But for paved streets, better schools, and improved sanitation, they had to look to Hillsborough Township; and Manville's pleas stirred little action. Although the new town had twice the population of the rest of the township, almost none of its inhabitants were eligible to vote.

Manville in the 1920s was known for good ball players, lively dances, and plentiful speakeasies. Scoffers loved to tell about the motorist who stopped there for a

The well-to-do Borough of Watchung boasted an actual castle in the early 1900s, known to the community as "Elsinore." Built by noted scientist and author Dr. Richard Modlenke in honor of his mother, this fascinating structure was located just off Valley Road. Courtesy, Margaret Demler

drink and found, on returning to his car, that a hen had laid an egg on the seat. What boisterous, backward Manville needed, according to some critics, was stricter enforcement of Prohibition and Sunday Blue Laws so the morals of its children would not be corrupted. Others simply smiled and shrugged. But Manville's shortcomings were not so comical when their fine, big fire truck got stuck in the mud and a house burned down. Laughter died away altogether once its people began taking out citizenship papers and influencing the outcome of local elections. The town of 5,000 and the township of 2,000, both, became eager for a parting of the ways, and a 1929 referendum brought it about—unanimously.

Although Somerset County welcomed growing numbers of blue-collar workers whose energy and thrift added substantially to local prosperity; old-timers, the expanding middle class, and the educated elite had no wish to mingle with these people. This was a class-conscious society that carefully cultivated the separation of "haves" and "have-nots." Formation of the Borough of Watchung in 1926 effectively served this spirit of aloofness. Tucked away behind the first mountain ridge were the homes of well-to-do commuters whose coachmen drove them each morning to the station in Plainfield.

In the 1920s congenial neighbors began finding their way by automobile into the pretty valley around the lake which had once been a millpond. The Borough of Watchung consisted of the little village of Washingtonville and about 600 people spread out over six square miles when it voted itself a separate existence from the Township of North Plain-

The Revolutionary Memorial Society was formed in 1896 to purchase and maintain the Wallace House in Somerville. In just one year this group raised sufficient funds to purchase the building, and it continued to maintain the facility until the historic site became the property of the state of New Jersey in 1947. Members of the society posed for a group portrait in front of the Wallace House on June 7, 1930. Courtesy, Special Collections/Alexander Library/Rutgers University

field. What was left of the township—the portion that was building up along the trolley line and new state highways—changed its name in 1932 to Green Brook.

The same year Watchung gained borough status, it also gained a golf course, built to replace North Plainfield's Hydewood, which was about to be transformed into building lots. Country club enthusiasts ceded two other golf courses to home builders as well: the Middle Brook in Bound Brook and the Somerset County course in Finderne. These were not going to be just ordinary homes though. Deed restrictions assured buyers the type of houses to be built would attract the "right kind" of people. As for golfers, they did not lack places to play. New links were being established. There were two in northern Somerset County: Penn Brook in Bernards and Somerset Hills in Bernardsville. And just outside Somerville was the popular Raritan Valley Country Club, a pet project of U.S. Senator Joseph S. Frelinghuysen.

A direct descendant of Somerset's Revolutionary War hero, Colonel Frederick Frelinghuysen, the senator owned some 900 acres, much of it inherited. Having made a comfortable fortune in the insurance business, he built up a huge model dairy farm in Raritan. It was so impressive that when the secretary of agriculture post was created in 1911, he was the natural choice to fill the position. While serving in the U.S. Senate (1917-1923), Frelinghuysen became a golfing buddy of Senator Warren G. Harding (later U.S. president) and on occasion invited him to spend a weekend playing the Raritan Valley course. A 1921 visit briefly made Frelinghuysen's Mansion in Raritan the focus of the national spotlight because it coincided with the end of U.S. Senate deliberations on terms for a treaty to end World War I. A messenger was dispatched from Washington to obtain the chief executive's signature as soon as possible. When he arrived, he was kept waiting two hours for the president to come in from his game, take out his fountain pen, and make peace official.

Reverend Edward Wheeler Hall, rector of St. John the Evangelist Episcopal Church in New Brunswick, was murdered in 1922, along with his paramour Eleanor Mills, a church member who was soloist for the choir. The bodies were found inside the Somerset County line, so the Widow Hall and her two brothers were tried in the Somerset County Courthouse. Among the evidence presented to the jury were the Panama hat and glasses of the Reverend Hall, shown here. Courtesy, Special Collections/Alexander Library/ Rutgers University

Significant political and historical events only rarely took place in Somerset. Outside of commuter towns the county was sufficiently out-of-the-way to appeal in Prohibition years to those producing illegal alcohol. Bootleggers had no difficulty renting unwanted farms where they could set up their stills and be within easy delivery distance of New York. Who was going to interfere, a township constable? The sheriff? The county prosecutor and his detective? A new state police force had been created to serve rural areas and had taken over the former Kenilworth Hotel in Pluckemin as its Somerset County barracks, but state troopers patrolled the highways, not backroads. Except when internal revenue agents called on local lawmen to back them up in a raid, there was little zeal for enforcing federal anti-liquor laws—except by white-robed members of the Ku Klux Klan.

Revived during the 1920s as a crusade against "the evil influences of Catholics, for-

The Somerville Fire Department celebrated its centennial on September 11, 1935, with community festivities and demonstrations of skill and bravery. Courtesy, Somerset Messenger-Gazette

eigners, and booze," the Klan easily attracted a following in Somerset. They burned crosses on the hillsides and established Owanamassie Country Club in Pluckemin as their headquarters. Somerville hosted a "Klanvocation" attended by thousands whose massed ranks paraded down Main Street, and 12,000 members from all over the Northeast assembled in Middlebush in 1923.

Also during the 1920s, sleepy Somerset proved to be the ideal milieu to dispose of a couple corpses. On September 16, 1922, just beyond the end of a New Brunswick trolley line, off DeRussey's Lane (Franklin Boulevard) in Franklin Township, two bodies were found under a crabapple tree. They were identified as the Reverend Edward Wheeler Hall, rector of St. John the Evangelist in New Brunswick, and Mrs. Eleanor Mills, his church choir's soprano soloist. Love letters the pair had exchanged were strewn around them.

By the time it was decided that the crime fell under Somerset jurisdiction and the county physician arrived from Somerville, thrill-seekers had overrun the site and obliterated any clues there might have been. For want of hard evidence, a Somerset grand jury returned no indictments. Four years later, in 1926, after renewed investigation by a special state prosecutor, the wealthy Widow Hall and her brothers were arrested and charged with murder. Two hundred reporters besieged Somerset County's stately courthouse throughout the month-long trial, turning it into a national sensation. The verdict was delivered after only five hours of deliberation: not guilty.

Outsiders who focused their attention on Somerset during this episode saw the county as being behind the times and backwards. But the county considered itself to be strong and vigorous and keeping pace in an era of progress. The new county government had heeded the mandate for paved roads; it had completely indexed all the records of the county clerk and surrogate; and it had added a home demonstration agent and a public health nurse to county services. A 1929 referendum approved the start of a county library; and in 1931, for the first time, freeholders approved a county budget exceeding one million dollars.

On the eve of the nation's Great Depression, Somerset could point proudly to 10 banks, nine savings and loans, seven newspapers, four high schools, six parochial schools, and 89 churches of 29 sects and denominations. There were two hospitals, one in Somerville, the other in Bound Brook. State highways crisscrossed the county east to west and north to south. Half of the 806 miles of roadway lacing the county together were classified as "improved," and of 150 miles of through roads maintained by the county, 50 were permanently paved. One person in five had a car.

Like all of New Jersey, Somerset was hard hit by the prolonged economic slump of the 1930s. Factories cut production and laid off workers. The woolen mills in Raritan and Bound Brook shut down for good. The Borough of Manville—which had gone heavily in debt to build schools, pave streets, lay sidewalks, install sewers and water, and build up a police department—defaulted on its bonds because it was unable to collect taxes from unemployed citizens. The state stepped in to supervise the running of the bankrupt municipality. But, bad as things were, the Manville National Bank never foreclosed a mortgage during the Depression; bank officers knew their people and knew they were good for the money just as soon as they got back to work.

Not all effects of the Depression were unfortunate. Federal make-work programs brought Somerset numerous capital improvements. Bridgewater received schools; Hillsborough, a township hall; Somerville and Manville, sewage treatment plants; Mt. Bethel, a fire-house; and dualization of Route 29 (Route 22) went forward. By 1938 the worst of the bad times were over, and renewing confidence lent extraordinary enthusiasm to the pageants and parties and giant parade marking Somerset County's 250th anniversary.

Athletics and other forms of local entertainment were popular diversions during the harsh years of the Depression as this spirited portrait of an unsung hero of Somerville's 1935 football season illustrates. Courtesy, Somerville Free Public Library

THE MOVE OUT OF TOWN

SOMERSET ANTICIPATED FRESH GROWTH AND DEVELOPMENT WHEN THE GREAT DEPRESSION of the 1930s began yielding to an improved economic climate, but no one foresaw the transformation this next boom would work on their county. Nor did they anticipate that the all-out national effort to win World War II would postpone the boom for an entire decade.

Unlike any previous war, this one meant much more than men going off to fight while folks at home contended with shortages and soaring prices. Somerset found itself very much a part of the war effort. Johns-Manville and Calco worked round the clock. Women manned assembly lines. All across the countryside volunteer airspotters of the Ground Observer Corps kept 24-hour vigil, in four-hour shifts, just in case of an enemy strike. Bluffs along the Raritan River in Franklin were the base for radio towers beaming Voice of America messages to occupied Europe. And all outdoor display lights and neon signs had to be turned off for the war's duration in a dimout ordered so glare from lights reflected in the night sky did not silhouette coastal shipping and create targets for submarines.

Proximity to the coast together with railroad arteries made Somerset the chosen location for two vast marshalling depots where war materiel was assembled for shipment overseas. Hundreds of acres at Roycefield and at Belle Mead were summarily seized by the United States government; without prior notice farmers were given only from Monday morning to Friday afternoon to remove their families, goods, livestock, equipment, and stores to make way for row after row of government warehouses. No housing was put up, though, for the 3,000 workers recruited to man these huge facilities. Somerville hotels

converted dining rooms into dormitories. Homeowners were petitioned to rent out spare rooms. The county jail was besieged nightly by pleas for a bed. Many workers simply slept in their cars.

Belle Mead Depot, by war's end also a prisoner-of-war camp for Italian soldiers, was taken over postwar by the U.S. General Services Administration and used for stockpiling the nation's reserves of strategic materials. South Somerville Depot was turned over to the U.S. Veterans Administration and used as a warehousing and distributing center.

Tumultuous victory celebrations in every town were a prelude to the return of thousands of servicemen eager to settle down and raise families; 236 did not return. After a time their families took down the red-bordered, gold star flags from front windows, and the world around forgot their names and faces. Only one, Raritan's hometown hero, Marine Sergeant John Basilone, awarded the Congressional Medal of Honor for resolutely manning machine guns on Guadalcanal in the face of unremitting Japanese attacks, is still remembered a half-century later, his bravery immortalized by a life-size, bronze statue at the west end of town. Raritan went mad with jubilation when "Manilla John" came home. The parade stretched for miles. Twenty thousand turned out to welcome him. But John Basilone, rather than face more crowds, chose to face more bullets. He was killed going ashore at Iwo Jima.

Most returning GIs had their dreams put on hold by lingering wartime shortages. There were no cars to buy; there weren't even tires for the relics still on the road. Worse yet, homes for newlyweds were impossible to find. A fortunate few were assigned places in

City leaders and local residents gathered for Somerville's Inspection Day Parade in 1948. Fire Chief Lou Spine led the way with Otto Leichtleitner, William McCrea, and John Carberry following close behind. Fireman Alex Tozzi is seen on the right driving the Lincoln Hose Company truck. Courtesy, Somerset Messenger-Gazette

the emergency housing developments that had gone up near war's end at the Belle Mead Depot and on the outskirts of Manville. Lots of couples moved in with parents. Some made do with converted garages or chicken houses. What good was a GI mortgage requiring almost no down payment if there was nothing to buy?

For the next few years builders enjoyed a bonanza; whatever they put up had a ready market. A new garden-apartment concept caught the fancy of young, upscale renters. Whole tracts of little, look-alike "Victory" homes rapidly sold out. Edward Chandler, an enterprising Somerville businessman, switched from making prefabricated garages to homes people could assemble themselves. When demand for his "Well Built" homes slowed down, Chandler cloned his factory building and created Somerset County's first industrial park, off Route 22 along Chimney Rock Road in Bridgewater.

Local Boy Scouts prepare for a canoeing expedition along the Raritan River in the quiet years of the 1920s. Courtesy, Somerset Messenger-Gazette

Builders of more conventional housing scarcely noticed a slowdown when the postwar surge had spent itself. A mass exodus from city to suburbs fueled markets for their "ranch" homes in the fifties and "split-levels" in the sixties. County population doubled between 1940 and 1960. Over the next decade the pace continued.

New York was emptying into New Jersey through the Holland and Lincoln tunnels. Old cities this side of the Hudson were adding more thousands to the stream of exurbanites in search of new beginnings. No longer dependent on railroads, people were willing to go wherever their cars could take them, and Route 29 (later Route 22), dualized as far as Somerville before the war, funneled the outpouring into Somerset County. People were spilling out of Plainfield and New Brunswick and Morristown, as well. And older towns within the county, while absorbing a great many newcomers, were seeing their own sons and daughters move out into surrounding townships. There, taxes were lower, and a larger lot cost less because farmers were glad to turn a dollar by cashing in some road frontage.

Thus, between 1940 and 1960, while North Plainfield, Bound Brook, and South Bound Brook, Somerville and Raritan, Manville and Bernardsville all experienced noteworthy growth; the populations of Warren and Bernards townships doubled; Branchburg, Bridgewater, Hillsborough, Franklin, and Watchung tripled; and Green Brook was engulfed by a four-fold increase.

Business was no less intent on moving out of town. Downtown parking space had become miserably inadequate, and introducing parking meters served only to compound

ABOVE: This view along Mine Brook Road (Route 202) in 1954 shows the flourishing growth Bernardsville was experiencing in the postwar years. Courtesy, Bernardsville Public Library

LEFT: Some Somerset County farmers clung to the old way of life even after the postwar boom in the midtwentieth century. Edwin W. Huff, Sr., shown here working his land in the late 1940s, ran a large sheep and dairy farm in Branchburg Township using horses to power his equipment. Huff maintained 10 teams of horses to cultivate his vast acreage. Courtesy, Special Collections/Alexander Library/Rutgers University

the annoyance. Flight to the highways accelerated as the fifties advanced. Two of New Jersey's early major shopping centers chose to locate within the county: Somerset Shopping Center, on the traffic circle where routes 202 and 206 converge; and Blue Star Shopping Center, on Route 22 in Watchung. Paradoxically, attaching the Blue Star name to a shopping plaza eclipsed public awareness of Blue Star Memorial Drive—a five-mile stretch of highway between Watchung and Mountainside planted with 8,000 flowering dogwood as a tribute to men and women who answered their nation's call to the colors during World War II. The memorial highway concept was initiated by the Garden Club of New Jersey with fond hopes of beautifying the entire length of this cross-state traffic artery and keeping it free of billboards and commercial ugliness.

To public officials eager to generate revenues by taxing businesses, a more appealing alternative to filling stations, hot-dog stands, and discount outlets was campus-style industry set in acres of green lawn. First on the Somerset scene was Johnson & Johnson (J&J).

They purchased most of Joseph Frelinghuysen's Raritan Valley Farms acreage and in 1947 sited their Ortho division in a sleek high rise on Route 202 in Raritan. Subsequently, J&J brought its Ethicon suture manufacturing operation to another part of the tract on the north side of Route 22 in Bridgewater. Lockheed Electronics moved its plant from Brooklyn to Route 22 in Watchung, and in 1955 RCA chose acreage on Route 202 in Bridgewater for its new semiconductor division. A few miles east on Route 22, Mack Truck Co. built a major parts-distribution center.

Off the highway other technology-driven companies moved into campus settings: Burroughs, in Warren, making electronic components; Research Cottrell, in Finderne, producing pollution control devices; and Hercules Powder Co., in Rocky Hill, manufacturing specialty fibers. Somerset could boast of two new homegrown success stories as well: Komline-Sanderson, in Peapack, making components for sewage treatment plants; and Frank W. Egan & Co., in Finderne, producing specialty machinery.

The old giants, American Cyanamid (Calco) with 3,200 workers and Johns-Manville with 3,700, were still the biggest employers in the county, but they no longer dominated its job market. Somerset had a diversity of large and small manufacturers of all sorts and an expanding retail and service sector. By 1960 more workers were commuting into the county than out.

Somerset's burgeoning industry, commerce, and population gained ground at the agricultural community's expense. Between 1954 and 1959 the county lost 28 percent of its remaining farmland. Even so, broad acres of crops and pastures invited Sunday drivers to leave main roads and enjoy rural vistas. There were still a few orchards and truck farms. Price supports and bulk milk systems were enabling some dairymen to survive, and poultrymen for a time profited from batteries of laying hens.

Many of the chicken farmers were city folk with a yen for life in the country who bought a few acres and went into the egg business. Quite a colony of them sprang up in

By 1957 U.S. Route 22 was more of an economic artery than U.S. Route 1, loaded with heavy trucks rolling between points west and east. The New Jersey State Police manned safety checkpoints to monitor the truckers and their loads. Courtesy, the Courier-News, *Bridgewater*

Franklin, near South Bound Brook. There were a good many in Hillsborough, too, along Sunnymead and Hillsborough Roads and over toward Neshanic. South Somerville Poultry Farm on Route 206 was one of the largest in the state. It pioneered the development of automated feeding and egg-handling and expanded egg production to previously unimagined volumes: at a time when a 10,000-bird operation was considered big, this farm housed 250,000 hens and sold eggs by the thousands of dozens.

Although there was still money to be made in agriculture, rising taxes were forcing farmers, one by one, to call it quits. The same paved roads that the preceding generation had fought for so they could transport produce to town were now bringing the town to the country, and with it the need for schools and police departments. Under New Jersey's system of property tax, a disproportionate share of the cost was pushed onto farmers. Relief came in 1964 when a statewide referendum approved a constitutional amendment allowing farmland tax assessments to be calculated on a differential basis, but it came too late to save very many of Somerset's family farms. The majority had already conceded defeat and sold out to land speculators who offered appetizing prices. Farmland assessments nevertheless preserved much of the county's rural ambience because "gentlemen farmers" mindful of tax advantages found it an attractive location for raising prize dairy herds and fine horses

Among the myriad duties carried out by country pastors was the tending of church stoves. Here, we see the pastor of the Pluckemin Presbyterian Church carrying his coal buckets, and though this photograph looks like an image from the 1890s, it was actually taken in the late 1940s. Courtesy, Special Collections/ Alexander Library/Rutgers University

and because speculators contracted to keep their acreage planted with crops until a time when development would prove more advantageous.

Increased development was inevitable, especially after federal highway engineers laid out the nation's interstate freeway system. The New York circumferential Interstate 287 was planned to loop around the western slope of the Somerset Hills and intersect the east-west Interstate 78 at Pluckemin. When these routes were announced in 1959, scouts from every major oil company came scurrying to Somerset in search of the best location at what was sure to be one of the crossroads of the East. But no neon nightmare of filling stations, eateries, and motels materialized; highway authorities and county and local officials agreed to make it a dry interchange with no immediate access to local roads. North-south Interstate 95 was also slated to traverse the county. Its route was laid out to run the length of Franklin Township, but reservoir plans compromised the alignment, and disagreements thwarted efforts to find an acceptable alternative.

Reservoirs also worked against plans for a political career Malcolm Forbes had launched in Somerset County by ringing 18,000 doorbells and upsetting the old country custom of choosing men with well-known family names and solid local reputations. Ambitious young Forbes possessed neither when he offered himself as a candidate for Congress in 1949; he was just

Somerville was enjoying the prosperous years of postwar America when this photograph was taken in 1949. Courtesy, the Courier-News, *Bridgewater*

one more veteran who had bought a home in Bernardsville and become a New York commuter. Passed over for that nomination, Forbes spent a solid year personally introducing himself to voters and effectively short-circuited political tradition to win Somerset's seat in the state senate the following year.

Voters loved a maverick on the campaign trail but lost enthusiasm when Forbes played the maverick in Trenton and disregarded his constituents' objections to damming Chimney Rock gorge in order to create a giant reservoir in the heart of the county. Forbes endorsed the plan because it appeared to be in the state's best interest, but his efforts to play the statesman failed to win him the governorship in 1957. A disappointed Forbes abandoned politics after that to concentrate on magazine publishing.

The search for alternative north-south highway alignments focused on the Millstone Valley in the sixties. Outraged at the prospect, citizens organized a coalition to call attention to the environmental sensitivity of this watershed, the historic significance of the Delaware & Raritan Canal, and the overall beauty of the area. Their tactics were similar to those employed to fight off a jumbo jetport that the Port of New York Authority wanted to build on the northeastern border of Somerset in the Great Swamp headwaters of the Passaic River. Jetport fighters succeeded in initiating the 7,000-acre Great Swamp National Wildlife Refuge. The Millstone Valley coalition won National Register recognition for the D&R Canal and convinced New Jersey to make it a state park, with a special commission appointed by the governor to safeguard its preservation.

Foiled highway planners tried again and, in the 1970s, achieved a consensus for Interstate 95 to parallel the Reading Railroad across Hillsborough and Montgomery and connect with Interstate 287 in Franklin, near South Bound Brook. But in the process of preparing detailed plans, the agreement unraveled. Protracted protests and squabbles all along the route finally convinced federal highway authorities to abandon attempts to build Interstate 95 across New Jersey and spend monies appropriated for it on other highway

The sprawling Johns-Manville complex, seen here in the 1970s, was one of the largest emloyers in Somerset County before the company relocated to Colorado. Courtesy, the Courier-News, *Bridgewater*

projects.

Hillsborough was not a bit pleased. It was anticipating industrial development along the Interstate-95 corridor and wanted the income that those businesses would generate. To overcome this disappointment county and state put forward a plan to build the stub end of the freeway from Belle Mead to Interstate 287 and call it Somerset Expressway. An alignment for this highway was still being studied in 1990.

Eagerness to attract industrial businesses had mounted as spreading suburbia pushed property taxes higher and higher. Schools were the biggest expense. The postwar housing boom obliged county districts to build four new high schools and 18 new elementary schools and to add to 27 existing schools by 1960. In the next decade six more high schools and 18 more elementary schools went up, plus 28 school additions. On top of these capital outlays, districts faced rising per-pupil costs as class sizes were lowered and curriculum was enriched to ensure quality education. As a result homeowners felt they were being clobbered, even though the taxes paid on the average home were less than the cost of educating its children.

Luxury homes on large lots might, on the other hand, enhance tax revenues. To this end fully half the county was zoned to limit housing development to one unit per acre, and many towns stipulated minimum floor area. Northern townships, which had been the playland of the super rich, sought to perpetuate their special quality of life by enacting even more restrictive codes. Far Hills zoned for 10-acre estates; Bedminster and Bernardsville adopted five-acre zoning; Bernards and Peapack-Gladstone set three-acre minimums.

Bedminster's five-acre minimum quickly came under attack, and in 1952 the NJ Supreme Court decided in favor of the township. Chief Justice Arthur T. Vanderbilt observed that although Bedminster lay only 40 miles from New York, it was still as rural as though it were 400 miles away. He said, "There would appear ample justification for the ordinance in preserving the character of the community, maintaining the value of property therein and devoting the land throughout the township for its most appropriate use." At the same time, Vanderbilt took note of urban problems and fine highways and warned, "Much foresight is required now to preserve the countryside for its best use." He concluded, "It

This aerial view of the Raritan River, downstream from the Albany Street Bridge, shows the remnants of the once thriving Delaware and Raritan Canal. Courtesy, the Courier-News, *Bridgewater*

must, of course, be borne in mind that an ordinance which is reasonable today, may at some future time by reason of changed conditions, prove to be unreasonable."

Justice Vanderbilt's prescience was confirmed when freeways began slicing through the lush countryside. Interstate 287 opened to Pluckemin in 1966, and cars began traveling Interstate 78 two years later. That same year developers unrolled plans for residential development on 1,500 Pluckemin acres, effectively serving notice that Bedminster was no longer on the western fringe of New York's suburbia. The long arm of the circumferential freeway had drawn Pluckemin into the East Coast megalopolis.

For the next several years Bedminster struggled to mitigate the impact of spreading development; it refused approval for a major shopping center, a college, and a giant industry. But in 1972 AT&T, the ultimate in desirable taxpayers, won consent for its Long Lines headquarters to employ 3,600. Subsequently a 1980 court order permitting townhouses to be planted 15 units to the acre in Bedminster cornfields enabled 4,000 people to move into "The Hills."

Many postwar advances soon proved obsolete under new development pressures. Among the buildings that were outgrown was the County Administration Building (CAB), which adjoined the courthouse. In 1950 construction of the CAB had represented a bold departure from the past. Somerville architect Jay Van Nuys had designed it in the linear international style introduced to Americans at the 1939 New York's World Fair with its "World of Tomorrow" theme. Spaciously housing every county function, including the library, under one roof, the CAB had been oversized enough to allot a penthouse suite to the Tuberculosis and Health League and still have room leftover.

Freeholders thought big, but they thought too small. By the seventies county government had taken on so many new functions and was serving so many more people that houses in the next block were being converted into offices, and in 1978 satellite service centers were opened in Franklin, Bernardsville, and North Plainfield. Building roads and bridges, maintaining a courthouse and jail, and recording deeds and mortgages were no longer the chief duties of county government. A referendum in 1957 authorized a park commission. Freeholders over the next decade added a county planning board, an office of economic development, consumer affairs services, a vocational-technical school, and a county college. In addition the State of New Jersey was making its counties administrative units for more and more programs—everything from mosquito extermination to child welfare, food stamps, mental health care, and services to the aged.

Although county government was adapting to changing times, it was scarcely in tune with the mindset of newcomers who enrolled their children in Little League, not Sunday School, joined Kiwanis, Rotary, and Lions instead of a lodge or grange, and owed no allegiance to either political party.

In 1959 voters handed a stunning defeat to C.I. Van Cleef, a cagey old farmer whose name had been a password in the courthouse for 20 years, and elected in his place Grace Gurisic, Somerset's first woman freeholder. Never mind that she was a candidate of the underdog Democrats, that her power base was the Borough of Rocky Hill, population 500, and that she was only 25 years old. "Gracie" was enthusiastic, confident, a college graduate, and she cared about people. In her wake came another upheaval.

The 1960 census counted 144,000 Somerset citizens and made the county eligible to increase its freeholder board from three to five. It was done in 1964, and Lyndon B. Johnson's sweep carried with it Democratic control of Somerset County for the first time since the small freeholder board was adopted.

Voters grew impatient for change at the municipal level as well, especially since New Jersey had foreclosed their option of breaking up a township into new units of government. The Balkanization process was halted right after World War II, and the state decreed it was now or never for those towns still retaining semi-independent commission forms of government. East Millstone and Raritan had, therefore, to choose in 1948 whether to become boroughs or rejoin their parent townships. East Millstone put itself back into Franklin, and Raritan cut loose from Bridgewater, giving Somerset County its current total of 21 municipalities.

In place of more local government units, New Jersey began to allow optional forms of government; voters could choose by referendum a system they believed suited their community. Franklin was the first to opt for change, electing in 1959 to replace its township committee with a council made up of both at-large and ward representation. Bridgewater in 1975 chose a nonpartisan council, elected at large. North Plainfield adopted a mayor-council plan in 1977.

Intermunicipal cooperation was another innovation. Rather than each building a separate high school, Warren and Watchung joined in forming a regional high school district. Even more far-reaching were cooperative efforts to combat pollution of the Raritan River.

In 1948 Middlesex County put forward the idea of a trunk sewer leading to central treatment facilities and stirred up a swirl of political currents. But there was no escaping the need to act. Treatment plants up and down the Raritan Valley were inadequate and becoming less sufficient every year. Out of the disputes two separate plans emerged. Somerset's downriver towns, Franklin and Bound Brook, and those along the Green Brook tributary, all tied into the Middlesex trunk sewer. Bridgewater, Somerville, and Raritan formed Somerset Raritan Valley Sewerage Authority to treat upstream sewage. American Cyanamid Co., which by itself was generating more wasteflow than the three towns combined, was a party to the discussions; however, it decided not to join the agency. Instead, a very unusual, cooperative agreement was worked out in 1957 whereby Cyanamid undertook to provide secondary treatment of wastes for the Somerset Authority, charging them only the additional operating costs incurred.

In years that followed, Hillsborough and Branchburg, Warren and part of Green Brook became customers of the Somerset Raritan Valley Sewerage Authority. Townships found themselves with no choice but to utilize sewers since one-acre lots proved unable to sustain large numbers of homes with individual wells and septic systems. Sewers were costly at one-acre densities, and alternatives to one-acre zoning were controversial. Hillsborough dared to try something different and in 1961 allowed one of the first cluster developments built in New Jersey—72 homes grouped together on 35 acres, leaving 40 acres of open space to be deeded to the township. The American Conservation Association called it "good esthetics and good economics."

Favorable reaction encouraged Hillsborough to try another experimental zoning concept: planned unit development (PUD), in which densities rather than lot sizes determined what could be built. PUD zones opened the way for townhouses and high rises as well as single-family homes and were such a magnet to condominium builders, Hillsborough had a 45-percent growth rate in the 1970s, the highest in the county.

One of the many corporations to take advantage of the surging industrial development in Somerset County in the 1960s and 1970s was American Hoechst. Located on more than 100 acres along Interstate 287 in Bridgewater Township, American Hoechst manufactures pharmaceuticals, chemicals, and fibers for textile and industrial use. Courtesy, Greater Somerset County Chamber of Commerce

Everywhere else residential building slumped sharply. A deep national recession was making mortgage money scarce and was sending New Jersey employment figures spiraling down to levels below the national average. Somerset County fared far better than the rest of the state. Its mix of industry and business provided a fairly recession-proof economy, and this prosperity amidst adversity, coupled with beautiful, wide open spaces, made Somerset singularly attractive, so much so it was dubbed "The Blue Chip County."

Industrial development continued at a robust pace despite bad times; a gain of 87 percent in industrial and commercial square footage was recorded in 1974, much of that attributable to the development of AT&T's $100-million, 150-acre headquarters in Basking Ridge. The communications giant had decided it made sense to be in New Jersey where most of its 3,400 New York office employees had their homes and selected Somerset as the location where the greatest number were concentrated. But AT&T was not the only company discovering Somerset's advantageous location. American Hoechst had moved its head office to 110 acres along Interstate 287 in Bridgewater in 1968 and was adding more buildings to its office and research complex. In 1974 RCA added a multistory office building. Numerous blocks of offices for rent went up along the highways; the largest, Bellemead

The United States Golf Association is headquartered in this handsome Far Hills mansion. A museum and library are maintained in the Golf House, which is open to the public daily. Photo by Carol Kitman

Development, on Route 202 in Branchburg, and Somerset Valley Office Center, next to Interstate 287 in Franklin, were harbingers of more and bigger to come. All told, 14 million square feet of industrial space were added in the decade, creating 15,000 new jobs, an increase of 52 percent.

The national slowdown did not impede expansion of county-wide services either. In the seventies Somerset went forward with construction of a permanent facility for its vocational-technical school in Bridgewater and completed the initial construction phases of its college campus in Branchburg. The county park commission added two more public golf courses, making four in all; built a tennis center; and launched an environmental education program in a unique, solar heated facility. Health needs, also, were better served than ever. Somerset Hospital put up a six-story addition, and the NJ College of Medicine and Dentistry decided to adopt a new hospital, which had opened in Green Brook as a teaching facility.

The population that benefitted by this proliferation of services expected no less. Their level of education was above average, so was their income, and most lived here by choice, having come from other states or other parts of New Jersey to find a better life. The prevailing mood of the county was upbeat, optimistic, and impatient.

THREE

HUNDRED

AND GROWING

THREE HUNDRED YEARS AFTER IT WAS ESTABLISHED, SOMERSET COUNTY CAN STILL BE described in much the same terms as those used by the first explorer: a region fertile with opportunity—a territory through which large numbers pass on their way north or east, making it suitable for all manner of business or trade. As it was when Cornelius van Tienhoven observed it in 1650, this area remains one of the handsomest and pleasantest places available for development.

In 1988, the year of Somerset's tercentenary, the county's vigorous economic performance confounded many observers. Despite both of the county's old industrial giants, Cyanamid and Johns-Manville, having phased out their operations, there were more job openings than ever.

Although manufacturing of all sorts clearly was on the wane, the loss was more than offset by new employment opportunities in service industries. There were big gains in the fields of finance, insurance, and real estate; law firms and technology consultants too found Somerset an attractive location.

Biggest of the big new companies in the county during the 1980s were Hoechst-Celanese in Bridgewater, Chubb in Warren, and Beneficial Management in Peapack. Beneficial's office plaza designed by the Hillier Group won a national architectural award.

Fully as important to the county's prosperity was expansion by large corporations previously established here: AT&T and the Johnson & Johnson family of companies, Somerset's biggest employers, both enlarged their operations and occupied new facilities during the decade. By this time there were more than 30 companies in the county with payrolls

exceeding 500 people. Even more significant to the overall upward momentum were several thousand small- and medium-size companies, a great many of them housed in over two dozen office complexes and industrial research parks which had sprung up along the highways and around freeway interchanges.

Somerset was riding the crest of a wave of national prosperity. Per capita income and the effective buying power of county residents were the highest in New Jersey and fourth-highest in the nation. Retailers were eager to profit from such a lush market, and plans were put forward for three enormous shopping malls. Just one materialized: Bridgewater Commons.

Occupying 63 acres in the center of Somerset, the Commons opened with a grand flourish in 1988. It is sited within the so-called Golden Triangle, which is bordered by Route 22, Route 202-206, and Interstate 287. The glossy allure of its 200 stores quickly became a magnet for both Somerset shoppers and shoppers from neighboring counties and states. Hahn Co., the developers, reported that in the first full year of operations Bridgewater Commons grossed more than any of their other regional malls across the country. Hahn has plans for a second phase of construction which will add to this site two eight-story office buildings, a 200-room hotel, and a conference center.

In doing so Hahn would be falling in line with a lot of other developers. All the major hotel chains discovered Somerset in a big way. In Franklin, for example, the towers of six—Holiday Inn, Marriott, McIntosh, Ramada Inn, Hilton, and Madison Suites—ranged themselves around the interchanges of Interstate 287, so when the Garden State Convention & Exhibit Center opened 34,000 square feet of leasable space in 1990, it was within walking distance of 1,200 rooms.

Somerset's skyline sprouted office buildings even faster than hotels. As the 1980s advanced, so did the optimism of speculators. No longer content to put up buildings of 20,000 and 50,000 square feet, they built blocks containing 200,000 and more. Clustered around ornamental lakes and fountains, these new buildings were set on campuses featuring heliports, health clubs, and highly dramatic designs. When supply exceeded demand, developers went right ahead pouring concrete and laying blacktop and conjuring up still more lavish layouts, intent on being ready to capture the next wave of renters to arrive by freeway.

Along with all this investment in commercial real estate, a housing boom hit Somerset County. The county's population grew at twice the rate of the state as a whole, adding in one decade an estimated 24,000 people—almost as many as the total population of the county when it was 200 years old. Franklin absorbed the most. Home buyers flowed in off Interstate 287 and along the old Lincoln Highway (Route 27), which forms the township's eastern border. Franklin caught the impact of explosive growth that was taking place in New Jersey's central corridor between New Brunswick and Trenton. Montgomery felt it too. At the other end of the county, Bedminster, Bernards, and Branchburg formed another growth zone along Interstate 78, as a result of greater accessibility gained by completion of that freeway's links to Newark on the east and Pennsylvania on the west.

Another important growth determinant was affordability. Bedminster's court-ordered "Hills" project and planned unit development zones in Hillsborough and Franklin provided opportunities for builders to put up rows of townhouses and clusters of small-lot homes for condominium buyers who found swimming pools and tennis and handball courts an acceptable substitute for broad green lawns they would have had to mow themselves; even these units were priced in a range which, for the most part, limited purchase to two-income families. Elsewhere in the county, builders were capitalizing on voracious demand for luxury homes, leaving would-be buyers of the average home to bid up the price of existing housing stock higher and higher. Price levels even in Raritan, historically a blue-collar town, climbed beyond the reach of ordinary people, and the town was found to fall short of the state's newly mandated quotas for affordable housing.

Thousands of new jobs pushed unemployment figures down to lows not experienced since World War II. Stores and restaurants all displayed signs inviting job applications. Recruiters tucked flyers under windshield wipers. High school sports enthusiasm waned; students were going out after paychecks, not varsity letters. By 1990 the scramble for housing and workers was making a commute from as far away as Pennsylvania's Lehigh Valley the way to go.

As a rurban county within the East

One of Somerset County's largest employers is AT&T, whose expansive administrative headquarters facility is located in Basking Ridge. Photo by Mary Ann Brockman

LEFT: The byways and turnpikes of yesteryear have been superceded by today's interstate freeways, carrying Somerset County residents and workers to their daily destinations. Pictured here is Route 78, looking west near the Interstate 287 interchange. Photo by Mary Ann Brockman

BELOW: Situated on 63 acres in the heart of Somerset County, the Bridgewater Commons mall features some 200 stores for the shopping enjoyment of area residents. Photo by Christopher Lauber

Coast megalopolis, Somerset was commuting, going and coming, in all directions. There was still a daily exodus by rail and bus to New York City, but its numbers were decreasing. Passenger service on Conrail (the old Philadelphia and Reading) was discontinued altogether in 1982 because there were too few riders. Most commuting involved a back and forth exchange with neighboring Middlesex, Union, Morris, and Hunterdon counties, and almost all traveled alone in their automobiles. At rush hours local traffic arteries were overloaded, and freeway ramp approaches clogged with long lines of waiting automobiles. An Alliance for the Future, formed by Somerset's large corporations, has set its sights on finding ways for employees to travel to and from work over existing highways without running into traffic delays, which cost businesses millions in lost man-hours. Traffic management options are being explored in cooperation with the County Planning Board and Somerset County Chamber of Commerce.

In a county where two out of three families had more than one car, traffic in the 1980s threatened to become a nemesis punishing greed for development profits. As for unplugging bottlenecks, the only major project scheduled by NJ Department of Transportation was construction of a Route 202 overpass to relieve the Somerville traffic circle. New Jersey's days of big new highway projects are over; and no one can predict when, if ever, the state will impose growth management controls effectively relating building approvals to road capacity. Somerset County has cooperated fully with the State Planning Act of 1985 in developing goals and objectives and taking part in discussions, but achieving statewide consensus on a final plan is still only a hope.

Named for a beloved pastor of the local church, the village of Harlingen in Montgomery Township grew up around its Dutch Reformed Church, which was first established in 1727. The present church building, pictured here encircled by colorful autumn leaves, was constructed in 1851 and is a graceful Greek Revival edifice designed by Charles Steadman. Photo by Mary Ann Brockman

During the 1980s business and government were well aware that continued growth was sustaining the buoyancy of Somerset County's economy. They were equally well aware that the quality of life in Somerset was a fragile asset. A county with excellent resources, beautiful surroundings—both natural and man-made—good services, proud traditions, and people who cared about their families, their homes, and their communities, it was one of the most desirable places to live within the New York region. Visually it was a pleasure: a countryside dotted with fine old farmhouses and handsome churches, towns abounding in Victorian elegance, winding roads, coursing streams, wooded slopes, and commanding heights offering spectacular views of broad plains spread out below. The country atmosphere remained despite the impact of development, and, hoping to preserve this character, Somerset became the first county in the state to utilize initiatives provided by New Jersey's 1983 Agriculture Retention and Development Act. Plans have been formulated to foster continued farming and agribusiness in selected regions in the north, east, and west.

An inventory of historic sites and buildings was completed in 1989. Municipalities are urged to consider the inventory's findings when approving subdivisions, demolition, or construction. In addition local historical organizations flourish in all parts of the county; they cultivate appreciation of a heritage and guard against laying waste what can never be duplicated. By steadfast opposition citizens persuaded freeholders not to tear down a century-old gothic church designed by William Appleton Potter to make way for a new courthouse. A foundation put together by concerned citizens has undertaken to preserve four historic houses in Franklin which were threatened with destruction. Public outcry won a reprieve for the 1896 lenticular truss bridge over the South Branch at Neshanic Station. Citizen initiatives have brought recognition and restoration to Washington Park in North Plainfield, raised money for an archaeological dig at Pluckemin, where General Knox and his artillery camped during the Revolution, and added, year by year, to National Register of Historic Sites listings throughout the county.

Adaptive reuse is preserving much more of Somerset's heritage. Some fine old buildings have been put to public use. The Van Dorn gristmill was turned into Bernardsville Town Hall, and the pre-revolutionary Vealtown Tavern into Bernardsville Public Library. The home of General John Frelinghuysen has been transformed into the Raritan public library. Bernards Township offices occupy a mansion built by John Jacob Astor, Jr., fifth to bear that name in a family of storied wealth. Somerville has for its town hall the elegant home New York businessman Daniel Robert had copied after the crowning gem on Bridgeport's Golden Hill.

Near Liberty Corner the magnificent summer home of the John Sloan family, a name synonymous with fine furniture on Fifth Avenue, was purchased by the U.S. Golf Association for its office headquarters and museum. The fieldstone residence built by stockbroker Frederick S. Mosely, Jr., along the Lamington River now graces Fiddler's Elbow Country Club. The U.S. Equestrian Team trains for Olympic competition at Hamilton Farms in Peapack, once the showplace estate of James Cox Brady, financier, industrialist, and philanthropist. "Stronghold," the country home of U.S. Senator John F. Dryden (1902-1907), founder of Prudential Insurance Co., was turned into Gill-St. Bernard School. Matheny School, nationally renowned for its work with cerebral palsy sufferers, has taken over the stables of "Blairsden," and the adjoining French chateau built high above Ravine Lake by C. Leyard Blair, onetime governor of the NY Stock Exchange, was made into a Catholic retreat house called St. Joseph's Villa. And these are just a few of many.

The Pumpkin Decorating Contest in Bernardsville is a favorite annual event. Photo by Carol Kitman

ABOVE: The sleepy hamlet of Peapack in northern Somerset County dates back to the early years of the 1800s. Photo by Carol Kitman

LEFT: Situated on the Delaware and Raritan Canal in Franklin Township, the Colonial Park Arboretum features the Rudolf W. Van der Goot Rose Garden. With approximately 4,000 roses of 275 varieties, this garden is an ideal setting in which to capture some special moments. Photo by Mary Ann Brockman

ABOVE: Considered to be one of the longest and most efficient canals built in the United States, the Delaware and Raritan Canal was inaugurated in 1834 and served as a major shipping route for more than 40 years. Now listed on the National Register of Historic Places, the canal is pictured here in the charming community of Griggstown in Franklin Township. Photo by Mary Ann Brockman

RIGHT: Most of the rural crossroad churches in Somerset County are Dutch Reformed because of the preponderance of settlers of that nationality in the Raritan Valley. This one in Pottersville was built in 1866 and is part of a National Historic District. Photo by Mary Ann Brockman

FACING PAGE: Somerset County still boasts more than 400 working farms, totaling some 74,000 acres of productive land. Photo by Mary Ann Brockman

ABOVE: The annual Midland Run in Far Hills attracts about 3,000 runners each year and benefits the Midland School. Photo by Christopher Lauber

RIGHT: Home to the United States Equestrian Team, Bedminster is well-known for its many and varied equestrian pursuits. The Essex Horse Trails, pictured here, is a favorite three-day event held during the month of May. Photo by Christopher Lauber

A picturesque spring day finds these two young boys preparing for an afternoon of fishing along the South Branch of the Raritan River. Photo by Carol Kitman

Somerset County still preserves a peaceful, rural style of living in beautiful surroundings. Photo by Christopher Lauber

The Somerset Hills adaptations serve not only to maintain irreplaceable buildings, but also help to keep alive the aura of privilege engendered by millionaires of the mountain colony a century ago. A far less ostentatious style of living prevails among wealthy individuals who continue to favor this vicinity as a place of residence. J. Mars Vogel of Bedminster, the candy billionaire, and Jane S. Englehard of Far Hills, widow of the "platinum king," rank among New Jersey's 10 richest, as did the late Malcolm S. Forbes of Bedminster, the magazine publisher who embarked on building a chain of Central Jersey newspapers not long before his death.

Abiding affluence in the Somerset Hills attracts big-spending foreigners like King Hassan of Morocco and newly rich individuals like Mike Tyson, when he became heavyweight boxing champion. However money has not been the sole source of fame for notables in northern Somerset County. Meryl Streep (Bernardsville High School Class of 1967) gained hers by winning Academy Awards for roles in *Kramer vs Kramer* (1979) and *Sophie's Choice* (1982). Ted, Gordon, Sara, Amy, and Abigail, the Kienast quintuplets of Liberty Corner, on the other hand, avoided fame and managed to grow up pretty much like all the other kids in Bernards Township.

The prevalence of money does not entirely explain what sets Somerset Hills apart from the rest of the world; what makes it truly unusual is a social climate and way of life which has kept intact some of the trappings and privilege of an earlier age. Wall Street financiers have continued to own a private club car they attach to the morning train out of Gladstone. Horses and hounds have not ceased chasing the fox to his lair on frosty mornings, and former first lady Jacqueline Kennedy Onassis has kept a country home nearby just so she can ride with them. The horsey set has also continued the tradition of Sunday games on the polo field along Burnt Mills Road. And footsloggers led by the Tewksbury Basset Hounds have persisted in sallying forth from the foot of Long Lane to hunt rabbits.

Located in the hills above Bernardsville is the estate of the late United States Senator John F. Dryden, who was president and founder of the Prudential Insurance Company. Dryden's former property now houses the Gill-St. Bernard's School. Known by the name of "Stronghold," the estate is shown here in this 1930s aerial view. Courtesy, Special Collections/ Alexander Library/ Rutgers University

Many people are naturally curious about these vestiges of Gilded Age glamor, and serious participants in such traditional activities do on occasion allow their sport to be turned into spectacle for worthy causes. The most famous such event is the Essex Hunt's race meet. For one afternoon every October as many as 30,000 people converge on Moorland Farm to goggle at one another and catch glimpses of steeplechasers going over the hurdles. Proceeds go to Somerset Medical Center.

The spacious meadows of Moorland Farm are invaded by tens of thousands again in the spring for the Midland Run, a very different sort of fund-raiser which caters to suburban enthusiasms by combining 15-kilometer championship races for men and women with a day of fun for everyone. The beneficiary is the Midland School at North Branch, a non-profit rehabilitation center for children with learning disabilities.

An entirely different type of annual crowd pleaser is the unique Somerset County 4-H Fair, which offers three days of free family fun during the second week in August. Exhibits, shows, and demonstrations under acres of gaily striped tents in North Branch Park showcase

A favorite annual event in Somerset County is the Far Hills Race Meeting. Held every October since 1920, this event attracts as many as 30,000 spectators, and the proceeds benefit the Somerset Medical Center. Photo by Carol Kitman

the accomplishments of 4-H members aged 7 to 19 and attract as many as 20,000 visitors.

Throughout the year every town and township has its own calendar of parades, carnivals, and festivals, but no other event comes close to the colorful excitement of the Tour of Somerville on Memorial Day. This 50-mile bicycle race, sponsored by the Jaycees, attracts riders from all over the world who come to compete for the Kugler-Anderson Trophy, named after Furman Kugler, winner of the first two Somerville races in 1940 and 1941 and Carl Anderson, winner of the third. This race is the country's most prestigious competition for cyclists, and the sustained enthusiasm it has generated for 50 years has resulted in Somerville being chosen as the location for a U.S. Bicycling Hall of Fame.

The good life in Somerset County has many other forms. The Audubon Society maintains a bird sanctuary in Bernards. There are two George Washington headquarters preserved as historic house museums—the Wallace House in Somerville and Rockingham in Franklin. Also gracing the county are three nationally renowned gardens: Rudolf van der Goot Rose Garden in East Millstone, with a display of 4,000 plants; Leonard J. Buck Garden in Far Hills, featuring rock formations covered with rare and beautiful specimens; and Duke Gardens in Hillsborough, where ecosystems maintained under glass allow visitors to take a tour through the gardens of the world. Within the county are 16 golf courses, six of them public. The county park system takes in 4,500 acres in 12 locations, and there are also state and municipal parks. In 1985 a 1,000-seat performing arts center was added to the county college.

The college's scope was expanded in 1987 by agreement with Hunterdon to make this the state's first bi-county college, henceforth to be known as Raritan Valley Community College. Another educational advance was a cooperative agreement between the college and the County Technical Institute to exchange credits for applied science degrees. For adults, there are also evening, weekend, and summer learning opportunities made available by Jointure for Community Adult Education, a consortium of nine communities.

Raritan Valley Community College is the state's first bi-county college, serving the educational interests of both Hunterdon and Somerset counties. Located in North Branch, Raritan Valley offers two-year degrees and certificates in a wide variety of subjects. Photo by Mary Ann Brockman

Throughout the 1980s the Board of Freeholders has steadily expanded county facilities and services, taking advantage of a growing base of revenue generated by businesses to cushion the load on individual taxpayers. A county library headquarters opened in Bridgewater in 1981. A new five-story courthouse was dedicated in 1987, and a 700-car parking deck opened that same year in the next block. Beside the parking deck a 200-bed jail is being built, slated for completion in 1990. Plans for a second administration building were recently approved. In addition the public works department was relocated to a new facility in Finderne.

Also sited in Finderne is a resource recovery operation that handles newspaper, corrugated paper, aluminum, glass, and plastics collected in a county-wide recycling program which has Somerset leading the way in meeting state standards for solid waste reduction. A trash transfer station was put into operation as well, to compact waste preparatory to shipping it out of county, and an agreement was negotiated for Warren County to incinerate wastes collected in Somerset.

Environmental protection remains a pressing concern. Because every square mile brought under development exacerbates storm water run-off, retention basins have been made a requirement for any major new land use. Despite this, stream corridors flood with increasing frequency and severity. Ground water too has begun to cause alarm; water tables have dropped, and pockets of pollution have shown up. Elizabethtown Water Company, the principal supplier within the county, has been steadily expanding its service area and lessening dependence on wells.

A far more urgent environmental concern is sewage. Development cannot proceed without the capacity to treat waste that will be generated, and local treatment plants have proved inadequate for increasingly stringent state standards. Over the years Branchburg, Hillsborough, parts of Green Brook and Warren, and, lastly, Manville have tied into Somerset Raritan Valley Sewage Authority. When its treatment facilities finally could not

Scenic roadways and picturesque vistas such as this one on Kline's Mill Road in Bedminster make Somerset County a delight for bicycling and hiking enthusiasts. Photo by Carol Kitman

handle the increased load, a moratorium on new tie-ins had to be imposed. Lifted in 1990, after being in effect for two years, the restriction while it lasted effectively put the brakes on a lot of construction plans.

If a national economic slowdown had not come about soon after the sewer moratorium, this restriction would have caused a lot more distress. As it was, the impetus for growth subsided for the first time in almost a decade, and the end of the eighties became a time for taking stock of accomplishments and considering what should come next. Perhaps the pause will prove a prelude to new trends like the last economic downturn in the 1970s.

In its tercentenary year, 1988, almost half of Somerset County was still open land. Thirteen major corporations were holding approvals for 11,000 more housing units. There were 24 new office complexes with a total of 3.5 million square feet of space slated for completion by 1990, and 15 more projects that would contain an additional 4.5 million feet were in the planning stages. Much of this went on hold, but these projects or others of similar magnitude are expected to go forward when the investment climate improves. More is sure to follow. After 300 years of progress Somerset County still has a lot of room left to grow.

PARTNERS IN PROGRESS

S OMERSET COUNTY HAS EXPERIENCED CONTINUOUS ECONOMIC GROWTH WHILE IT RETAINS
its natural beauty, from the Watchung and Sourland mountains to the Raritan, Millstone,
Lamington, Passaic, and Neshanic rivers. Its economic assets as a thriving business community are strengthened by its scenic countryside, working farms, strong local school systems,
and progressive municipal government.

Somerset County's rich past can be seen in its many historic sites, monuments,
and beautifully renovated colonial and Victorian homes. The area's historic charm combined with its economic expansion make it a highly desirable place to establish a home
or business.

Somerset County's 21 municipalities comprise 35 square miles. Its network of major
highways and central location equidistant between Philadelphia and New York City attract
major corporations whose office buildings, corporate parks, and retail businesses dot the
landscape throughout the county.

The roots of the county's current growth began with the establishment of its railway
system in the mid-nineteenth century. Churches, schools, hospitals, and municipal services
flourished to accommodate the influx of New Yorkers who sought a less urban environment
in which to raise their families. While Somerset County is still a bedroom community for
many business commuters, the county has come into its own as a source of employment for
local residents.

As a result of economic development that has made it a major employment base, the county's population and housing growth far exceeds national and state growth rates. A study conducted by the the U.S. Department of Commerce cited Somerset County as among the top 10 areas in per capita income in the nation.

Further housing construction and commercial development are foreseen. However, as the first county in New Jersey to establish a central planning board and local planning boards in each of its municipalities, Somerset County has achieved a pattern of controlled growth in which its infrastructure and community services have kept pace with land development.

To improve local educational programs ranging from adult literacy to academic skills for young people, county businesses and schools have formed the Business/Education Partnership of the Greater Somerset County Chamber of Commerce. Acting on a study it conducted of business and education's mutual needs, the partnership's goal is to blend the educational objectives of county schools with the work force needs of the community.

The organizations whose stories are detailed on the following pages have chosen to support this important literary and civic project. They illustrate the variety of ways in which individual citizens and their businesses have contributed to the area's growth and development. Their commitment to active community involvement has made Somerset County an excellent place to work and live.

Participants in the great American pastime, the Somerville High School baseball club posed for a team portrait in the early 1920s. Courtesy, Somerset Messenger-Gazette

GREATER SOMERSET COUNTY CHAMBER OF COMMERCE

Networking is just one of the many benefits enjoyed by Greater Somerset County Chamber of Commerce members. Expo '89 enabled member companies to showcase their products and services to a variety of contacts.

The chamber's annual luncheon is always a highlight. The 70th annual event featured Steven Forbes as keynote speaker. From left: David Linett, Richmond Shreve, Marguerite Chandler, Steven Forbes, Bill and Kim Fraser, and Barbara Roos.

Founded in 1919, the Greater Somerset County Chamber of Commerce is dedicated to making the entire county an even better place in which to live and work.

On the occasion of its 70th anniversary in 1989, the chamber of commerce initiated a plan that will affect its activities as a proactive organization for years to come. As part of its mission, the chamber is expanding its traditional business-oriented functions to encompass matters of broader interest to the county. Greater interaction between business and community groups is needed as the issues involved become more complex. Recognizing this fact, the chamber will investigate issues such as tax structures, education, the environment, child care, affordable housing, and transportation.

Two chamber initiatives to be launched in the 1990s are conducting a county-wide "town meeting" on the environment and establishing

a special education committee, which will be a partnership between leaders in business and education. This committee's goal will be to improve the dialogue between Somerset County school officials and area businesses.

To keep pace with the progressive Somerset County business environment, the chamber computerized its operations. This helps the staff work more efficiently in meeting the members' needs. The chamber informs members of important issues, trends, and seminars through the quarterly *Somerset Business* magazine, a monthly *Chamber Update*, and periodic program notices.

The chamber conducts many educational programs throughout the year, which address a variety of business concerns. Topics cover regulatory, tax, personnel, and marketing issues. Educational awareness information is also available to members who seek more details on topics of interest.

Striving to meet the demands of its members, the chamber conducts an annual wage and benefit survey in conjunction with several other area chambers, in addition to sponsoring a job fair. Its Expo, the only trade show to highlight Somerset County businesses, enables companies to showcase their products and services to a wider variety of contacts. The chamber also holds many functions that provide great networking opportunities for members.

Another important aspect of the chamber is that it offers people the ability to voice their concerns to legislators and community leaders. By participating in decision-making forums, members can help shape policies that will improve the community and provide a return on their investment in the chamber.

Annual chamber events include the Outstanding Citizen of the Year awards dinner, a golf and tennis outing that serves as both a social event and a chamber fund-raiser, the Recognition of Outstanding People awards, and the annual meeting, which features a notable keynote speaker.

The chamber itself is an active organization of more than 700 member businesses that range from home-based operations to large corporations. The members shape the chamber's agenda and programs with an eye to meeting not only their own business needs, but also the needs of the growing community.

With its plans and strategies ready for the 1990s, the Greater Somerset County Chamber of Commerce continues its work as the only business organization in the county working full time to improve the economic climate and the quality of life in Somerset County.

CELGENE CORPORATION

Biotechnology represents a leap forward that may prove more significant than the conquest of space or the development of the microchip. It will have a huge impact on health care, agriculture, and industry. Somerset County is emerging as one of the important centers of the biotechnology revolution. One of these companies is Celgene Corporation, a chemical biotechnology company located in Warren. It is a spin-off from a major chemical company, Celanese (now Hoechst-Celanese Corp.), also headquartered in Somerset County.

At its technical center in Summit, New Jersey, Celanese began to apply biotechnology to new processes for commodity chemicals. Its accomplishments indicated that biotechnology was particularly applicable for new specialty chemicals, but that new, competitive processes for the huge commodity chemical sector were beyond reach. With these results Celanese saw the value of establishing a new biotechnology company focused on specialty chemicals.

Celgene became an independent company in 1986 and raised $37 million in stock offerings its first year. It is led by John L. Ufheil, president and chief executive officer, and a board of directors that includes Louis Fernandez, chairman (and the company's first president and chief executive officer), and other top executives from some of the nation's largest corporations. Nobel laureate David Baltimore, Ph.D., president of New York City's prestigious Rockefeller University, chairs Celgene's scientific advisory board.

Initially, 25 Celanese employees joined Celgene and began the process of building a new company. At the Powder Horn Corporate Center, 44,500 square feet were outfitted for offices, laboratories, and a state-of-the-art pilot plant, which opened in 1987. Within three years the employment level doubled, and teams of researchers and commercial development specialists were focused on the development of products in chemical intermediates for pharmaceuticals and agricultural chemicals; new monomers for polymers; and the biological treatment of hazardous chemical wastes.

All of Celgene's research and development projects are based on biocatalysis—a technology that marries biology and chemistry to harness the many unique chemical reactions that occur in living organisms. Biocatalysis has three major advantages over conventional chemistry-based technologies. It offers improved product quality; it can reduce production costs; and it also offers protection to the environment by elimination of the waste products generated in high-temperature, high-pressure manufacturing processes.

Celgene's unique combination of scientific talent has helped the young company establish alliances with some of the world's top chemical and pharmaceutical firms. In 1989 Celgene announced two joint programs with major firms in the state: American Cyanamid and Schering-Plough Corporation. Celgene also has agreements with Yukong, Ltd., a major South Korean energy and chemicals company, and with RTZ Chemicals, Ltd. (United Kingdom).

In the coming years Celgene Corporation will focus all of its resources on bringing to the marketplace proprietary products based on its core technology of biocatalysis.

The Celgene team pictured in the lobby of the company's headquarters at the Powder Horn Corporate Center in spring 1990.

SUBURBAN NATIONAL BANK

Suburban National Bank in Hillsborough came into existence because a group of local bankers and businesspeople recognized the need for an independent, locally owned bank.

The bank organizers believed there was a real demand in the marketplace for bankers sensitive to the needs of the local community. Mergers, consolidations, and change had been the order of the day in the decade preceding the formation of Suburban National Bank. Long-term relationships between customers and their bankers were disrupted when locally owned financial institutions were merged into larger organizations.

The officers who formed the nucleus of Suburban were all locally oriented bankers living and working in Somerset County. All were strongly committed to the idea of community banking.

Once the decision was made to form the bank, necessary paperwork was filed with appropriate governmental agencies, and the busi-

A former fine arts school was renovated to provide this modern facility for Suburban National Bank, one of the most successful independent banks in Somerset County.

ness of funding the bank was begun. "While we were required to raise only one million dollars in capital," says Joseph Sullivan, president and chief executive officer, "we decided we wanted $4 million to start off in the best possible way." The necessary stock was sold during the fall of 1987, one of the worst times for the sale of securities of any kind in recent history. The shares were sold primarily to local businesses and residents. In addition, eight months after the initial offering, another offering of $1.75 million was successfully sold to finance expansion.

Directors for the new bank were chosen with care. "We wanted an active board," says Sullivan. "It was our belief that an involved board of directors would be the best board for Suburban. We wanted people who would not only give us their business and personal accounts, but would be active in the community, soliciting other business for us." Consequently, all of the bank's directors have strong ties through business and, in most instances, through their residence.

The location for the bank was selected with great deliberation as well. Sullivan says, "We wanted a headquarters that our customers could get to easily and would feel comfortable visiting. We also wanted a building that would grow with us as we grew." Bank headquarters at 32 New Armwell Road had previously housed a school of fine arts. The bank's sleek, modern offices are an attractive addition to the Hillsborough area.

The bank opened for business in January 1988 with 25 employees, 19 of whom had worked together at another bank in Hillsborough. The five officers at the time of the opening were Michael Cinelli, Joseph Sullivan, Sara Behory, Helen Mason, and John Oliver.

By the end of 1988 the bank had more than $73 million in assets. According to Sullivan, a number of factors were responsible for this phenomenal growth. "First, we were known in the community because of our long experience there. Second, we were at the right place at the right time. By that I mean that many new customers came to us with the belief that at our bank they would receive the kind of personal service they wanted and deserved. Their former banks and perhaps their contacts with those banks were gone. Loan approval was no longer local. Delays were bothersome. Service was negligible. And there we were with our local experience, our local lending authority, and our people who knew them. It was ideal."

The bank's business accounts include many local retailers, small manufacturing firms, professional associations, and owner-operated businesses. Interestingly, 79 percent of the bank's stockholders are also customers of the bank. While most customers are from Somerset County, other customers come from Hunterdon, Middlesex, and Mercer counties as a result of referrals. Hillsborough comprises 40 percent of the bank's customer base. The remaining 60 percent represents a mix of surrounding areas.

Suburban National Bank offers consumer loans, commercial and residential mortgage loans, money market accounts, statement savings, and a variety of certificate accounts. For customers based out of the area, the bank has bank-by-mail service.

"We're fortunate to be based in Somerset County, where the economic situation is strong. There's plenty of room for more expansion, and we expect area growth to continue," says Sullivan. "Our own plans include opening new branches and continuing to be innovative in the services we offer to customers. As an example, we are presently looking at expanded electronic banking services."

One of the newest banks in Somerset County, Suburban National Bank has become one of the most successful. "We are optimistic about the future," Sullivan says. "We are looking forward to an infusion of new capital to support our growth, and we are determined to maintain our high-quality customer service. We are pleased with our progress so far, and we are enthusiastically looking to a bright future. Our commitment will always be to position our bank for long-term growth, stability, and success."

LEFT: Joseph Sullivan, president and chief executive officer.

BELOW: Suburban National Bank has established itself as a positive force in the economic life and growth of Somerset County.

BOTTOM: Suburban National Bank officers provide more than 100 years of combined banking experience. Standing, from left, are Daryle Biunno, assistant vice president; Debra Minier, assistant cashier; Joseph Sullivan, president and chief executive officer; Dolores West, auditor; and Helen Mason, assistant cashier/branch manager. Seated are John Oliver, vice president, and Sara Behory, senior vice president.

FORBES NEWSPAPERS

The late world-renowned publisher Malcolm Forbes' love for good journalism spanned the international and national newsfront of *Forbes* magazine to the local newsbeat of Forbes Newspapers.

A resident of Bedminster, Forbes bought the newspaper chain in 1987 from the Bateman family following the death of publisher Palmer Bateman. This was not Forbes' first venture into local news. Upon graduating from Princeton, Malcolm Forbes worked at a midwestern community newspaper, which he eventually bought.

After serving in the U.S. Army during World War II, he decided to join his father's company, which publishes *Forbes* and *American Heritage*. "The best business decision of my life was going into my father's magazine business," Forbes once said. By acquiring the newspaper chain, Forbes returned to his roots in community journalism.

Forbes plied what he called his "capitalist tools" to fine-tune the operation. Today the company has grown from six to its current 14 publications, and its circulation is larger than all but two daily newspapers in the state.

One of the first moves Forbes made was to sell the company's sheet-fed printing operation to concentrate efforts on the newspaper business. The company moved to a new executive headquarters on Route 206 in Bedminster, home for *The Hills-Bedminster Press* as well as the company's circulation and accounting departments. The company also installed a $1.5-million state-of-the-art computer system at its Somerville facility, home of flagship newspaper, the *Somerset Messenger Gazette*. Future plans call for adding more press capacity and increased use of color.

Lending both his publishing expertise and the mystique of the Forbes name to the newspaper, Malcolm Forbes attracted a top-notch staff, which has grown from 110 to 200 people since his acquisition. A hands-on publisher, he maintained constant touch with the chain's staff, critiquing each week's newspaper and frequently visiting the office.

The publication policy of Forbes Newspapers is based on maintaining editorial excellence within a highly successful advertising format designed and marketed to reach the upscale portions of Somerset, Middlesex, and Union counties.

"Our forte is community journalism. You won't read about Noriega and Gorbachev unless they're visiting here," says publisher and president John O'Brien. " But if no garbage truck is coming because of a local strike, you'll hear about it from us. We want to provide our readers with all the news that affects their everyday lives."

Forbes newspapers are circulated every week to nearly 150,000 households in Somerset, Union, and Middlesex counties. These three counties comprise a market area that now ranks among the top 10 nationally in all demographic categories. This attractive market is regarded by the retail community as one of the premier growth areas of the entire Northeast.

To help advertisers target their markets, Forbes Newspapers conducted extensive research regarding the demographics, shopping preferences, and purchase patterns of area residents. The chain's 12 award-winning community newspapers, along with its two shoppers, provide advertisers with more than 100 possible advertising combinations that both large or small advertisers are able to use to their best advantage.

Forbes Newspapers offers blanket coverage for large advertisers or a highly cost-effective targeted approach for small advertisers. Advertisers can run ads in all publications, individual newspapers, or any combination. Preprint insert users can have inserts delivered by zip code to the most desired markets for a particular business.

Forbes Newspapers also offers advertisers a free cooperative advertising service to bring customers additional advertising dollars. Forbes' staff researches an advertiser's suppliers to determine if the advertiser qualifies for co-op money. Personnel then tracks the co-op budget and sends in reimbursement claims. Advertisers using this service have been able to increase their ad budget by as much as 35 percent or more at no additional cost to them.

In addition to having help-wanted and merchandise ads, the classified advertising department offers graphic production and media planning for real estate brokers and automotive dealers.

Every week Forbes Newspapers includes local community news such as religious events, the police beat, municipal court, sports, life-style, arts and entertainment, calendar of events, and meetings. "The newspaper is committed to the communities we serve. We are active in retail trade groups, local chambers of commerce, and we encourage our staff to be active in the community," says O'Brien.

One example of the newspaper's community involvement is its active role in the Somerville to Summerville emergency aid effort to help Summerville, South Carolina, victims of Hurricane Hugo in 1989. In addition to the newspaper soliciting local contributions, Malcolm

Forbes took a personal interest in this local effort by supplying the company's private jet to send money and supplies.

The Forbes Newspapers includes the *Somerset Messenger-Gazette, Bound Brook Chronicle*, and *Middlesex Chronicle, Piscataway-Dunellen Review, Metuchen-Edison Review, South Plainfield Reporter, Green Brook-North Plainfield Journal, Highland Park Herald, Hills-Bedminster Press, Cranford Chronicle, Franklin Focus*, and the *Scotch Plains-Fanwood Press*. Its two total advertising publications are the *Middlesex County Shopper* and the *Somerset County Shopper*, which are mailed to nonsubscriber county residents within the circulation area to achieve saturation market coverage.

Somerville's first newspaper was the *New Jersey Intelligencer*, published by John C. Kelly. It remained in business until 1820, when it was sold and the name changed to the *Somerset Messenger*.

The *Messenger-Gazette* was also derived from two other early newspapers, the *Somerset Unionist Gazette* and the *Somerset Democrat*. The *Somerset Messenger-Gazette* first appeared January 6, 1931, after the *Somerset Messenger* merged with the *Unionist Gazette* and the *Democrat*, political newspapers that lambasted each other on their front pages.

Plans for the future include expanding to publish more newspapers while keeping them contiguous. Says O'Brien, "We will continue to expand. New Jersey is growing. We're going to be part of that growth."

The late Malcolm Forbes (left), chairman and editor-in-chief of Forbes, *inspects a front page with Forbes Newspapers president and publisher John J. O'Brien in the Somerville newspaper production center.*

ZEUS SCIENTIFIC INC.

Standing, left to right: William McDowell, Joseph Turner, Donald Tourville, and William Cleary. Seated, left to right: Jean Steele, Peggy Stocker, Betty Rogozinski, and Marion Cleary.

Zeus Scientific Inc. began in 1976 with a 900-square-foot office and one employee. Today more than 50 employees work in its newly expanded 22,000-square-foot building, producing 27 medical test kits that enable physicians to test patients for autoimmune diseases, infectious diseases, sexually transmitted diseases, and breast cancer.

Zeus' test systems are distributed and used in the common-market countries of Europe, the Middle East, Canada, Japan, Mexico, and Korea, as well as other countries. Zeus Scientific test kits are distributed in the United States by Wampole Labs, a division of Carter-Wallace. Bayer Diagnostics is its exclusive distributor overseas, and Miles Diagnostic distributes in Canada.

According to company founder, chairman, and chief executive officer Dr. Donald R. Tourville, "We knew we had the wherewithal to produce quality products and that there was a need for pre-standardized diagnostic kits that could be manufactured and commercially distributed to hospital labs, large reference labs, and also to private labs."

Zeus created diagnostic test kits to aid in the diagnosis of connective tissue diseases, such as systemic lupus erythematosus (a potential multisystem disorder), liver disease (hepatitis), thyroid diseases, infectious diseases such as syphilis and toxoplasmosis (parasite infection), herpes simplex, and Legionnaires' disease (a type of pneumonia).

Tourville completed his post-doctoral fellowship in Buffalo, New York, from 1966 to 1969, when he studied under Dr. T.B. Tomasi in one of the highest-caliber labs at that time for research in the areas of immunology, allergy, and autoimmune diseases. During Tourville's career he has published more than 40 papers in academic journals.

"During 1969 I was named chief of immunopathology at St. Barnabas Medical Center in Livingston, New Jersey, where I remained until July 1979," says Tourville. "Zeus Scientific was a major breakthrough for me because I knew, based on my professional experience at the hospital, that developing diagnostic test kits would be well received by pathologists." During that year Zeus Scientific obtained the exclusive rights for a patented breast cancer test known as Fluoro-Cep®, which is noted for providing oncologists same-day results.

Zeus Scientific is known both domestically and internationally as a leader in the medical health care field for fluorescent antibody test systems. Zeus is recognized as having the broadest range of IFA test kits and applications available from a single company.

As new technologies and methodologies are developed, Tourville and his research and development staff are developing new test systems. During 1989 Zeus Scientific introduced 13 new test systems worldwide using a method known as the ELISA assay. This stands for Enzyme Linked Immuno Sorbent Assay, a method for finding antibodies in the patient's serum that are associated with a particular disease. ELISA methods are well suited for large-volume labs because the testing can be automated and thus be made more cost-effective.

In response to a nationwide health crisis, Tourville and his staff have manufactured several diagnostic test kits for Lyme disease. Zeus Scientific was a leader in obtaining Food and Drug Administration clearance for a Lyme test kit that aids the physician in the diagnosis of this disease, which some experts currently consider to be one of the most medically significant infectious diseases, second only to AIDS.

"This has been one of our most successful products," says Tourville. "The news media have played a very important role in making known that this desease is transmitted by ticks. Lyme disease is a potentially devastating disease that has raised many concerns, especially in certain areas of the northeastern United States where the disease is endemic. Lyme disease has now been reported in all 50 states."

Tourville is also involved in working on a diagnostic test for AIDS. "Scientists have learned the peptide sequence of the most common antigenic areas representative of the AIDS virus. We can make these peptides synthetically in a test tube that conveys the same antigenicity that we would find in the intact virus."

The success of Zeus Scientific was acknowledged by the U.S. Department of Commerce and the Small Business Administration (SBA) in May 1984, when Tourville received two nationally acclaimed awards. He was the first individual to be recognized as Exporter of the Year by the SBA. The second award, the President's "E" Award, was presented to him in recognition of Zeus Scientific's significant contribution to U.S. efforts to increase exports. The award was presented to Tourville by former President Ronald Reagan.

Tourville was singled out for the honor because of Zeus' successful export record. His company began exporting its products in 1979. Exports have traditionally represented 35 percent of Zeus' annual sales, with the firm's products now sold in 20 countries.

"I had been involved as a consultant for other companies before starting my business, and I knew even then that there was a fairly good overseas market for our products. We are fortunate enough to work with a company, Bayer Diagnostics, that has a very aggressive marketing policy," Tourville says. To win the award, Tourville first had to win on the state level. On the national level, he was judged with other companies that had been nominated by each state association.

One of nine children, Tourville credits his perseverance and ambition to the example set by his family. That family tradition of hard work and achievement is being carried on by his two sons: Scott, the company's controller, and John, its operations manager. Tourville's wife, Vicki, whose background is in diagnostic-equipment sales, provides him with solid support and feedback for his ideas. Joseph B. Turner, company president, who is noted as an excellent salesperson, communicator, and administrator, shares Tourville's working philosophy.

"Our future holds for an expansion, and presently we have a dedicated staff of more than 50 individuals, from Ph.D's to technicians and typists, who are carefully selected for the rigid standards set by Zeus," says Tourville.

Dr. Tourville anticipates that Zeus Scientific Inc.'s business will double through the 1990s. Everything he has set out to accomplish, he has done so with hard work, the help of good employees, and a little luck. But it seems there is no ending to what this successful, talented man can commit himself to—and to what he can accomplish.

Donald R. Tourville was presented the president's "E" Award by Ronald Reagan at the White House Rose Garden in May 1984.

HOCKENBURY ELECTRICAL COMPANY, INC.

RIGHT: J. Carl Hockenbury, Sr., founded the Hockenbury Electrical Company in 1922.

ABOVE: Jeffrey Craig Hockenbury is the third generation of the family to be involved with the Hockenbury Electrical Company.

RIGHT: J. Carl Hockenbury, Jr., became the firm's president in 1980.

A partial list of jobs completed by Hockenbury Electrical Co. Inc.

Ethicon
Ortho Pharmaceutical
Muhlenberg Hospital
Somerset County Vo-Tech
Johnson & Johnson Hospital Ser.
Hillsboro High School
Salem Industrial Park
Chandler Industrial Park
Azoplate
Immaculata High School
New Jersey Savings Bank
Raritan Savings Bank
FNB of Central Jersey/Rt. 22
FNB of Central Jersey/Somerville
FNB of Central Jersey/Hillsboro
St. Mary's Parish—Hillsboro
St. Bernards School—Bridgewater
St. Francis Cabrini Church
Stillman School
Somerset Residence

Over the course of three generations and nearly 70 years, Hockenbury Electrical Company, Inc., has grown from a small electrical fixture store to a large electrical contracting firm, serving major business clients and residential customers. The firm provides design/build services for electrical installation, including telephone systems, fire alarms, and sound systems. The company provides its clients with a set of electrical-construction drawings to meet local and state building requirements.

Among the firm's major projects is the Central Jersey Industrial Park, which required work on 52 buildings. The firm also completed all of the electrical work for the Salem Industrial Park's 11 buildings. As part of a major renovation project to enlarge the Muhlenberg Hospital and Medical Center in Plainfield, Hockenbury Electrical Company converted the hospital's electrical system from 4,160 to 13,000 volts. The firm also served as the prime contractor on the new Ortho Pharmaceutical Administration Building—a $3.1-million project managed by firm supervisor George "Buck" LaFever.

Carl Hockenbury says, "We take pride in what we do, and we stand behind every job."

The firm was founded in 1922 by J. Carl Hockenbury, Sr., son of John and Ida Hockenbury of Glen Gardner. Carl Hockenbury's company was originally known as Carl Hockenbury,

Electrical Contractor. To get his start in business, he went to New York Electric School during the day and worked at a New York post office at night.

He opened a fixture showroom on Division Street in Somerville, which was operated by his wife, Meta. Carl Hockenbury finally established his office and residence at 29 East High Street in Somerville, where the office is still located. He started out by convincing groups of home owners to sign up for a conversion from gas to wiring, and then Public Service extended poles for electrical service because there were several customers concentrated in one area.

In 1948 the founder's son, Carl Hockenbury, Jr., and Buck LaFever, Carl Jr.'s high school friend, went to New York Electrical School together. Upon completion they joined Local 262 IBEW electrical union, with whom Hockenbury Electrical Company, Inc., is still affiliated. To manage a rapidly growing business, in 1966 Carl Hockenbury, Jr., began primarily focusing his efforts on overseeing the office operation, and LaFever became field superintendent.

Carl Hockenbury, Jr., became president in 1980, and his son, Jeffrey Craig, has joined the firm as an apprentice electrician. An active member of the community, Carl Hockenbury has served as president of the Somerset Valley YMCA, president of the Somerville Kiwanis Club, and is a member of the Greater Somerset County Chamber of Commerce.

"When my father started the business, we just handled residential accounts. Today we also manage commercial and industrial accounts. The economic growth of Somerset County helped expand our business," says Carl Hockenbury.

SOMERSET MEDICAL CENTER

Somerset Medical Center in Somerville pledges to link medical expertise and technology to human needs. The medical center is a nationally accredited 374-bed acute care and teaching hospital affiliated with the University of Medicine and Dentistry of New Jersey. It serves central New Jersey residents, using the most progressive medical technology and a caring, dedicated professional staff.

The medical and dental staff, comprised of more than 350 physicians in all the major medical and surgical specialties, must meet strict criteria regarding education and experience. As a result, Somerset Medical Center has one of the highest percentages of board-certified physicians in New Jersey. Board certification requires physicians to pass stringent tests in their specialty.

The nursing staff, dedicated to the individual rights of its patients, delivers patient care efficiently and compassionately. Many nurses on the staff hold advanced degrees and are certified in various nursing specialties. The support staff delivers professional expertise, talent, and energy in making Somerset Medical Center an outstanding leader in New Jersey health care; many are certified in their various specialties and have advanced degrees.

Emergency services include a Mobile Intensive Care Unit (MICU) and an Emergency Department, both open around the clock. The MICU is an emergency room on wheels that works with the Emergency Department. More than 3,000 MICU calls are answered annually, and more than 26,000 patients are received in the emergency room.

In the Same Day Center surgical and nonsurgical procedures are conducted on an outpatient basis. General services include cardiology, the Center for Diagnostic Imaging, a clinical laboratory, speech and hearing, and laboratories for EEG, gastroenterology, pulmonary function, and noninvasive vascular procedures. The Center for Diagnostic Imaging includes digital subtraction angiography (DSA), a mammography suite, ultrasound, nuclear medicine, and computerized tomography (CT). The gastroenterology laboratory is the largest and most comprehensive lab of its kind in the state. Critical care for patients is administered in the Coronary Care Unit, the Special Care Unit, and the Progressive Coronary Care Unit.

Family-Centered Maternity Care offers a full range of family-centered services and education and a Regional Level II neonatal intensive care nursery. Located in the Pediatrics Department is the Sunshine Suite, a day-care center for ill children.

Special services include the Center for Lasers Surgery, which offers laser treatment for cardiovascular disease, ophthalmology, neurosurgery, urology, gastroenterology, and gynecology; the Diabetes Treatment Center; and the nationally accredited Oncology Center. Somerset Medical Center participates with other New Jersey hospitals in the Garden State Community Dialysis Center and the New Jersey Kidney Stone Treatment Center.

Other medical center services include the Center for Mental Health, Eating Disorders Program, STAR (Specialized Treatment for Addictions Recovery) Program, Social Work Department and its Hospice Program, Department of Physical Medicine and Rehabilitation, Cardiac Rehabilitation Program, Blood Donor Program/Blood Bank, Homebound Communications Program, Educational Services, and a physician referral service.

"As Somerset Medical Center is progressively recognized as one of the stronger, more viable health care institutions in New Jersey, we reaffirm our responsibility and pledge our best efforts toward continuing our delivery of a superior health care system," states William J. Monagle, president.

Somerset Medical Center is designated as a Regional Level II neonatal intensive care nursery and is staffed by a neonatologist as well as certified nurses who give optimal care to premature infants and ailing newborns.

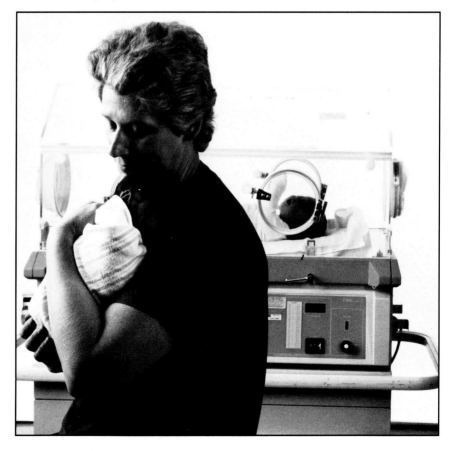

SOMERSET WOOD PRODUCTS CO.

Somerset Wood Products Co. has grown considerably since its start in 1967 as a modest custom cabinet shop with five employees in a 3,000-square-foot facility. Today this highly sophisticated 65,000-square-foot architectural-woodwork firm employs more than 50 employees. Its headquarters, among the most modern in the industry, serves as a showcase for the company's beautifully crafted woodwork designs.

This success story is the result of the efforts of president Lester Bloch and his wife, Dorothy "Dottie" Bloch. After serving eight years as general manager and turning the company around into a profitable operation, Brooklyn natives Lester and Dorothy Bloch bought Somerset Wood Products from the original owner, Paul Henderson, in 1976.

The firm transforms the concepts of architects and interior designers into interior furnishings, finished wall panels, furniture, cabinetry, reception desks, molding, and more. Somerset Wood Products is a turnkey operation starting with the process of drafting and design to manufacturing raw materials into finished products.

The employees of Somerset Wood Products bring a combined total of more than 200 years of experience to producing architectural woodwork for schools, hospitals, institutions, and corporate facilities. The company has worked with many of the country's leading architecture and interior-design firms.

Among Somerset Wood Products' most notable projects are the courtrooms and judges'

Somerset Wood Products' own executive offices (below) and conference room (above right) are examples of the beauty of a polished wood design.

chambers for the Supreme Court of New Jersey, a new building by world-renowned architect I.M. Pei in New York's Mount Sinai hospital complex, the ABC television studios in New York, Somerset County Courthouse, and the restoration of Mead Hall at Drew University.

As part of the restoration team for Ellis Island, Somerset Wood Products refurbished most of the facility's woodwork, including doors, frames, and interior paneling. The project required retaining as much of the original material as possible, which entailed a painstaking matching process so that old and new woods could be placed side by side. As a result of this work, the company is recognized by the New York Landmark Commission as qualified to deal in the restoration of historical woodwork. Bloch attributes the company's success to maintaining his commitment to personalized service while expanding its product line and improving production methods.

"We began as a mom-and-pop business, and we still apply a hands-on approach to our work," Bloch explains, crediting Dorothy, chief administrative officer, with the company's ability to meet all the increasingly complex legal and contractual requirements of the construction industry.

Lester Bloch's management approach was greatly influenced by his experience as an evening student in the Bernard Baruch College production management BBA program and the MBA program in entrepreneurial management at Rutgers University.

As part of the strategy to expand his business, Bloch recognized the need to expand beyond wood and plastic laminate to glass, metals, and other architectural materials. The company now offers stock wood doors, post-formed plastic laminates, wood molding, and custom and production-run cabinetry and paneling. The firm is also a licensed UL door fabricator and one of the largest woodwork fabricators of Dupont Corian in New Jersey. The plant produces these

LEFT: *The ABC lobby and reception desk in New York shows off Somerset Wood Products' fine woodworking skill and expertise.*

BELOW: *The company is responsible for all the woodwork in the courtrooms of the Somerset County Courthouse.*

non-wood products with the same skill and care in fabrication it gives to wood.

"The trend among large clients is to put total responsibility with a single source," Bloch says. "In order to meet this demand, we must offer all related items, including marble, fabrics, architectural metal, accessories, and architectural hardware in addition to wood and plastic laminate. To meet the needs of the construction industry, for example, we stock thousands of dollars worth of birch, red oak, white oak, and walnut doors."

Bloch established financial controls and cost-management measures usually associated with corporate giants to his small firm. He also reinvested profits into improving the company's capabilities by buying new innovative equipment five to 10 years before they became standard in the industry.

"I felt strongly that it was necessary to improve production methods to increase efficiency while still maintaining our custom capabilities," Bloch says.

Somerset Wood Products is one of the few woodworkers in the metropolitan area that operates its own molder, which enables the company to maintain control over quality and delivery on each job. The firm creates its own patterns, grinding the required knives and finally running the raw wood into finished molding.

Its latest innovation is a new automated finishing facility that adopts furniture manufacturing techniques to custom work. Wood products are moved assembly-line style from a spray booth to a drying oven. To reduce labor costs and increase productivity, the system enables fewer

people to do more work. Several other areas of the shop are also semiautomated or computerized.

"As important as technology is, you can't run machines without people," says Bloch. "We are able to respond to customers' needs because we treat our employees with respect, and they take pride in their work."

Somerset Wood Products Co. has instituted a training program to carry on the tradition of fine craftsmanship while simultaneously teaching workers new technology. The firm as well as its principals are active members in the Architectural Woodwork Institute (AWI), an organization in which Bloch once served on the board of directors.

According to Bloch, "Our mainstay is that we seldom say we can't do something. We try to accommodate the customer with short time schedules and difficult requirements."

REBTEX, INC.

With an industry-wide reputation for its expert and imaginative work, Rebtex ranks among the nation's top leaders in textile dyeing.

Rebtex of Somerset County ranks among the nation's top leaders in textile dyeing, serving textile converters from coast to coast. During its many years in business, the firm has dyed millions of yards of material that grace today's fashions and homes.

The firm's family atmosphere starts with its president, Robert Brandell, and the more than 100 employees, who all take personal pride in every yard of fiber they dye.

Brandell takes a personal interest in every member of his staff. He and his wife, Frances, the company's secretary and treasurer, have worked side by side with employees for more than 40 years, keeping close tabs on how they and their families are doing. The result of this close interrelationship is loyal employees, some of whom have been with the company for 10 to 35 years. The quality of the company's dyed products is a direct reflection of the care the Brandells and their employees give their work.

The firm's roots began in 1919, when Robert Brandell's father-in-law, Andrew J. Ackerman, helped a French company set itself up for the dyeing of greige goods for veils, which were then, and for decades after, a major high-fashion embellishment in millinery (women's hats).

Two years later Ackerman established his own business with 15 employees, the United Veil Dyeing and Finishing Company. In its many years of operation the company has consistently

maintained an enviable industry-wide reputation for its expert and imaginative work.

Because of this reputation the word "veil" in the company's name has been retained, in spite of the fact that veils have been almost entirely eliminated in recent years. This occurred when former First Lady Jacqueline Kennedy and others among the world's best-dressed women introduced the pillbox hat, which revolutionized millinery fashion.

In 1939 Ackerman left Paterson and reestablished in Jersey City. Robert Brandell joined the family business in 1955, after serving in the armed services.

During the 1970s United Veil Dyeing and Finishing Company decided to diversify its business and directed its experience and sophistication toward textiles for better home furnishings, and it has progressed steadily to a position of leadership in that industry.

When the Jersey City location had to be expanded, the family moved the home-furnishings products operation to Somerset in 1985, where they started a new company called Rebtex. Brandell's two sons, Robert and Thomas, both played a leadership role in setting up the new Somerset operation. Brandell's daughter Michelle is also active in the business.

Brandell and his family converted the former National Lockwasher Plant that produced automobile parts to an operation that dyes home-furnishing products such as shower curtains,

LEFT: Modern equipment and employee care ensure a perfect dyeing job every time.

BELOW: Rebtex utilizes state-of-the-art technology, including computerized dyeing systems.

draperies, and tablecloths. The structure of the building was well suited to be adapted for Rebtex's needs. Experienced employees from the Jersey City location helped set up the Somerset operation and trained new employees in the highly specialized techniques for fabric dyeing.

The shift to the home-furnishings market was a natural evolution of the firm's capabilities in the clothing industry as it uses lace to create home furnishings. The home-furnishing products are made radiantly beautiful by the unique dyeing processes that the firm uses. The Jersey City plant continues to dye and process lingerie and outerwear fabrics.

In a few years the Somerset plant was expanded from its original 65,000 square feet to 120,000 to keep pace with an increased demand for Rebtex dyed products. The Somerset location was ideal because it provided easy access to New York City for customer meetings and product shipments to major clients in fashion and home furnishings.

The Somerset location has the latest equipment, including computerized dyeing systems. Rebtex, Inc., is one of the few independent, small dyeing businesses in the country to use state-of-the-art technology. The equipment enables the firm to dye an increased number of goods per hour and to match colors more accurately.

"To ensure our clients are 100 percent satisfied with our work, every piece of linen has to be dyed to the designer's specification. We used to do it by eye before, using a process called spoon dyeing, but we can now avoid errors in mixing colors by using the computer, which gives the exact tone," says Robert Brandell.

"Essentially we work for converters. The converter buys the greige goods from knitters,

turns them over to us for dyeing, and then does the selling. Our plant does a great deal of dyeing, with many thousands of webs, or rolls, each week. Even so, we continue to cater to minimum orders," he explains. "A two-web minimum order is somewhat unique in an industry that generally deals in bulk orders. However, we understand our customers' needs and problems, and we do all in our power to cooperate with them."

JOHNSON & JOHNSON

A spectacular, three-story atrium is the hallmark of the Ortho Pharmaceutical Corp. headquarters on Route 202 in Raritan.

During the early development of business and industry in our country, few people thought of corporations as being "caring." But in more recent years, companies have found that business can not only be caring, but it can even reflect the personalities and emotions of people.

In the case of Johnson & Johnson the development of a tiny handful of individuals in New Brunswick more than 100 years ago to the world's largest health care company today is a story of a collection of people who work together and have developed a personality that is reflected not only in its products but in the concerns of the communities in which they work and live.

Somerset County Johnson & Johnson is part of a larger organization that is actually not one company but 160 entities in 55 countries. Together these companies represent the largest and most diversified health care company in the world, and it is the only corporation serving all 23 medical specialties, from anesthesiology to urology.

As it has often been in the health care industry, the local Johnson & Johnson company was in the forefront in the development of Somerset County as one of the most attractive locations in the country.

JOHNSON & JOHNSON IN SOMERSET COUNTY

Somerset County abounds with J&J companies. When Ortho Pharmaceutical Corporation located in Raritan in 1946, oral contraception was truly in its infancy.

When ETHICON moved to Bridgewater Township a decade later, it was to consolidate five different surgical-suture locations that had scattered in and around Johnson & Johnson holdings in the New Brunswick area.

In subsequent years other J&J companies adopted Somerset County, including Ortho Diagnostics Systems Inc., a leading-edge diagnostic laboratory systems producer, and Johnson & Johnson Management Information Center, hub of the worldwide computer network for J&J. Both companies are located in Raritan.

More recent additions are Johnson & Johnson Consumer Products Co. in Skillman, producing the familiar line of consumer baby products, and Devro, Inc., of Somerville, a producer of natural protein sausage casings, a spin-off of ETHICON research into artificial sutures.

As Somerset County has mushroomed into one of the fastest-growing counties in the state over the past decade, the Johnson & Johnson companies in Somerset County have also reflected dramatic growth. More than 6,000 employees representing a broad spectrum of technical, scientific, and professional training now comprise the response team to the ever-broadening and unprecedented health care needs of the world.

THE CREDO

Several national publications have described this growth as remarkable—yet there has been a unique continuity—a guiding path represented by a set of beliefs embodied in the Johnson & Johnson Credo. Authorized by the late General Robert Wood Johnson in the mid-1940s, The Credo is an internationally known declaration of corporate responsibility that has proved to be an enduring document.

The Credo continues as evidence of General Johnson's remarkable vision in foreseeing the need for business to accept its multiple responsibilities to its customers, employees, shareholders, society, and the community at large.

Some 2,300 ETHICON employees spell out "Pride!"—the motto of Quality Improvement Process—on the lawn of the Route 22 plant.

Recently the company announced a precedent-setting corporate initiative, the Work and Family Program. It includes a comprehensive set of policies, benefits, and services to help meet the wide and continually evolving range of family needs.

Perhaps the most visible tenet of the credo is that which charges each company and each employee to assert community responsibility. The call for all employees to loan their talents to the communities in which they reside, coupled with management initiatives to direct attention to community problems and projects, have had a profound impact on Somerset County.

As J&J board chairman Ralph Larsen says, "The Johnson & Johnson credo is a great deal more than a collection of words. We believe in it, we are serious about it, and we work at supporting its principles."

J&J employees have been part of the very substance of community endeavors, from leadership roles in youth shelters, elder-care groups, mental-health and learning-disability entities, trusteeships on hospital boards, school boards, first-aid squads, and volunteer firefighters. The corporate commitment is almost legendary. J&J Somerset County companies matched employee giving in the United Way of the Somerset Valley and became the first company in United Way history to top the million-dollar mark.

Capital campaign contributions of $300,000 to Somerset Medical Center and $200,000 to Hunterdon Medical Center were both area record breakers. Commitments of $100,000 to PeopleCare Center, Rolling Hills Girl Scout Council, and Somerset Valley YMCA were also major leadership responses.

The Somerset County commitments are an important contributor to the national recognition of Johnson & Johnson, which was selected by *Fortune* magazine as the number-one corporation in the country in the Community and Environment category, for the third consecutive year.

While J&J employees from different Somerset County companies often join together in their community endeavors, the products and services generated by the respective companies are widely diversified.

ETHICON, INC.

When Johnson & Johnson published its first product catalog in 1887, four catgut and four silk sutures were listed. Today, under the banner of ETHICON, Inc., more than 3,000 different types of sutures and needle combinations and mechanical staplers are represented in the product listing

of the world's largest producer of wound-closure products.

Chances are that anyone who has had an operation has had some blood vessels tied with ETHICON ligatures or an incision closed with ETHICON sutures or mechanical devices.

Over the years ETHICON sutures have changed to keep pace with the dramatic strides made in fields like microsurgery and cardiovascular surgery. For example, in response to surgeons performing valve-replacement surgery, ETHICON developed a line of polyester sutures. For the microsurgeon, sutures three times finer than a human hair have been produced.

The vast majority of ETHICON sutures are attached to surgical needles, thus eliminating the need to thread suture material through a needle. ETHICON needle technology is among the finest in the world, and the company is the only suture manufacturer that produces both the needle and suture within its own control processes.

ETHICON's commitment to mechanical wound closure came with introduction of the Proximate disposable skin stapler in 1978. Since then a number of products has followed, including the Proximate linear stapler, combining the benefits of reusable staples with design advancements and disposability.

The Proximate linear cutter allows the surgeon to cut and join tissue throughout the gastrointestinal tract and thoracic cavity. It is used not only to remove diseased portions, but to bring the remaining healthy ends back together.

As ETHICON product lines have expanded, so have its facilities. In addition to Somerville headquarters, which includes administrative research and production facilities, other

Ortho Diagnostic Systems, Inc., has a full line of blood-typing reagents produced by the use of monoclonal antibodies.

This microsurgery needle produced at ETHICON, Inc., shown alongside the head of a match, is used with a suture one-third the diameter of a human hair.

The ETHICON Worldwide Headquarters' surgical-suture plant, located on Route 22 in Bridgewater, was the winner of a "Factories Can Be Beautiful" national contest.

domestic locations include operations in Chicago, Illinois; San Angelo, Texas; Albuquerque, New Mexico; Cornelia, Georgia; Cincinnati, Ohio; and San Lorenzo, Puerto Rico.

ETHICON leadership is evident in the worldwide scope of its operations, with products manufactured in 13 countries: Canada, Mexico, Brazil, Venezuela, France, Germany, Italy, Scotland, Sweden, India, Pakistan, South Africa, and Australia.

ORTHO PHARMACEUTICAL CORP.

A single product for family planning and improved female health led to the birth of Ortho Pharmaceutical Corp. 50 years ago. The formation of Ortho Products Inc. in 1940 was preceded by the first prescription contraceptive jelly for women and was followed by its second product, a vaginal cream. These pioneering products led to extensive growth that necessitated a new facility, and the first of a series of buildings was constructed in 1946 on Route 202 in Raritan.

Through the years Ortho scientists have introduced some historical innovations into medical science. During the 1940s a diagnostic test called the Pap smear was introduced to detect cervical and uterine cancer and is still in use today.

Work on another diagnostic preparation to test the blood of newborns of the Rh-negative mothers led Ortho researcher Dr. Philip Levine into medical history by identifying the problem and its cause. The breakthrough in 1968 for RhoGam, the first product for prevention of Rh hemolytic disease, has been credited with saving the lives of thousands of children born to Rh-negative mothers.

The introduction in 1951 of the first vaginal contraceptive for use without a diaphragm, Preceptin Vaginal Gel, led its developer, Dr. Carl Hartman, to further research in reproductive physiology that became the springboard for modern birth-control methods. As early as 1957 Ortho scientists began investigating hormone combinations to prevent pregnancy, and in 1963 Ortho-Novum 10 milligrams, known worldwide as "the Pill," was introduced.

Today Ortho is a diversified company with products in contraception and female therapeutics, dermatology, and biotechnology. As the leader in oral-contraceptive therapy, Ortho markets a variety of oral-contraceptive dosage strengths to meet a wide range of needs, includ-

A leader in monoclonal antibody technology, Ortho's Biotech Division was the first to discover, produce, and market monoclonal antibodies for therapeutic use.

ing the most widely prescribed oral contraceptive in the United States. Ortho also manufactures the most widely prescribed contraceptive diaphragm, and it is a leader in female therapeutic products with vaginal creams and suppositories. Other prescription products nearing the United States marketplace include a treatment for infertility and an oral antibiotic.

Ortho's Dermatological Division markets products to treat a range of skin problems. Leading products are Retina-A Gel/Cream, Spectazole Cream, and Monistat Cream.

Assuming a leadership role in biotechnology, Ortho introduced the first monoclonal antibodies for research and diagnostic use in 1980. In 1986 the Biotech Division marketed a treatment to reverse the body's rejection of a newly transplanted kidney, the first monoclonal antibody for therapeutic use. Today, as a newly organized separate operating company, Ortho Biotech is developing a treatment for anemia, and until it receives Food and Drug Administration marketing approval, the division provides its product at no charge through the FDA Treatment IND program to patients suffering AIDS-related anemia.

To meet today's competitive research environment, Johnson & Johnson pharmaceutical companies have coordinated their research and development groups to form the R.W. Johnson Pharmaceutical Research Institute.

Through PRI, Ortho maintains active research programs in a broad range of therapeutic categories. Research continues in contraception and female therapeutics. In dermatology,

Ortho is a leader in topical retinoid research. Biotechnology research centers on monoclonal antibodies and substances that promote the growth of specific blood cells, known as hematopoietic growth factors. Major research efforts are under way in cardiology, immunology, and infectious diseases.

Today Ortho's worldwide headquarters occupies a 203-acre site in Raritan. Other facilities include a distribution center in Franklin Township, manufacturing sites in Puerto Rico and the United Kingdom, and a diaphragm manufacturing facility in Geneva, Illinois. The company's products are marketed in more than 100 countries worldwide.

ORTHO DIAGNOSTIC SYSTEMS INC.

Holding a position of preeminence in its field, Ortho Diagnostic Systems Inc., located on Route 202 in Raritan, provides diagnostic reagent and instrument systems to hospital laboratories, commercial clinical laboratories, and blood-donor centers worldwide.

An independent subsidiary since 1974, following earlier operations as a J&J division, ODSI achieved early commercial success in the 1960s with the development and introduction of the RhoGAM Rho(D) Immune Globulin (human), an immunoglobulin solution that prevents diseases in newborns.

With the influx of the AIDS virus, ODSI researchers developed the HIV-1 ELISA Test System in 1986, screening for the HIV antibody, which is associated with AIDS. The Ortho assays offer very sensitive and highly specific results in a convenient micro-well format supported by automated procedures for test manipulation.

In late 1989 Ortho Diagnostics joined in a landmark agreement with Abbott Laboratories and Chiron Corporation, agreeing to collaborate in developing and supplying the world's first hepatitis C diagnostic products for blood banks, hospitals, and laboratories. The hepatitis C virus is transmitted predominantly by blood transfusions and affects as many as 175,000 in the United States and 700,000 people worldwide each year.

Other agreements will result in diagnostic products for patient self-screening, monitoring, and diagnosis of disease not served by existing products.

A more definitive focus on the AIDS scourge is represented in the early 1990 agreement to join with Chiron in the purchase of Du Pont's AIDS and hepatitis blood-screening business. The newly combined business results in one of the major suppliers of such tests worldwide.

The ever-changing business climate re-

Technicians at Ortho Pharmaceutical Corp. undergo elaborate sterilization procedures before entering an area especially designed to protect filled glass ampules from impurities.

sulted in a corporate restructuring that combined the former Johnson & Johnson Baby Products Company and two other subsidiaries, Johnson & Johnson Dental Care Company and Johnson & Johnson Health Care Company, into a new entity, Johnson & Johnson Consumer Products Company. All operations are locating at the Skillman plant formerly occupied by J&J Baby Products.

CONCLUSION

In the ensuing years from Johnson & Johnson's founding in 1888, the one accolade that keeps being repeated is the simple but meaningful statement: "It's a good place to work." Perhaps the most important reason is that the company has always been able to attract quality people.

The formula equates to quality people attracting other quality people, and over the years Johnson & Johnson has evolved into the largest and most versatile health care company in the world— with firm roots anchored in Somerset County.

This multistory, glass-paneled structure anchors the Ortho Pharmaceutical Corp. headquarters complex in Raritan.

LOWENSTEIN, SANDLER, KOHL, FISHER & BOYLAN

Attorneys with Lowenstein, Sandler are well versed in litigation and business, banking, real estate, bankruptcy, and environmental law, although all general matters of law are handled in the office. Conferences regarding client matters involve the participation of law specialists, such as (from left) William Munday, Stuart Yusem, Steven Fuerst, and Phyllis Pasternak. Photo by Nat Clymer

Modern offices in Raritan house work space for 60 lawyers, paralegals, and support personnel. Lowenstein, Sandler has a state-of-the-art legal library with computer access to case information retrieval systems. Photo by Nat Clymer

"Lawyers serving the business community" was the goal set when Lowenstein, Sandler, Kohl, Fisher & Boylan was founded in 1961. It still is the preeminent role the firm plays in New Jersey's business/industrial community with a dramatic record of growth and success.

Built on a solid base of practice by its founders, Lowenstein, Sandler has become one of the largest banking and corporate law firms in New Jersey, with 125 lawyers, 27 paralegals, and a total staff of 325 people. The firm's impressive and diversified list of clients includes a number of New Jersey corporate and financial giants, but also many mid-size and small businesses, both publicly owned and closely held. The number of out-of-state clients continues to expand as national awareness of the firm's capabilities to serve business has increased.

To expand into the growth areas of central New Jersey, Lowenstein, Sandler opened a full-service office in Somerville to complement its headquarters in Roseland. The managing director in Somerville is Steven B. Fuerst, former president of the Somerset Bar Association. A specialist in business, banking, and real estate law as well as litigation, Fuerst started a Somerville-

based firm in 1973 and joined Lowenstein, Sandler in 1982.

The Somerville office has a full-range practice with its primary focus on commercial development, real estate, litigation, tax law, and white-collar criminal defense. The office is noted for handling complex litigation cases as well as land use issues.

Lowenstein, Sandler has been a catalyst with other major New Jersey law firms in shattering the long-held belief that New Jersey businesses had to turn to New York or Philadelphia for high-powered corporate legal services.

The firm's capabilities to offer specialized services necessary for today's dynamic business climate include staff specialists to meet the most-current client needs in mergers and acquisitions, state and federal taxes, corporate and public finance, securities law, environmental law counseling and litigation, and in the growing area of corporate employee ownership.

The range of specialized services and the quality of professional expertise are shown by the various departments of Lowenstein, Sandler. Business attorneys provide the broad range of expertise to act as general counsel for a wide variety of companies. Health care attorneys serve both proprietary and nonprofit clients. Litigation attorneys provide assistance to the firm's business clients in litigating both criminal and civil matters. Environmental attorneys provide expertise in all phases of environmental law for clients across the country. Real estate attorneys assist clients in contracting, financing, zoning, site planning, subdivision, environmental, and tax aspects of real estate transactions. Securities attorneys offer broad expertise in all phases of securities law, from representing issuers of public offerings to going-private transactions, including leveraged buy outs. Tax attorneys provide highly specialized tax planning services. Employee benefits attorneys assist clients in designing and implementing employee compensation programs. Lowenstein, Sandler, Kohl, Fisher & Boylan's estate planning and administration attorneys provide sophisticated estate and income-tax planning for individuals and stockholders of closely held corporations.

"As time goes by there will be more and more businesses availing themselves of this area's resources. We plan to continue to serve existing businesses in the area with a full range of legal services and provide services to new businesses as they establish themselves here in keeping with the Lowenstein, Sandler commitment to be 'Lawyers serving the business community,'" says Steve Fuerst.

3M

Tiny colored granules of rock that have helped to beautify rooftops throughout New Jersey and the eastern United States are produced at the 3M Industrial Minerals Division facility on Sourland Mountain in southern Somerset County.

The multicolored granules that cover the surface of roofing shingles are one of the more than 50 major product lines made by 3M—everything from famous Scotch-brand tapes and Post-it notes to sandpaper, fiber-optic connectors, high-technology adhesives, and health care products.

Located along Route 601 southwest of Belle Mead, the Somerset facility is one of five 3M operations in New Jersey that employ a total of nearly 1,000 people. The Belle Mead site, which began operations in 1961, covers 1,300 acres.

Most of the acreage is maintained as an environmental preserve, with forestland and abundant wildlife. A small portion, approximately 60 acres, is used as a quarry to mine the area's unique diabase rock found on Sourland Mountain, and for processing facilities where the rock is crushed and colored before being shipped to roofing manufacturers. The by-products are sold for other useful purposes, such as highway paving material or ballast for railroad tracks and breakwaters.

The quarry, which is more than a half-mile from the nearest public highway, has a series of steep winding roads through a heavily wooded area. Inside the quarry, diabase is broken up by sophisticated drilling and blasting techniques. Quarry trucks, with tires as high as a pickup truck, transport the boulders to modern, automatic crushing facilities that reduce the rock to granule size.

When screened and graded to proper specifications, the raw granules are transported to a nearby coloring facility, where the drama of the entire story takes place. Under a patented 3M process, the granules receive a durable, colorfast ceramic coating. This is the color that has transformed the rooftops of America. It has given home owners the opportunity to choose from a wide range of roof colors to harmonize with exterior design and trim. The selection runs from pure white to solid black and includes the new pastels as well as the 3M-developed brilliant colors.

As with all 3M products, a vast amount of research and quality control has gone into every pound of roofing granules. And while research has led to advancements in product and process technology, other improvements also have been made at the Belle Mead facility over the years. The most recent changes have reduced noise and dust and have helped to protect the environment.

In 1971 3M Belle Mead made a generous gift of 650 scenic acres of woodland to the Somerset County Park Commission, helping to preserve a lovely and historic area for future generations to enjoy. The acreage is spectacularly rugged with fine forests and some of the most attractive mountain views in the state. 3M Belle Mead also donated one of the oldest houses in the county to the Van Harlingen Historical Society. The house is located just south of the main entrance to the 3M site.

The Belle Mead facility is one in a family of nearly 100 3M manufacturing locations in the United States. 3M corporate headquarters is located in St. Paul, Minnesota.

For many years 3M has ranked as one of the nation's most admired companies, especially for its research and innovation, financial management, and environmental leadership.

The 3M quarry atop Sourland Mountain, where diabase rock is broken up by sophisticated drilling and blasting techniques. Large trucks carry the boulders to modern, automatic crushing facilities at the 3M Belle Mead site that reduce the rock to granule size. The granules are then colored in a range of attractive hues.

The multicolored granules are shipped to manufacturers of shingles, which are used to protect and beautify roofs throughout New Jersey and the eastern United States.

THOMAS & BETTS CORPORATION

Thomas & Betts Corporation is an expanding international *Fortune* 500 firm engaged in the design, manufacture, and marketing of electrical and electronic components and systems.

T&B's products are used for connecting, fastening, protecting, and identifying wires, components, and conduits. The corporation operates throughout North America, Western Europe, and the Far East.

Thomas & Betts was founded in 1898 by Robert McKean Thomas and Hobart D. Betts, electrical engineers who had been classmates at Princeton. Selling electrical wires and raceway tubes (for enclosing and protecting electric wires) on a commission basis, the two men formed Thomas & Betts Company in New York City. A third partner, Adnah McMurtrie, developed products that later launched the firm's manufacturing activities.

The business was quite profitable from the start. By 1910 T&B had acquired the Standard Electric Fittings Company of Stamford, Connecticut, which had been making most of its products. T&B moved the operation to Elizabeth, New Jersey, built a factory, and, in 1916, officially became a New Jersey company, designing, manufacturing, and selling electrical raceway accessories.

The relocated company had 125 employees and still retained an office in New York City. T&B soon built a second New Jersey plant, and in 1928 it established Thomas & Betts Ltd. in Canada.

T&B's product line continued to expand, with several company innovations in solderless terminations. This technique greatly improved methods of connecting and terminating wires and cables by eliminating the more expensive and less reliable soldering operations. In 1934 T&B introduced the Wedgeon®, the first solderless copper connector, and the Tightbind®, a cast-copper connector. Both won wide approval in the industry.

During World War II Thomas & Betts products were widely used in the wiring of aircraft, ships, submarines, tanks, and other armaments. T&B received the Army/Navy "E" Award for efficiency in war production five times.

In 1959 T&B revolutionized wire tying with its TY-RAP® cable ties and straps. The TY-RAP® reduced labor time, cut the weight of the material used, and was more reliable. TY-RAP® cable ties are still a growing and highly profitable product line. Also in 1959 T&B, which had been a closely held company since its formation, went public.

During the 1960s Thomas & Betts products went into space on the TelStar satellite and other space vehicles. T&B introduced its flat conductor cable and connectors, which also were lighter in weight, easier to install, and more reliable than conventional wiring, making them a natural for the space program.

In that same decade the company became multinational, moving into Europe and the Far East. Today T&B has two plants in England, two in France, two in Germany, and one in Luxembourg, as well as sales companies in England, France, Germany, Italy, Sweden, and Spain. T&B also has both sales and manufacturing operations in Japan, Taiwan, Singapore, Australia, and Canada.

The firm moved into the electronics business in the late 1950s with the development of flat cable for NASA, followed later on by insulation displacement connectors for flat cable. Electronic products then comprised less than 5 percent of the business; today electronics represents more than 40 percent of sales and continues to grow. In 1987 Thomas & Betts moved to its current headquarters, a modern complex in Bridgewater, New Jersey.

Thomas & Betts, a Fortune *500 company, is headquartered in this impressive structure in Bridgewater.*

T&B's five core product lines are fittings, terminations, electrical fastening products on the electrical side, insulation displacement connectors (IDCs), and chip capacitors on the electronics side. The company is a market leader in all five of its core product lines.

New proprietary products are continuously developed by the firm. Its insulation displacement connectors, two-piece connectors, opto-electronics connectors, and insulation products for the telecommunications industry are just a few examples of its recent innovations.

Thomas & Betts has introduced a major new product family every 10 to 15 years, the result of money well spent on research and development and market research, and it owns hundreds of patents. While the electrical industry as a whole spends about 1.6 percent of sales on research and development, Thomas & Betts allocates about 4 percent.

The company's main electronic markets are electronic office equipment, factory automation, and automotive electronics, as well as others. Electronic sales are through distribution and sold directly to major accounts.

Today two-fifths of Thomas & Betts' total business is international, and three-fifths is domestic. T&B's domestic electrical business comprises about 40 percent of sales and domestic electronics represents about 15 percent. The company's international operations, divided between electrical and electronics products, account for the remaining 45 percent of total business.

Since T&B went public in 1959, it has provided an almost 15 percent average yearly total return to shareholders, composed of 2.7 percent in dividends and the balance in stock appreciation. It has paid dividends every year since 1934, and for the past 10 years it has averaged an 11 percent after-tax profit on sales, nearly three times the national average. Company philosophy has always stressed the long-term benefit to the shareholder.

Though Thomas & Betts is a mid-size company, it has continued to play an important role in its industry. Three of its officers have served as chairman of the National Electrical Manufacturers Association.

WOODGLEN GRAPHICS

Centrally located at 56 Old Camplain Road in Somerville, Woodglen's 6,000-square-foot facility offers complete printing services.

This five-color perfector is one of six presses that enable Woodglen craftsmen to achieve the finest lithographic production.

Twelve years ago a commercial printing company opened shop in Somerset County with only one press and a lot of optimism. That company was Woodglen Graphics, and today it boasts six presses, including a five-color perfector housed in a new facility designed specifically for print production. The secret of Woodglen's growth, according to Jack Holthaus, company founder and president, is customer service. Years of experience in the printing trade provide the background.

As a young man during college summer vacations, Holthaus worked at a printing company where his father was plant superintendent. Upon graduation he worked as a plant manager for two printing companies, where his experience was instrumental in bringing those firms to multimillion-dollar business levels.

He then decided to go into business for himself, and he began as an independent print broker before starting Woodglen Graphics in 1978.

In keeping with the tradition established by his father, Holthaus' two sons serve as production manager and bindery foreman. Holthaus' wife helps with administrative duties.

Since the company's founding, its customer base has grown steadily, along with the necessary equipment and services to satisfy that base. In addition to the presses, Woodglen Graphics has a complete pre-press operation, including camera and stripping operations and bindery.

"We are a full-service printing operation that produces everything from business cards to full-color process brochures and magazines. Our growth has been achieved through a total dedication to customer service. Today our client list includes such blue-chip accounts as AT&T, the Cosmair Division of Loreal Cosmetics, Cross Publishing, Johnson & Johnson, Mid Jersey National Bank, Tandy Electronics, and numerous advertising agencies," Holthaus says.

Holthaus also believes his Somerset County location has contributed to the growth of Woodglen Graphics, Inc. "I like the area because its central location makes it easy to reach our customers," he explains. "For the future, we plan to double the size of our facilities to accommodate a complete art studio, typesetting, and additional storage space. This expansion will enable us to continue to provide our customers with the service they expect, well into the 1990s."

PYMAH CORPORATION

More than 20 years ago Paul M. Hanafin and his wife, Marcella, established PyMaH Corporation in their Branchburg home. The company quickly grew and moved twice to different locations in Somerset County before settling in its current facility. Today, from its corporate headquarters on Route 206 in Somerville, PyMaH manufactures and distributes medical products to health care professionals worldwide.

The highly specialized technology and manufacturing expertise developed by PyMaH is used to produce devices that accurately measure vital signs and monitor hospital sterilization processes. It was, however, Paul Hanafin's extensive research and experience in blood pressure measurement that served as the catalyst for the founding of the company on July 17, 1969.

It was this experience and research that allowed PyMaH to produce scientifically accurate products to overcome the problems associated with inaccurate blood pressure readings. As a

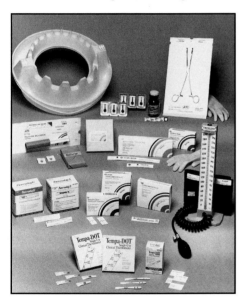

result of the Hanafins' dedication to excellence, the TRIMLINE™ Sphygmomanometer and Pre-Gaged® Cuff were born. Later additions to the PyMaH blood pressure line of products were the BALANCED Bladder and Merc-Loc® Top. Each feature was added to increase the accuracy and safety of blood pressure determinations.

The PyMaH plant, once known as Raritan Valley Farms, was adapted to function as a main headquarters and manufacturing facility for the growing company. Today there is still some evidence of the former dairy—the white tile of the cheese-processing room now decorates the sewing department. The facility is home to nearly 100 of PyMaH's 300 employees.

In 1973 the Hanafins' global vision became a reality. PyMaH Ltd. was established in the Republic of Ireland and began producing blood pressure equipment for European markets.

Between 1982 and 1984 PyMaH acquired two other companies: Info-Chem, the hospital products division of Organon; and Biomedical Sciences Co. Both are headquartered in Fairfield, New Jersey. By this time PyMaH technology encompassed far more than blood pressure. The Tempa-DOT® Single-Use Clinical Thermometer and SteriGage® Sterilization Integrators were being produced and sold worldwide. Four years later, in early 1988, PyMaH acquired ATI, a California-based company. This acquisition added a full line of sterilization monitoring products and indicator inks technology to PyMaH's increasing manufacturing capabilities.

Throughout the years PyMaH products have been designed to meet or exceed recognized industry standards and guidelines for performance and safety. Raw materials and components are carefully selected and tested to exacting specifications prior to being used.

Somerset County has served well as the headquarters for PyMaH Corporation. Having grown up in Long Island, Paul Hanafin was charmed by the small-town character he found in Somerville. Until his death in May 1988, he left the office every morning on his daily run to the post office to personally pick up the mail. He enjoyed his daily excursions and used them for a chance to catch up on some of the local gossip.

Today Marcella Hanafin serves as chairman of the board, and her son, Bernard, one of the Hanafins' five children, serves as president. As the worldwide growth of PyMaH continues, the mission remains unchanged—to provide accurate, safe, and reliable health care products that improve medicine and reduce health care costs.

ABOVE: PyMaH Corporation's headquarters, located on Route 206 in Somerville.

LEFT: PyMaH manufactures products that monitor or measure vital signs and sterilization procedures.

HAINES LUNDBERG WAEHLER (HLW)

Van Dorn Mill 1842

HLW HAINES LUNDBERG WAEHLER ARCHITECTS ENGINEERS AND PLANNERS

Haines Lundberg Waehler's Basking Ridge office is located in a converted gristmill. Photo by Keith Mascheroni

The history of Haines Lundberg Waehler (HLW) dates from 1885, when the Metropolitan Telephone Company commissioned architect Cyrus L.W. Eidlitz to design its new headquarters in lower Manhattan. Subsequent commissions from the telecommunications industry spurred Eidlitz to combine the disciplines of engineering and architecture during the design process. At the turn of the century, he established a partnership with engineer Andrew McKenzie and formed a solid foundation from which the firm grew to prominence.

This emphasis on both technology and design has kept HLW a leader in developing advanced building concepts for labs, clean rooms, communications buildings, medical facilities, and, more recently, automated offices. HLW's broad range of services enables the company to help clients in all phases of their building programs, serving as a single facility planning and design resource.

The firm's clients include small and medium-size organizations as well as many of the world's largest. In addition to architecture and a full range of industry-related engineering

services, the firm offers planning, urban design, interior design, and landscape architecture. It specializes in assisting management with strategies and operational procedures to comply with safety, health, and environmental regulations.

HLW has been designing corporate headquarters and research and development facilities in New Jersey for more than 50 years, beginning in the 1920s with the construction of New Jersey Bell Telephone Company headquarters in Newark, now a noted art-deco landmark. The original Bell Tel Labs complex in Murray Hill, constructed in 1942, is another significant New Jersey project designed by the firm. HLW opened its first New Jersey office in Newark in 1966 and moved to Bernardsville in 1979.

HLW has designed more than 50 million square feet of space for research and development. Projects include the Florham Park Exxon Research Center, completed in the early 1970s; Allied Chemical Corporate Services Center in Morristown in 1975; Dun and Bradstreet's data center in Berkeley Heights in 1975; and the CIBA-GEIGY safety evaluation facility in Summit. Other New Jersey projects are Hoffmann La

Roche's quality-control lab in Belvidere in 1980; the Roche Institute of Molecular Biology in Nutley in 1972; two office buildings for P.I.C. Realty, a subsidiary of Prudential Insurance Co. in the Forrestal Center in Princeton, in 1981 and 1989; and Galaxy Towers in Guttenberg in 1981.

HLW clients also include real estate developers building corporate office parks throughout New Jersey, among them Prudential Realty Group, Lincoln Property Company, Mitsui Fridosan Inc., and Lanid Corporation. The firm's experience in laboratory design has been applied to university clients such as Rutgers University, Ramapo College, and the University of Mississippi.

In order to handle the large volume of corporate and industrial businesses in New Jersey, in 1981 the firm opened a new, larger office in Basking Ridge that could accommodate added staff.

The firm's New Jersey headquarters—the completely refurbished Van Dorn Mill—is a testament to its ingenuity, creativity, and dedication to fine design. Leevi Kiil, managing senior partner in charge of the branch office, says, "The mill afforded us a marvelous challenge to restore a unique, historic building. It is not only an inspiring home for HLW's New Jersey personnel but a showcase of our dedication to sensitive design."

The mill is on the National Register of Historic Places. By renovating the landmark building, vacant since 1941, HLW saved the old stone mill for the community by restoring its architectural integrity, while providing the firm with unique and interesting space suited to architects' contemporary needs.

HLW restored the exterior to retain the original design. The deteriorated interior was designed to provide for modern drafting and office space, while preserving the past by retaining as large a part of the original power and working machinery in place as possible.

When Ferdinand Van Dorn built his mill in 1842, he paid local stone masons 75 cents per day. The construction lasted a year and cost $5,000. The mill paid for itself within its first operating year. HLW's restoration also lasted a year, but the construction cost exceeded $500,000—100 times the original cost.

Several staff members have been active in the New Jersey Society of Architects. The award-winning, landmark restoration has attracted many community groups to the mill, and HLW's staff has hosted tours and meetings for numerous community groups.

In New Jersey HLW clients are served by the staff of HLW-Basking Ridge, a team of archi-

tects, planners, engineers, and designers who devote themselves almost entirely to projects within the state. As specialists in New Jersey, the firm's team has been a major participant in the state's recent dramatic economic growth.

Haines Lundberg Waehler's team is strengthened by its association with HLW's international headquarters in New York City, which when necessary provides specialists and extra resources for projects that require them. A computer link to the New York office enables the New Jersey office to offer clients the benefits of the latest computer-aided design technology. In keeping with the hands-on philosophy of the firm's management, a managing partner heads each team.

"We take pride in our work in New Jersey and the reputation for service to clients that the men and women of HLW-Basking Ridge provide. Our dedication to our professional disciplines is matched by our knowledge of New Jersey and our commitment to meeting the needs of our clients," says Carl Muskat, the partner in charge of the New Jersey headquarters. "As a small, cohesive staff made up of New Jersey residents, we have been praised for our ability to provide the kind of attentive and thorough services that help clients achieve their goals without wasting time or money or sacrificing quality. It is the kind of service that can only be provided by an organization that understands its environment as well as its clients. We believe good architecture is good business. Our service provides aesthetically pleasing, soundly managed, and cost-effective architecture to the business community."

A skylit drafting area on the top floor of the Basking Ridge office is pleasantly interrupted by the mill's old gears and antique beams.

From left: HLW's general manager, Richard Sparks; Carl Muskat, partner in charge of the New Jersey office; managing partners Leevi Kiil and Theodore S. Hammer; and designer Yu-Heng Shang review a complex project.

THE CHUBB CORPORATION

Hendon Chubb (1874-1960), who was elected to the Insurance Hall of Fame, was a major force in developing marine insurance business in the United States.

Nestled in the rolling hills of Warren Township is the world headquarters of The Chubb Corporation, a diversified holding company principally engaged, through its subsidiaries, in property and casualty insurance, life insurance, and real estate development.

Ranked by *Fortune* magazine as the 42nd-largest diversified financial organization in the nation, Chubb is New Jersey's ninth-largest employer and the fourth-largest employer in Somerset County. Chubb employs nearly 2,200 people in its Warren Township headquarters and more than 1,000 staff members at its Bridgewater, Murray Hill, and Princeton locations. Additional Somerset County offices are under construction in Branchburg and Pluckemin. Throughout the world Chubb maintains 58 branches in the United States and Canada, and it staffs 32 offices in Europe, South America, and the Pacific Rim.

Chubb moved to its Somerset County home in 1983, after consolidating and relocating its corporate headquarters from Short Hills, New Jersey, and New York City to the 150-acre Warren Township site. This site, and its other Somerset County locations, were selected for their attractive landscapes, accessibility to major roadways, inviting municipalities, talented labor pool, proximity to Newark International Airport, and opportunity for future growth and expansion.

The 525,000-square-foot headquarters houses a gift shop, dry cleaner and shoe repair service, fitness center, cafeteria, dining room, a branch of the Warren Township library, a branch of the Summit Trust Company, and an art gallery that exhibits the work of local artists. Eight classrooms and an amphitheater are used for training employees as well as for special meetings. Many of the instructional videos used in these sessions are produced in Chubb's own video production studio, also located in the Warren facility.

Chubb carolers serenade patients at Lyons Veterans Hospital.

Recognizing the impact commuting employees have on the local area, Chubb has created a van pool and ride-sharing program. Approximately 300 people commute to work in a fleet of 26 company-supplied and -maintained vans. An additional 25 percent of Chubb employees commute by car pooling. In 1987 the New Jersey Department of Commerce and Industry recognized Chubb for its outstanding efforts to alleviate the state's traffic problems.

An active participant in the community, Chubb has supported public television for more than a decade and is the corporate underwriter of the award-winning "American Playhouse" series on Public Broadcasting Service stations. With donations and volunteers, the company actively supports the Watchung Arts Center, Watchung Hills Regional High School, Bonnie Brae School, Raptor Trust, Somerset County Special Olympics, United Way, American Cancer Society, Salvation Army, Association for Retarded Citizens, and Warren Recreation League, Fire Department, and Rescue Squad.

In addition, Chubb employees serve on the advisory boards of various local civic, charitable, and community service organizations. Because of all of the above-mentioned activities, the Greater Somerset County Chamber of Commerce gave Chubb its 1987 "New Good Neighbor" award.

Founded as a partnership in 1882 by Thomas Caldecot Chubb and his son, Percy, Chubb & Son began as an insurer of sailing ships and cargo, representing the New York Marine Underwriters (NYMU).

Chubb & Son emerged 19 years later as general manager of Federal Insurance Company, a property and casualty insurance company incorporated in Jersey City by a group of NYMU managing partners, including Percy Chubb and his older brother, Sydney.

Over the years Chubb & Son has expanded its operations beyond marine and cargo insurance through the acquisition and management of other property and casualty insurance companies. These companies, referred to collectively as Chubb Group of Insurance Companies, are today among the most highly regarded in the insurance industry.

In 1967 Chubb & Son Inc., along with the companies it manages, became a wholly owned subsidiary of The Chubb Corporation. Today Chubb operates three principal subsidiaries: Chubb LifeAmerica, headquartered in Concord, New Hampshire; Bellemead Development Corporation, located in Roseland, New Jersey; and Chubb Group of Insurance Companies, operating from the Warren Township headquarters, the largest contributor to the corporation's consolidated assets.

Throughout its century-old history, Chubb has been known as an innovator. In addition to providing traditional business, property, and liability insurance coverages, Chubb provides an array of products and services for clients with special insurance needs. All of these activities are supported by expert loss control services, a reputation for prompt and equitable claim handling, and a state-of-the-art computer network. Clients are served worldwide by a staff of more than 9,000 people in 58 branch offices in the United States and Canada, and by an international operation found in more than 100 countries.

One example of the company's bold and innovative decision making occurred while Thomas Caldecot Chubb was quite young. A sailing ship carrying more than one million dollars in gold was reported several days overdue.

As days went by and no reports of the vessel's whereabouts were received, the original insurers tried desperately to reinsure the cargo. No one would consider the offer except Thomas Chubb. After looking through his atlas and finding the place where the ship was last sighted, he decided to reinsure the vessel when no one else would.

Two days later the clipper sailed gracefully into port, after having been delayed by a storm. When people congratulated Thomas Chubb on his good fortune, he replied, "It wasn't luck. From studying the charts I saw that the clipper would be in shallow water from its last-sighted point to its home port. The premium I charged was high enough to cover the costs of diving for the cargo and salvaging the ship if she had gone down."

Chubb moved to its 150-acre world headquarters in Warren Township in 1983.

Chubb supports the Raptor Trust, a private center for the preservation and well-being of birds of prey.

OZZARD, WHARTON, RIZZOLO, KLEIN, MAURO, SAVO & HOGAN

The offices of Ozzard, Wharton, Rizzolo, Klein, Mauro, Savo & Hogan are located at 75-77 North Bridge Street in Somerville.

The law firm of Ozzard, Wharton, Rizzolo, Klein, Mauro, Savo & Hogan maintains a broad general practice with particular emphasis on commercial litigation, corporate activities, environmental law, financial institutions, municipal representation, as well as commercial and residential real estate. The firm has been involved in a number of bank mergers and acquisitions and is recognized for its work in general negligence, product liability, and toxic-waste defense cases.

Today the firm numbers 31 attorneys, 6 paralegals, and 46 support personnel. Its practice is primarily concentrated in Hunterdon, Middlesex, and Somerset counties and served by offices in Somerville.

The firm greatly expanded and it increased its scope of services in 1986, when two of the areas's oldest law firms—Ozzard, Rizzolo, Klein, Mauro, Savo & Hogan and Wharton, Stewart & Davis—merged to form the firm that today practices as Ozzard, Wharton, Rizzolo, Klein, Mauro, Savo & Hogan.

The firm has its roots in three renowned leaders of the bar, Alvah A. Clark, Clarence E. Case, and Daniel H. Beekman.

During his nearly 50-year career started in 1864, Clark guided the careers of many of the bar's future leaders and served in Congress from 1876 to 1880.

Three years after his admission to the bar in 1903, Case formed a partnership under the firm of Clark and Case. Daniel Beekman commenced practice in the Somerville area independently in 1898.

T. Girard Wharton became associated with Clarence Case in 1925 and continued that association until Case was appointed to the state supreme court. William E. Ozzard became a partner of Beekman & Beekman in 1952.

During the 1950s and 1960s, many of the firm's partners distinguished themselves in public service. Fredrick W. Hall was appointed to the New Jersey Supreme Court; Joseph Halpern was appointed to the Appellate Division of the Superior Court of New Jersey as was John W. Fritz. William E. Ozzard was elected to the state senate and served as both president of the senate and acting governor, in addition to chairman of the Public Utilities Commission. Other current partners of the firm have made outstanding contributions to public service. Victor A. Rizzolo served both as an assistant prosecutor in the state assembly and as a County Court Judge. S. Philip Klein was formerly Deputy Attorney-General of the State of New Jersey. George A. Mauro served as counsel to Branchburg and Somerset counties. William B. Savo continues to serve as Deputy County Counsel to Somerset County.

According to senior partner William E. Ozzard, current Somerset County Counsel, "The history of the firms that merged to form the current partnership reflects our still-active role in the development of Somerset and surrounding counties. We will continue to contribute to the growth of the area by taking an active role in the community, supporting the judiciary process and the law, and by providing comprehensive, specialized services to our individual, corporate, and municipal clients."

PHILIPS LIGHTING COMPANY

The Philips Lighting Center.

Philips Lighting Company has installed lighting systems at some of America's most famous infrastructures, from Kennedy Airport in New York City to Dodger Stadium in Los Angeles.

The firm was founded in 1935 as the Radiant Lamp Corporation. Its first plant was on Sherman Avenue in Newark. In 1942 World War II had begun, and the military needed incandescent lamps—especially aeronautical lamps. Radiant Lamp Corporation provided the lamps, and the company's production facilities were then expanded considerably.

In 1959 five men with varying business experience purchased Radiant Lamp Corporation. By 1961 it had posted annual sales of $2 million and had a total of 200 employees. Among its notable installations in the early 1960s were the Pittsburgh Civic Arena, Kennedy International Airport (then called Idlewild), the Bronx-Whitestone and the Tri-Boro bridges, and the Tishman Building at 666 Fifth Avenue.

Nearly 400 New York City playgrounds also were using Radiant Lamp-designed R52 lamps. Other lamp installations included the Lincoln Road Mall in Miami Beach and the 1962 lighting of the new Dodger Stadium.

Radiant Lamp Corporation was acquired by Consolidated Electronics Corporation in 1968. A year later the parent company name was changed to North American Philips Corporation. That development occurred through the merger of Consolidated Electronics Industries Corporation and North American Philips Company.

In December 1970 Radiant Lamp Division of North American Philips acquired the companies of the Lighting Products Division of Lear Siegler, Inc., including Verd-A-Ray, Penetray, and Par Light.

In December 1972 the firm completed construction of a 105,000-square-foot warehouse in South Brunswick. Two major acquisitions from the International Telephone and Telegraph Corporation in 1973 were the Large Lamp Division in Lynn, Massachusetts, and the Lustra Lighting Division in East Rutherford, New Jersey.

In 1974 North American Philips Lighting Corporation's sales reached $40 million. Four years later a new 105,000-square-foot warehouse was built at South Brunswick, adjacent to the firm's existing facilities. In 1980 the company posted annual sales of $105 million, and its work force numbered 1,670 employees.

With the 1980s came new expansion. During this period the company acquired Solar Electric Corporation of Warren, Pennsylvania. By 1981 North American Philips Lighting Corporation's sales had eclipsed the $110-million mark. In 1982 the firm created a fixture division, a separate arm of the company concentrated on lighting fixtures. And by the end of that year the entire corporation's sales had reached $120 million.

In 1983 the company acquired the Westinghouse Electric Lamp Division, at the time the nation's third-largest seller of lamps. Six months later the company acquired the Danville, Kentucky, glass plant from Corning Glass Works of Corning, New York. In September 1983 the Philips Elmet Division of North American Philips Corporation—a separate manufacturing facility—was assigned to Philips.

Through the years the firm has had a tradition of diversification and continued expansion. Today Philips Lighting Company is one of the top companies of its kind in the United States.

NEW JERSEY SAVINGS BANK

New Jersey Savings Bank opened for business in 1871 in the "Ten Eyck House" on the southwest corner of Division and Main streets in Somerville.

New Jersey Savings Bank's history has spanned more than a century. The bank began its operations in 1871 as a state-chartered mutual savings bank and became a public company in 1987.

The impetus for the bank began when several local citizens realized the need for a savings bank, where average wage earners could invest their small savings safely and at a profit—a bank where women, children, and even the many newly arrived immigrants would feel at ease. In 1871 New Jersey's governor approved an act of the state legislature to incorporate the Somerville Dime Savings Bank.

By December 31 of that year 102 accounts were opened for total deposits of $6,795. Before the end of 1872 the officers were able to make the bank's first investment—$3,000 of City of Elizabeth bonds.

In less than 10 years the bank's deposits had increased to $83,590. Over the years the bank continued to show steadily growing deposits, maintaining its stability even through the Depression.

Since 1871 industrial growth and improved transportation have contributed to the increase in population of Somerset and neighboring counties and resulted in demands on New Jersey Savings Bank for the financing of homes, cars, higher education, commercial development, and civic improvements.

The bank, founded in 1871 to serve the Somerville population of 3,000 people, now serves depositors and borrowers throughout the state, with offices in Somerset, Hunterdon, and Mercer counties. Total assets were in excess of $282 million on December 31, 1989.

New Jersey Savings Bank became a wholly owned subsidiary of Bancorp New Jersey, Inc., in a 1988 reorganization. Formation of the holding company offers the institution attractive and competitive approaches to various financial markets in the coming decade.

New Jersey Savings Bank is headed by Beatrice D'Agostino, president and chief executive officer. In 1976, when the bank chose D'Agostino to direct its role in the developing economy of New Jersey, she became one of three women to head banks in the United States. Over the years she has received many accolades for her business acumen.

In 1989 and 1990 she was honored as a policymaker by the Executive Women of New Jersey, received the Five Worlds of Girl Scouting Women of Achievement award, and the Somerset Business and Professional Women's Woman of the Year award. In addition, she received a citation from the General Assembly of New Jersey for her "extraordinary record of community service and civic leadership."

D'Agostino attributes much of the bank's growth and success to its management dynamics, commitment to responsible citizenship, and sound business ethics. The bank's management and the members of its board are active in many community organizations, including the Somerset Alliance for the Future, Greater Somerset County Chamber of Commerce, Somerset Valley United Way and its member agencies, Somerset Medical Center, Raritan Valley Community College Foundation, and Rotary Club.

The bank's outstanding financial record has led to it being cited by analysts as one of six outstanding banks in New Jersey, based upon its asset quality, management strength, and ability to maintain credibility in interest margins.

"Economic cycles are ever present in our financial markets and should be managed with prudent judgment and flexible strategies that provide stability and favorable returns to depositors, shareholders, and other users of the bank's services, with the foremost objectives being performance and profitability," says D'Agostino.

Today the bank's principal business consists of attracting deposits from the general public in the form of certificates of deposit, business and personal checking and savings accounts, and Individual Retirement Accounts. It then invests these deposits in mortgages, commercial and consumer loans, and home equity lines of credit.

Other securities, primarily U.S. government and agency obligations, are also included

Corporate headquarters of Bancorp New Jersey, Inc., and New Jersey Savings Bank is located at 10 West High Street in Somerville.

in the bank's investment portfolio. The bank is a member of the MAC and Plus ATM systems and offers VISA/MasterCard credit cards.

Implementation of innovative but conservative growth strategies has led to significant accomplishments for New Jersey Savings Bank. A major factor in its earnings performance is substantial activity in mortgage financing, with a focus on the origination of conventional one- to four-family residences, construction, and other real estate loans. The bank delivers a professional and personalized level of service to a real estate market with increasingly diverse and sophisticated credit requirements.

The bank's other lending activities are concentrated on consumer borrowing through a variety of lending products, including equity lines of credit, commercial loans, and business financings. The diversified commercial portfolio of the bank includes loans for construction, plant expansion, and equipment purchases, as well as working capital lines of credit for various industries, such as metalworking and fabricating, plastics, retailing establishments, and the medical and legal professions.

In response to the expanding population base in its market area, a continuing emphasis for New Jersey Savings Bank is attracting funds from commercial and retail customers. Its strong deposit base, which includes personal and business checking, is achieved by providing customers with competitive rates and innovative products.

New Jersey Savings Bank is enhancing its integrated data-processing products with a sophisticated computer system to take advantage of advanced capabilities and improved delivery services. The mortgage, commercial, and consumer loan divisions have successfully completed improvements to its loan portfolios computer systems. The bank will realize time-saving benefits through the use of this more economical and multipurpose computer equipment and software.

"We strongly believe that, by all measurements, New Jersey's economy is headed for continued development. Bancorp New Jersey, and its subsidiary, New Jersey Savings Bank, are positioned to participate fully in this favorable environment. Building strong relationships with our customers and long-term value for our franchise by enhancing our ability to compete in a broadened market environment is our core strategy for growth," says D'Agostino. As the decades move forward, the bank will embrace challenge and opportunity and maintain the strong position it has enjoyed in its history.

Beatrice D'Agostino is the president and chief executive officer of Bancorp New Jersey, Inc., and its subsidiary, New Jersey Savings Bank.

RONSON CORPORATION

Since Ronson's 1885 founding in Newark, New Jersey, by Louis V. Aronson as Art Metal, Inc., the company, later becoming Ronson Art Metal Works, Inc., in 1928 and Ronson Corporation in 1953, has been identified with the finest in precision craftsmanship.

The world's first automatic pocket cigarette lighter, the Banjo, with its patented action, was introduced in 1928 and was the start of a very successful worldwide lighter business. It was also in that year that the company became public when it joined the American Stock Exchange. Ronson has remained a public company since that time. During the past several years, Ronson Corporation has been listed under RONC on the National Association of Securities Dealers (NASD).

Over the years, through the maintenance of high standards of quality, Ronson has built up one of the world's best-known brand names. Not until 1954, however, did Ronson initiate its program of diversification. In this effort the company has capitalized on its greatest asset—the internationally respected brand name of Ronson itself. Today, with its corporate office located in Somerset, Ronson Corporation has four wholly owned subsidiaries (three in the United States and one in Canada): Ronson Consumer Products Corporation, Ronson Hydraulic Units Corporation, Ronson Aviation, Inc., and Ronson Corporation of Canada, Ltd.

Ronson Consumer Products Corporation operates in a modern 40,000-square-foot manufacturing plant in Woodbridge, New Jersey. This plant produces Ronsonol and butane refills and flints. In addition, the company produces and markets Ronson Multi-Lube, a lubricating spray, and Ronson Kleenol Spot Removal, a complete cleaning kit containing two cleaners. Kleenol

RIGHT: Louis V. Aronson II is president and chief executive officer of Ronson Corporation.

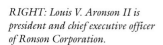

BELOW: Before 1953 Ronson Corporation was called Ronson Art Metal Works, Inc., known for the manufacture of lighters and other metal products.

Ronson Aviation, Inc., is a general aviation sales and service company headquartered at the Mercer County Airport in Trenton.

also is offered in a personal-size package for home or travel.

Recently, Ronson introduced three new products—the Ronson Typhoon windproof lighter; the Ronson Varaflame ignitor, used for lighting fireplaces, barbecues, camping stoves, and candles; and the new Ronson Refil-A-Lite, a low-cost refillable butane lighter.

Ronson Corporation of Canada, Ltd., has its sales and distribution center for Ronson Consumer Products Corporation in Mississauga, Ontario. This company markets and distributes Ronson consumer products throughout Canada.

Ronson Hydraulic Units Corporation was formed in the early 1950s to meet the growing demand of the aerospace industry for precision hydraulic and pneumatic components. Ronson's 77,000-square-foot Charlotte, North Carolina, facility is equipped with technologically advanced numerical control machining centers. These machine-tool centers are complemented by lathes, mills, drills, grinders, laps, hones, and related finishing equipment. Research and development plays a vital role at Ronson Hydraulics, with engineering personnel qualified in up-to-date hydraulic and pneumatic design technology, including the use of computer-aided design systems. Ronson has continued to invest in both engineering and manufacturing state-of-the-art equipment.

New proprietary designs include a cargo-door hydraulic system to retrofit Boeing 727 aircraft, a spoiler manifold system for the Canadair Regional Jet, and a hydraulic actuator assembly for the U.S. Air Force's rail garrison system. In addition, Ronson received major contract awards for the U.S. Navy's vertical launch system and the C-17 landing-gear damper assembly. Ronson's hydraulic products are in service worldwide on commercial and general aviation aircraft, helicopters, and space programs.

Formed in 1965 and headquartered at the Mercer County Airport in Trenton, New Jersey,

Ronson Aviation, Inc., is a general aviation sales and service company operating airplanes and helicopters and providing services that include air charters, maintenance, fueling, hangaring, parts sales, aircraft sales, and flight training. Ronson Aviation's 22-acre facilities include a 52,000-square-foot hangar and office complex, 24 airplane storage hangars, a 60,000-gallon fueling complex, and maintenance and test equipment for repairing both turbine and piston engine airplanes and helicopters.

Ronson Aviation is an authorized agency for Beech Aircraft Corporation and sells Beech parts and equipment to other aviation facilities servicing Beech aircraft. The company is an authorized service agency for Bell Helicopter, Allison, Pratt & Whitney, and Garrett turbine engines. Ronson Aviation operates six twin-engine aircraft and three helicopters that provide air-taxi and air-cargo services to the general public and various government agencies.

According to Louis V. Aronson II, president and chief executive officer of the company since 1953, "We intend to capitalize on the renowned Ronson brand name in consumer products with new products and to encourage the growth of our aerospace and aviation businesses. We feel strongly that the efforts of our employees, combined with our strategy of growth through diversification, will contribute to a bright and successful future."

Ronson Consumer Products Corporation operates from a modern manufacturing plant in Woodbridge.

CENTRAL JERSEY INDUSTRIAL PARK

Edward A. Chandler, founder of Central Jersey Industrial Park.

Ed Chandler's daughter, Marguerite (right), and son, Edward (below right), now manage the business that he founded.

Central Jersey Industrial Park provides its tenants easy access to major highways, flexible clear span space, competitive rates, and many support services. It is the legacy and vision of a unique family business founded by Ed Chandler.

Ed Chandler is the definition of the word "entrepreneur." During the Depression, Ed Chandler came to New Jersey on the back of a freight train with 75 cents and a goal of making a million dollars. After working as an operations troubleshooter for Johns-Manville, he started his own construction business, and 11 years later he realized his monetary goal.

Chandler took his first step toward establishing his own business after he built a prefabricated garage. Neighbors asked him to build garages for them, and Chandler was in business. He left Johns-Manville in 1938 to work solely in his prefabricated home and garage business, called the Well Built Manufacturing Company. He was joined in business by his brother, George, after World War II.

From the original garages and small cabins, Edward Chandler branched out into houses and roof trusses for industry, restaurants, and other commercial establishments. Besides diversification of product, he also moved into vertical integration, at both ends of the business, owning a lumber mill in Oregon that provided high-quality lumber, creating a mortgage company to help customers finance their homes, and organizing a system of dealerships that represented Well Built nationwide.

The early years of Well Built coincided with World War II. The U.S. Army was keenly aware of the asset that lay in an efficient, weather-independent mode of building construction.

Eventually the Well Built Manufacturing Company grew to be a business with a volume of $13 million in annual sales and one million dollars in yearly profits. In its heyday it employed 150 people who built eight houses per day. Such productivity put increasing pressure on the physical plant, and by 1950 Edward Chandler expanded his factory space, and in doing so created his next opportunity.

After Chandler built a new building to expand his business, General Robert Johnson, head of Johnson & Johnson, inquired about the possibility of renting the space for a warehouse. Chandler agreed, and he set about constructing another building for Well Built. Representatives from the Standard Brands company then rented this second building, and Chandler began to sense the potential for providing warehouse space.

With his gambler's instinct, Chandler decided to build several large buildings without having tenants lined up. After banks told him this venture was too risky, Chandler decided to use his own risk capital derived from the profits of Well Built, and he proceeded to create one of the first industrial parks in the United States at the intersection of Routes 22 and 28 and Interstate 287.

Where the Well Built operation had used wood, the park was built using innovative concrete construction techniques that revolutionized the concrete building industry. Between 1950 and 1975, one or two warehouses were added per year. As the park expanded through local land acquisitions, it grew to 80 acres, 1.3 million square feet of floor space, with 40 buildings,

ranging in size from 22,000 square feet to 207,000 square feet.

In 1956 Edward Chandler created the Edmar Corporation, named after his two children: Edward, then 15, and Marguerite, then 13. He anticipated that they would one day inherit his business.

Both Edward and Marguerite worked at the park while growing up. Marguerite graduated from Syracuse University with a degree in accounting. Edward graduated from Georgia Tech with a degree in engineering. By the mid-1970s both were working for the company.

The younger Edward had learned a great deal about facilities management through hands-on experience in every aspect of the park, from sewer work to roof construction. Choosing a career in architectural engineering prepared Edward well for his present role as president of Chandler Realty, a company that owns one-half of Central Jersey Industrial Park and takes care of the construction and structural maintenance of park buildings. Several loyal crew members who worked for his father still work with Edward today.

Taking an active role in the community, Edward Jr. serves on the Somerset Medical Center Board of Directors and has served as chair of the Somerset County Council on Alcoholism.

Marguerite Chandler, president of Edmar Corporation, has distinguished herself both in business and in humanitarian efforts. She is noted for founding the PeopleCare Center, a day-care facility. She is also the founder of the FoodBank Network of Somerset County, which distributes donated food to families in need, and World Works Foundation, which provides funding and organizational support of projects to end hunger and promote world peace. She is a volunteer and major contributor to the Hunger Project, a movement to inspire people in their individual participation to feed the needy. She also provided leadership for the Governor's Blue Ribbon Committee for Ending Hunger, which studies the issue of hunger in New Jersey. In 1987 she received the Presidential Outstanding Achievement Award from Ronald Reagan for her vision, initiative, and leadership in ending hunger.

Her many professional and volunteer accomplishments include working as a tax accountant with the Peat, Warwick & Mitchell accounting firm, establishing a boiler maintenance and energy-management business, and serving on the board of directors of the United Way in Somerset Valley and the New Jersey Council of Churches. She is the chair of the Greater Somerset County Chamber of Commerce.

Richmond Shreve (below right) is Edmar Corporation's chief executive officer.

In 1980 Richmond Shreve, Marguerite's husband, left his position as head of marketing research at Sandoz Pharmaceuticals to join the family business. He became chief executive officer of Edmar Corporation in 1988. Marguerite became a candidate for the United States Congress in 1990.

The senior Edward Chandler died in 1986 and is survived by his wife, Jacquelyn Hay Chandler. His first wife, Marguerite Moore Chandler, died in 1975.

The professional careers of his children, Edward and Marguerite Chandler, are perhaps the best expression of Ed Chandler's spirit in their dedication to the community, innovation in business, and continuation of their father's dream.

Central Jersey Industrial Park has grown with Somerset County.

BENEFICIAL CORPORATION

Beneficial Corporation is one of the world's largest consumer financial services companies, with assets totaling more than $8 billion. Its subsidiaries maintain diversified operations throughout the United States and three foreign countries.

Beneficial Corporation subsidiaries offer a variety of financial products through more than 1,000 consumer credit offices, banks, mortgage and escrow companies, sales finance companies, and insurance companies. Finance receivables currently total $7 billion.

The foundations of Beneficial Corporation began in 1914, when the Beneficial Loan Society opened an office in Elizabeth, New Jersey. The founder was Colonel Clarence Hodson, a descendant of the Hodson family of Maryland's eastern shore.

Hodson practiced law in Baltimore, began his financial career as a banker in Crisfield, Maryland, and was director for more than 40 banks, mortgage and trust companies, and public utilities. Working with the Russell Sage Foundation, Hodson lobbied for small-loan legislation. His efforts led to the 1913 passage of the first Uniform Small Loan Act in New Jersey.

The Beneficial Loan Society made its first loan on August 18, 1914. Expansion came quickly as other states enacted small-loan legisla-

tion similar to New Jersey's. By 1919 Beneficial had 17 offices in seven states.

When Hodson died in 1928, Beneficial had more than 200 offices throughout the United States and more than $30 million in loans outstanding. That same year a credit life insurance division was formed.

Beneficial common stock was listed on the New York Stock Exchange in 1933. By then the company had extended operations into Canada, opening offices in Ottawa and Toronto under the name Personal Finance Company. By the end of 1934 Beneficial had $53 million out in loans, marking the first time any American system of loan offices had passed the $50-million mark.

In 1935 new quarters were opened at 15 Washington Street, Newark, for management and supervisory personnel. These offices remained in Newark for 20 years.

Beneficial subsidiaries began purchasing installment notes from merchants covering their retail sales, which provided the basis for what is now Beneficial's installment sales contract business. By 1948 Beneficial subsidiaries had made more than one million loans, and in 1949 had more than 500 offices throughout the United States and Canada.

Finn M.W. Caspersen, chairman and chief executive officer of Beneficial Corporation.

In the mid-1950s the single name "Beneficial Finance" was established across the United States and Canada. A remarkable milestone occurred in 1956—the opening of Beneficial's 1,000th office.

In 1959 Beneficial formed Guaranty Life Insurance Company of America, which became the first of the Beneficial Insurance Group companies. That same year Beneficial opened its first office in London, England.

Beneficial was growing and diversifying by leaps and bounds, and needed a headquarters for Beneficial Management Corporation, its management subsidiary in New Jersey. Beneficial Management Corporation purchased 5.5 acres in Morristown, and a million-dollar, four-story, colonial-style building was ready by September 1955. The Beneficial Building, with 80,000 square feet for some 300 employees, was located at 200 South Street, Morristown.

However, 200 South Street was no match for Beneficial's astounding growth rate. By 1965 the company's assets had passed the billion-dollar mark, and additional space was leased for Beneficial Management Corporation at other Morristown locations.

In 1970 Beneficial established a data-processing network called Bencom, linking most Beneficial offices to a computer center at its New Jersey management headquarters. By 1972 Beneficial had passed the $1.5-billion mark in net cash invested.

Beneficial Finance Co., the parent company, became Beneficial Corporation in 1980, a move reflecting the firm's diversification into banking, income tax preparation, and various insurance programs.

Meanwhile, Beneficial Management Corporation had been busy planning a new corporate complex. A site had been chosen in the Borough of Peapack and Gladstone in 1978. Construction began in 1979, and in 1982 the new Beneficial Center was ready,

Beneficial Center resembles a European village with its 88-foot European-style clock tower, brick walkways, elegant colonnades, formal gardens, cobblestone courtyards, and Renaissance architectural details.

TOP: *Bradley A. Firle, group vice president, Southwest Group.*

ABOVE: *Allen L. Wehrhahn, vice president/acquisitions, business development department.*

RIGHT: *The first office of the Beneficial Loan Society opened in Elizabeth in 1914.*

bringing together Beneficial employees from more than a dozen locations.

Beneficial Center is truly a unique corporate complex. Sometimes compared to a college campus, it is more like a European village, with its 88-foot European-style clock tower, brick walkways, elegant colonnades, formal gardens and cobblestone courtyards, and Renaissance architectural details.

With six buildings no more than three stories tall, the complex enhances the rural character of the historic Somerset County area. Its Old World exteriors combine with high-tech interiors, creating a striking corporate environment. Beneficial Center includes more than 30 acres, 550,000 square feet of office space, and accommodates 1,000 employees.

Restructuring in the 1980s returned Beneficial's focus to the company's roots:

consumer financial services. And the accent remains—as it has for 76 years—on service, according to Finn M.W. Caspersen, Beneficial chairman and chief executive officer since August 1976.

"As it has been for decades, consumer lending continues to be one of America's truly wonderful businesses," says Caspersen, "generating high returns on investment year after year—for those who manage it prudently and with a strong customer orientation. If commitment to credit quality is the heart of our consumer lending culture, service to the customer is the soul."

Beneficial Corporation is based in Delaware, while Beneficial Management Corporation is located at Beneficial Center in Peapack. Beneficial Management Corporation furnishes management and supervisory services

TOP: Michael J. Mayer, vice president, business development department.

ABOVE: Patrick R. Boney, assistant vice president, human resources.

LEFT: None of the six buildings of Beneficial Center are more than three stories tall. The complex's Old World exteriors combine with high-tech interiors, creating a striking corporate environment.

to the Beneficial Consumer Finance System and other Beneficial subsidiaries.

Beneficial Consumer Finance System, the cornerstone of Beneficial's business, has more than 1,000 offices throughout the United States and in the United Kingdom, Canada, and Germany. It is one of the nation's largest providers of second-mortgage lending and provides other financial services including personal loans, first mortgages, and revolving equity credit.

SEAL-SPOUT CORPORATION

From the homes of consumers to the reaches of outer space, the products manufactured by Seal-Spout and its sister company, American Aluminum, have touched the lives of millions.

Seal-Spout's origins began in 1896, when company founder Henry Brucker's experience in aluminum fabrication led him to the New Jersey Aluminum Company, where he worked for 14 years. He received a medal for his work at the Louisiana Exposition in St. Louis in 1904 for his development of new ways to shape aluminum and his pioneering work in production methods.

In October 1910 he started a small aluminum business. His brother, Oscar B. Brucker, helped on a part-time basis. In 1911, with Henry Brucker's new business partner, Joseph

RIGHT: Henry J. Brucker, chairman of the board.

BELOW RIGHT: Robert J. Brucker, president and chief executive officer.

Klausmann, the American Aluminum and Metal Specialties Manufacturing Company was incorporated with $25,000 of capital.

The product line was expanded and included some sifting cans, milk-bottle lids, and salt and pepper shakers. As World War I began, American Aluminum provided aluminum boxes for medical supplies, buckles, and cups.

During the late 1920s one of the salt companies approached Henry Brucker to create a replacement for salt plugs, a device used to prevent moisture from getting to the salt. It wanted a device that was more efficient and would not be lost as easily or as often as salt plugs.

Brucker created a fully formed pouring spout that was inserted manually as the box was being filled. With the increase in volume of packaged salt and the increasingly high cost of hand labor, it was necessary to insert spouts automatically. In 1927 Brucker patented a pro-

cess for making automated spouts in a continuous strip. Brucker's key patent for this process, one of his more than 25 patents, was many years before its time.

Today, using Brucker's manufacturing concept, spouts are threaded through machines, clipped off, and driven into packages at a rate of five spouts per second. The inserting machines are high-precision pieces of equipment with close tolerances and the ability to work efficiently without service for long periods of time. The company's reclosable pouring spout has become a recognized consumer packaging component for a wide range of powdered and granular products, including baby foods, detergent powders, and pet foods.

The company remains innovative today with its addition of the plastic spout, which features the same basic design as the aluminum original. Metal and plastic Seal-Spouts are used today by such major food giants as Procter & Gamble, H.J. Heinz, and Gerbers Baby Food. A major factor in both companies is the employment of vertical integration, so all manufacturing processes are efficiently completed under one roof.

The company prides itself on its family of loyal employees. American Aluminum has had six employees retire with 50 years of service. In addition to chairman Henry Brucker with 52 years of service, veteran Seal-Spout personnel include Alfonse "Sonny" Giordano with 46 years, Artie Smith with 37 years, Willie Hyder with 36 years, Fred Plaessmann with 31 years, Hans Fleck with 29 years, and George Faber with 28 years.

"Seal-Spout is a small machine shop that is an extremely clean, well-lit operation. We have rarely had a problem finding skilled people, because we provide a good workplace for employees," says Ed Duggan, the company's

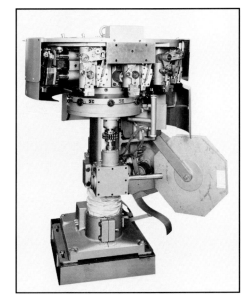

executive vice president. His father served as the company's senior counsel for many years.

Although the plant for making insertion machines and spouts is a separate operation from its sister company, American Aluminum, both companies have experienced impressive growth since Seal-Spout was originally established.

In 1939 Henry J. Brucker, the founder's son, joined the company, eventually became its president, and today serves as chairman of the board.

In World War II American Aluminum diversified by working for the defense industry. Five Army/Navy "E" Awards reflect the truly dedicated performance of the company during those war years. It manufactured thousands of airplane nose cones and engine baffles. The armed forces turned to American Aluminum to solve one of its major problems. The propeller nose spinners used in the original design of fighter planes could not stand up to wear and tear from the sand found in North Africa and the South Pacific. American Aluminum developed the technique of forming heat-treatable aluminum alloys so that the spinners were as hard as mild steel yet lightweight.

Another problem was that radial aircraft engines had insufficient cooling on the cylinder bank. This caused the plane's rear cylinders to burn up. The engines were fitted with a baffle designed and produced by American Aluminum Company. This part, though small and inexpensive, was very significant in the operation and success of the radial engines.

After the war there was a large pent-up demand for heavy commercial cookware. During the 1950s increasing productivity with new methods and machines became an important goal of the company. To facilitate the company's expansion, it relocated its operations from Newark to Mountainside, New Jersey. The new plant was more efficient and helped increase production and on-time delivery.

Space and defense items became an increasingly important part of the production output in the 1960s. NASA sent quite a number of sophisticated instruments out into space housed in the company's aluminum cases.

The 1970s produced great changes for American Aluminum Company in products, management, and corporate structure. Seal-Spout moved to a new plant built in Liberty Corner, New Jersey, and the founder's grandson, Robert J. Brucker, became company president. Custom contract work of sophisiticated metal assemblies became the company's primary focus in the late 1970s, and this direction continues today.

"Today American Aluminum's products include a wide range of consumer, industrial, and defense-related products, and Seal-Spout Corporation continues to produce both metal and plastic spouts for use with many consumer products, " says Robert Brucker. "We expect continued growth and profitability for both companies throughout the 1990s."

ABOVE LEFT: Made of lightweight, high-strength alloys, Seal-Spout's Model 15 machine is the fastest on the market.

ABOVE: Spouts come in many sizes and shapes to accommodate various powdered materials in round or rectangular cartons.

Seal-Spout is located in this rural setting in Liberty Corner.

HIGHLAND PACKAGING LABS, INC.

Highland Packaging Labs, Inc., has been in business under ownership and management of Mildred and Stuart Campbell since December 1983. In late 1987 the company changed its name from Drug Concentrates, Inc., as it had been known since first incorporated in Connecticut by previous owners in 1962.

Today Highland Packaging Labs is an ultramodern state-of the-art manufacturing and packaging facility that is Food and Drug Administration registered and state health department licensed. There are strict in-house quality controls, good manufacturing practices, independent laboratory testing for raw materials, and in-process materials and finished goods.

As company president, Mildred C. Campbell possesses a wealth of experience in management with 20-plus years in operating-room nursing. She designed and supervised construction of a major heart institute. She also served four years as a full-time consultant to a leading health care business.

H. Stuart Campbell has 22 years experience with Johnson & Johnson; he retired in 1982 as chairman and chief executive officer of eight subsidiary companies, domestic and international. He also serves as director on three other company boards, including chairman of a biomaterials company.

The business was founded and is based upon the Campbells' operating principles of high-quality products and procedures, outstanding service to customers, timely deliveries, and orientation to employee satisfaction and motivation.

The fourth operating principle—providing an exceptional working environment—is the key to the company's success. "The workplace for our family of employees constitutes an environment that is pleasant for working and that represents a place of opportunity for us all to realize the gratification of productive employment, meet economic needs, and fulfill ambitions. We feel the caring we give to employees comes back tenfold. They ultimately determine the quality of what we produce and that results in satisfied clients," say the Campbells.

Before the Campbells took over, the company had one product, a powdered mouthwash called Sip n' Rinse®. To diversify the business the Campbells started a contract packaging operation. Highland has the capability to design packaging, or adapt customers' ideas to produce packages that meet their needs.

Highland Packaging Labs, Inc., can formulate and mix powders, liquids, gels, lotions, or creams for a variety of product uses, including foods, vitamins, minerals, food supplements, pharmaceuticals, and cosmetics.

Products are blended in machines that look like giant food processors. Each packaging room is self-contained, unlike other packaging laboratories, providing a clean environment meeting state and federal regulations. Materials are packaged in humidity-controlled environments, and the machines are meticulously washed down after each job is completed.

"Our goal was not to become just another contract packager with a commodity approach. Instead, we have developed a unique facility and a high-quality approach to packaging premium products," says Mildred Campbell.

According to Stuart Campbell, "It is the fulfillment of a dream to take a small business and grow it to this level. Just as importantly, we have been able to share the experience with each other and with our family of employees."

ABOVE RIGHT: Stuart and Mildred Campbell have owned and managed Highland Packaging Labs, Inc., since 1983.

RIGHT: Highland Packaging Labs, Inc., is a state-of-the-art manufacturing and packaging facility primarily serving the food, pharmaceuticals, and cosmetics industries.

TAYLOR OIL COMPANY

Taylor Oil Company provides contractors and industrial equipment users throughout New Jersey and the Northeast with cost savings, increased productivity, and the convenience of on-site fuel and lubricant supply. Taylor provides customers with fuel servicing of road construction equipment, structural cranes, boats, or storage tanks, marinas, and entire fleets of trucks.

From two operations centers and eight terminals, Taylor Oil Company provides petroleum products on a programmed system available 24 hours per day, seven days per week. This enables customers to have maximum use of their machinery while reducing operating costs for refueling.

According to company president George Taylor, "Strict scheduling is the key to servicing the contractor before start-up, during lunch break, or after shutdown. Our customers have lower operating costs because they don't have to purchase and maintain fuel storage and handling equipment."

With more than 50 years of service and experience, Taylor Oil Company is the largest on-site service company in the fuel and petroleum business. Its system of high-volume purchases assure low competitive rates while providing quality petroleum products from Texaco, Hess, Exxon, and Lubriplate.

Taylor's professionally trained drivers—averaging eight years experience—are dependable and knowledgeable. All drivers and vehicles are fully insured. With 65 radio-dispatched vehicles, the company assures its customers prompt service and rapid response in emergencies. When special or emergency fueling is required, a radio-dispatched vehicle can usually be on the job within an hour.

Special services include installing above-ground tanks and underground tanks. Taylor Oil Company complies with the new EPA regulations governing underground storage tanks. In some cases Taylor Oil Company can actually eliminate the need for underground tanks with on-site refueling service. Taylor also offers skid-mounted above-ground tanks, ranging in size from 300 to 10,000 gallons. Taylor provides a full range of products, including motor oil (bulk and in cases), hoses, pumps, and special lubricants.

The delivery of gasoline, diesel fuel, motor oil, and bulk lubricants directly to the job site was conceived and organized in the early 1960s by George Taylor III, grandson of the firm's original founder. According to Taylor, "My goal was to be flexible and adaptable to the needs of the contractor. I felt that we had to combine fueling experience with clever dispatching in order to provide an economical service to the contracting industry."

The construction job-site service phase was organized by George Taylor III, who began as a lubricant jobber in 1909, and son of George Taylor, Jr., who operated the retail fuel oil end and the sale of fuels to trucking companies. David Taylor joined the firm in 1964 and heads the environmental operations.

Taylor Oil Company's construction fueling operation was established in 1960, and the service has spread throughout the region to where it now provides exclusive field service to many heavy construction firms in New Jersey, Pennsylvania, Delaware, New York, and Massachusetts as well as to many of the container-handling firms in Port Elizabeth and Port Newark.

Company founder George Taylor (second from left) in 1934.

Today Taylor Oil Company is owned and operated by George Taylor III (left) and David Taylor, brothers and grandsons of founder George Taylor.

UNION CARBIDE

Union Carbide is a worldwide corporation active in 36 countries, and New Jersey has played a major role in its growth and development. The root of what is today Union Carbide's largest business group—chemicals and plastics—began in New Jersey in 1910.

It was then that Dr. Loe Baekeland, a pioneer in the discovery of phenolic plastics, formed the Bakelite Company. Many industry experts equate the founding of Bakelite with the dawn of modern plastics. Bakelite became America's leading plastics-manufacturing company, producing phenol-formaldehyde resins and related products. In 1931 Bakelite moved to its present location on River Road near Bound Brook, and in 1939 it was acquired by Union Carbide.

Today this Bound Brook facility is the largest of Union Carbide's New Jersey operations. Since becoming part of Union Carbide, the Bound Brook plant has grown from a small group of buildings on an 80-acre site with 270 employees to a 275-acre complex with 30 major buildings. Some 900 people work at Bound Brook in manufacturing, engineering, research and development, and administration. Bound Brook today is considered one of Union Carbide's major chemicals and plastics-manufacturing facilities worldwide, producing more than 100 million pounds of plastic resins, compounds, and chemicals monthly.

Activities at Bound Brook have spearheaded Union Carbide's surge into specialty chemicals and thermoplastic resins. This evolution has helped create the "new" Carbide, an evolving company moving into new areas and stressing quality products, safety and environmental commitment, and increased customer services.

The plant produces hundreds of different products within several basic families of plastics. Marketed to industries as raw materials, these

RIGHT: Loe Baekeland originally formed the Bakelite Company in Perth Amboy.

BELOW: Union Carbide's new research and development complex is located at Weston Canal Center in Somerset.

products comprise polyethylenes, phenolics, and phenoxies. They are used to insulate wires and cables, for videotape and industrial coating, for space shuttle products, and for synthetic thickeners for the paint.

Over the years research and development at Bound Brook has resulted in plastic and chemical products that have improved the quality of life and provided new jobs. Developments have included new plastics, substitutes for wood and metal, and artificial heart components. The research center has received numerous industry awards for its outstanding technical achievements. Current work with new water-soluble polymers for personal products, mining, and petroleum drilling offer exciting possibilities for Union Carbide.

New materials for coatings include solvents that are compatible with environmental concerns. High solids water-borne resins and new cross-linking agents and radiation cross-

The Bound Brook facility is the largest of Union Carbide's New Jersey operations.

linking resins for cured coatings are current contributions to Union Carbide's sales portfolio.

Bound Brook is by no means the only Union Carbide facility in New Jersey. Other operations include production and distribution facilities for oxygen and nitrogen gases in Keasby and a coatings and materials plant in Somerset. One of the world's largest marine terminals, at Carteret, supplies Union Carbide with raw products from plants on the Gulf Coast, Puerto Rico, and Europe.

A new complex at Weston Canal Center in Somerset specializes in fulfilling the research and development needs of the polyolefins division. In addition, the center has the division's customer service operation and New Jersey-based sales operations and a regional corporate training center.

Union Carbide recently streamlined its operations in order to become more customer responsive. Four major business groups have been creating the restructuring: specialties and services, carbon products, chemicals and plastics, and industrial gases. The four groups each have a president and worldwide responsibility for their product lines. This simplified structure has eliminated several layers of organization within the corporation.

Union Carbide has ongoing programs to safeguard New Jersey's environment. Water used at Bound Brook for processing and cooling, sani-

tary sewage, and rain runoff are discharged into the Middlesex County trunk sewer for treatment and disposal. In compliance with New Jersey Department of Environmental Protection guidelines, the Bound Brook plant uses low-sulfur oil, noise suppressors, and air-pollution control devices. Union Carbide has spent hundreds of thousands of dollars on these measures to clean and protect the state's atmosphere as well as its rivers and streams. In addition, a cogeneration unit was put on stream to effectively generate utilities for the site. All of Union Carbide's plants have aggressive emissions-reduction programs. For example, the Bound Brook facility accomplished reduction from the years 1987 to 1988 by 43 percent.

Union Carbide and its employees play an active role in the New Jersey community, participating in civic activities. The firm's New Jersey Public Affairs Committee evaluates legislation affecting its business and involves itself in community activities. Each year the committee sends more than 10 New Jersey high school students to a week-long seminar in Washington, D.C., where they join 125 other students sponsored by Union Carbide sites from around the nation, meeting with senators and representatives and learning firsthand how America's system of government works. The PAC also sponsors safety-awareness programs, particularly for schoolchildren, providing educational materials and school presentations.

SOMERSET TRUST COMPANY

Somerset Trust Company's oldest office is located at 50 West Main Street in Somerville.

The Somerset Trust Company, established in 1864 as the First National Bank of Somerville, is a full-service commercial bank. Somerset Trust Company provides a full range of banking services, including trust and investment services, consumer banking, private banking, and corporate banking.

In 1984 Somerset formed its holding company, Somerset Bancorp. Inc., and was acquired in 1988 by The Summit Bancorporation, a $3.8-billion New Jersey bank holding company.

As a member of The Summit Bancorporation, Somerset Trust Company retained its name and local identity. In 1990 Somerset Trust Company expanded its geographical region when it consolidated operaions with Town and Country Bank, also a member of The Summit Bancorporation. The bank has 375 employees and 18 full-service branches.

The bank has benefited from the significant growth in commercial and residential real estate, particularly in Somerset County, where a number of national firms have located their offices. Somerset Trust Company is strategically positioned to effectively compete and grow in its marketplace while maintaining its strong earnings performance.

The bank's policy is to take on an active role in such community organizations as the chamber of commerce, service clubs, and local business organizations. Somerset Trust has always prided itself in its strong employee and officer involvement in the communities they serve.

Somerset Trust Company is one of seven community banks which comprise The Summit Bancorporation. Customers benefit from the convenience of having access to 80 branch offices spanning New Jersey from Ocean County to Warren County. The holding company has enabled each community bank to offer more services and achieve a greater lending limit for its corporate customer base.

According to Somerset Trust Company president Mortimer J. O'Shea, "A significant benefit of the Summit structure is our ability to deliver the best of both worlds. Our customers receive the quality service which is the hallmark of a small community bank while enjoying the diversity of services associated with a $3.8 billion organization."

ADIDAS

In the early 1920s in a little town 40 miles west of Nuremberg, West Germany, Adi Dassler designed his first pair of athletic shoes using a bicycle like milling cutter driven by the muscle power of an assistant. It was from these modest beginnings that Adi Dassler created the largest sporting-goods company in the world.

An avid sportsman himself, Adi Dassler believed that "good tools are half the work," and designing the best possible athletic shoes for all kinds of sports became his life's devotion.

By 1967 adidas was beginning to complement its extensive shoe range by manufacturing training suits. Today adidas produces apparel for all types of sports, having pioneered the wearing of fashion sportswear for any leisure activity.

Today adidas is headed by Swiss-born Rene Jaeggi, who was brought to adidas by Horst Dassler in 1986 to oversee sales and marketing. The largest family-owned sporting-goods business in the world, adidas employs more than 10,000 employees worldwide, exports to more than 150 countries, and owns more than 700 worldwide patents and registered trademarks. The firm has subsidiaries and licensor commissions in more than 40 countries and manufactures 280,000 pairs of shoes per day.

Its research and development facilities are located throughout the world, with the main R&D location in Lucerne, Switzerland. U.S. headquarters is located in Somerset Hill Corporate Center

Horst Dassler poses beside a portrait of the founder of adidas, Adi Dassler.

in Warren, New Jersey. Approximately 70 employees make up the corporate, marketing, sales, service, and footwear divisions. Adidas USA has a team of marketing managers who work closely with their international counterparts to design both shoe and apparel products for the North American market.

The company has a long history of outstanding athletes succeeding while wearing its shoes in competition. In 1932 Arthur Jonath won an Olympic bronze medal in the 100-meter race, and in 1936 Jesse Owens won four gold medals in Berlin. Both men wore individually designed Dassler shoes. At the 1952 Helsinki Olympic Games, adidas was the athletic shoe of choice for more athletes than any other sport-shoe company. In 1954 Germany's soccer team won the World Cup wearing Adi Dassler's screw-in stud soccer shoe.

Other adidas sports notables include Wilma Rudolph, winner of three gold medals in the 1960 Rome Olympics; Edwin Moses, Los Angeles Olympics gold-medal winner and world-record holder; Jackie Joyner-Kersee, one of the world's best athletes; Olympic marathoner Greta Waitz; tennis champions Steffi Graf and Stefan Edberg; and football hero Herschel Walker.

After 60 years of its name being synonymous with soccer, adidas will sponsor the United States Soccer Federation through the 1994 World Cup, and the U.S. national soccer team will proudly wear adidas products in the 1990 World Cup tournament.

Throughout its history, adidas philosophy has been that "only the best is good enough." To live up to this credo, adidas continues striving to design the best possible athletic footwear and apparel for every type of sports activity.

ABOVE: Swiss-born Rene Jaeggi, president and chief executive officer of adidas AG.

LEFT: The Etrusco collection is a new line of adidas soccer apparel. The U.S. national soccer team will proudly wear adidas products in the 1990 World Cup Tournament.

EGAN MACHINERY DIVISION/ JOHN BROWN INC.

Egan Machinery Company was founded in 1946, starting as a partnership in Bound Brook, New Jersey, home of the late Frank W. Egan with his two sons, Edward and Lawrence. From its beginnings as a locally based company, Egan has become an international leader in process technology for the plastics extrusion and converting industries.

The initial business of Egan was the design and manufacture of converting machinery used to coat paper, film, and foil webs. Within two years the founders sensed the coming importance of extrusion coated products and launched a line of equipment that today makes Egan one of the largest suppliers in the world.

In 1951 Egan developed its own plastics extruder technology and entered into other extruder-based product lines, including film, sheet, and resin compounding. Also in 1951, manufacturing facilities were added to meet the increasing business. The company remained in Bound Brook until 1955, when increased sales dictated an expansion move to its present office and manufacturing site in Somerville. During this period sales were $1.5 million and the company had 100 employees.

Through the late 1950s and early 1960s, Egan added technology for rotogravure printing presses for decorative laminates and floor coverings, a screw plasticizer for injecting molding called the Reciproscrew, and pressroom equipment to its product lines. In 1969, with sales over $18 million and with 555 employees, the company became a publicly held corporation to finance further expansion.

In December 1977 Egan Machinery Company was acquired by the Leesona Corporation. John Brown, PLC, of London, England, acquired Leesona in 1980, which positioned the company well to penetrate and serve markets internationally with manufacturing facilities in several countries and sales offices worldwide. Founded in 1837, John Brown employs more than 8,000 people in 14 countries, with its main business activities in engineering and construction for the process plant, oil and gas, and petrochemical industries; machinery for plastics processing, textile handling, and factory automation industries; power system engineering; and special engineering services for heavy manufacturing. Trafalgar House—a United Kingdom-based, real estate development, international construction, engineering, oil, and transportation group—acquired John Brown in 1986.

Today Egan is one of eight companies that together form the Plastics and Automation Sector

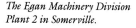

The Egan Machinery Division Plant 2 in Somerville.

Machinery Group of John Brown, PLC. The plastics manufacturing division of John Brown Inc. is a world leader in the development and supply of equipment for the processing of plastics and converting machinery, also providing a single source for the design and installation of complete systems.

Egan Machinery leads its industry in producing extrusion and converting equipment and associated control systems for production of films, sheets, laminates, and coated materials for uses such as food packaging, protective wrappings, magnetic tapes, photographic products, and pressure-sensitive labels.

Egan continues to expand its capabilities through acquisitions to attain its goal of becoming a major shareholder in selected market segments in the high-quality, high-performance converting marketplace. To that end Egan acquired the Wisconsin facilities of Hayes Technology, renamed Egan Converting, to establish a firmer position in the converting marketplace. Through its facility in Stroud, England, Egan offers sales, service, parts, and engineering backup staff to better serve customers in the U.K. and European market.

The company has maintained long-term relationships with Japanese licensees to provide

continuous service to the Far Eastern market. Teijan Seiki is licensed to produce converting machinery products while Modern Machinery is licensed for extrusion coating and cast film products. Chugai Boyaki Co., Ltd., is a trading company that sells Egan equipment in Japan.

The company philosophy is to invest in market-led product development to ensure client industries get state-of-the-art machinery and controls, with quality and reliability to match. Its objective is to provide Egan customers with cost-effective process equipment. Whether it is utilizing the latest technology in computer-aided design, investing in more productive manufacturing equipment, or upgrading the CMR controls it produces, Egan is always searching for new and innovative ways to serve the market. Egan products are engineered, manufactured, and serviced to help its customers consistently meet the product quality and productivity levels necessary to gain market share.

Egan's highly skilled, carefully trained professionals set the company apart from its competition. From machinists to assemblers to computer engineers to design engineers to experts in process technology—all work toward producing the world's finest extrusion and converting systems.

Egan's Somerville facilities are comprised of more than 250,000 square feet of space devoted to the engineering and manufacturing of complex plastics processing machinery. The facilities include an on-site technical center equipped with versatile Egan processing lines for film, sheet, extrusion coating, compounding, and reclaim. These can be configured for clients to demonstrate Egan productivity and value and to help customers validate the commercial viability of their project.

Quality control measures include inspecting all raw materials and components closely before manufacturing, using only the finest, most up-to-date machinery. The company utilizes extensive quality checks at every step in manufacturing. Egan's specially designed plant and computer-integrated manufacturing provides an exceptional production environment for the manufacture of precision, high-quality equipment. From design to manufacture to final assembly it can all be done at the Somerville facility.

With its roots in Somerset County, Egan Machinery has extended its reach to become an international leader in plastics extrusion and conversion, serving customers in Japan, England, Germany, Argentina, Russia, Spain, Mexico, and many other countries worldwide.

THE CLAREMONT COMPANIES

The Claremont Companies—Claremont Painting & Decorating Co., Claremont Wall Systems Co., Inc., and Claremont Interior Contractors, Inc.—is a group of affiliated companies that provide builders, developers, and institutions with a full range of construction finishing services.

Claremont Painting & Decorating Co., the first of the Claremont Companies, was founded in 1947 by Dominic Sciaretta, and within 20 years the company developed from a one-man residential painting business into one of the largest interior construction firms in the United States.

The Claremont Companies has achieved a preeminent position in the industry with emphasis on quality, cost control, on-time performance, and responsive management. As a result, The Claremont Companies has maintained relationships for more than three decades with many *Fortune* 500 companies.

Today The Claremont Companies employs more than 100 people in two New Jersey

Three examples of The Claremont Companies' work: Trump's Castle Hotel and Casino in Atlantic City (right), the Beneficial Finance Complex in Peapack, New Jersey (below), and East Brunswick, New Jersey's Tower Center (bottom).

offices and in excess of 1,100 field employees. It serves the interior construction needs of many of the largest commercial builders and developers in the world. Its projects range from regional shopping malls, hotel/casinos, hospitals, corporate headquarters, and government facilities to nuclear power plants.

Claremont Properties, Inc., the real estate development and management arm, develops fine residential and commercial properties in northern and central New Jersey. Founded in 1987, Claremont Properties has the resources to handle every step of the development process

from site acquisition through design, construction, and management.

Claremont Properties has already developed a wide range of commercial and residential properties, including office complexes, industrial and flex space, mixed-use projects, single-family homes, multifamily townhouses, and mid-rise condominiums.

Courthouse Square in Somerville features two similar buildings of 40,000 square feet and 50,000 square feet of prime office space. Phase I of these modern office structures has attracted corporations and organizations who desire a downtown business-district location by the courthouse and county offices.

Other Claremont Properties developments include the Somerset Hills Hotel, adjacent to the Somerset Hills Corporate Center, a joint venture with the prestigious Boyle company; Grande Commons at Bridgewater, a two-building 318,000-square-foot corporate office complex developed in joint venture with Bellemead Development Corp.; The Gladstone House, a 14-unit condominium complex built in the 50-year-old former Ellis Tiger industrial building, an area landmark; the Gladstone Shoppes, a mixed-use building divided into five retail stores; the 400-acre Morris County-based Long Valley Run, a single-family residential development; and Roxbury Office and Research Center, a 50-acre office/flex space development near the Foreign Trade Zone in Mount Olive.

A leader in its industry and its community, The Claremont Companies has made a substantial contribution to the economic development of central New Jersey and Somerset County.

ELIZABETHTOWN WATER COMPANY

Elizabethtown Water Company, one of the largest investor-owned water companies in the country, serves drinking water to 46 municipalities in six central New Jersey counties. On an average day Elizabethtown produces more than 136 million gallons of water to meet the needs of more than a million New Jersey residents.

Elizabethtown was founded in 1854 to serve the city of Elizabeth, New Jersey. In 1855 a pumping station was established at Harris Brothers Grist Mill on Golden Street to pump water from the Elizabeth River.

Over time, Elizabethtown grew through a series of mergers with, and acquisitions of, surrounding companies. In 1904 the Somerville Water Company became a subsidiary of Elizabethtown.

In the 1960s Elizabethtown added the Bound Brook, Plainfield-Union Water Companies, and many smaller companies located throughout central New Jersey. Presently, all of the companies have been merged into Elizabethtown.

Elizabethtown currently draws water from both surface and ground supplies. Its surface treatment plant is located in Bridgewater, Somerset County, at the confluence of the Raritan and Millstone rivers and adjacent to the Delaware and Raritan Canal.

There is little ostentation about the R-M plant, as it is called. Several of its squat brick buildings were put up more than 50 years ago. Its 100 acres once contained Tunis Huff's farm. In 1750 this was the site of Kell's Hall, summer home of Cornelius Van Horne, a mayor of New York.

The Raritan-Millstone plant in Bridgewater in the summer of 1931.

As Elizabethtown expands its facilities and equipment, it continues to be recognized as a leader in industry. Elizabethtown has a very sophisticated water treatment laboratory. Using some of the most advanced analytical equipment available, skilled operators continuously test water going into and leaving the R-M plant to ensure that Elizabethtown meets or exceeds every bacteriological and chemical standard set by state and federal government agencies.

Elizabethtown Water Company continually looks to the future and is ready to handle the tremendous growth within New Jersey. Its computer-aided planning department projects population and water-demand growth through the year 2020.

The people of Elizabethtown are proud of their history and continuously growing relationship with Somerset County and look forward to a successful future.

Today 85 percent of Elizabethtown Water Company's water is treated at the Raritan-Millstone plant.

SHIVE/SPINELLI/PERANTONI & ASSOCIATES/ARCHITECTS

Shive/Spinelli/Perantoni & Associates, Architects & Planners, offers a comprehensive range of architectural and planning services, including project feasibility studies, budgeting, comparative site analysis and selection, conceptual design, site specifications and drawings, and construction project management.

The firm was founded in 1891 by Peter C. Van Nuys, one of the first licensed architects in New Jersey. During the 1930s the original firm was expanded to include Jay Van Nuys, the son of the founder. This set an important precedent as the firm made its first organizational change to maintain continuous, dedicated professional services on behalf of its clients.

During the 1950s Adolph Scrimenti, James Swackhamer, and Frank Perantoni became associates of the firm named Jay Van Nuys and Associates. The firm earned national recognition for its designs for educational facilities. With the death of Jay Van Nuys in 1957, the firm was restructured as Scrimenti, Swackhamer & Perantoni, Architects.

The impact of the baby-boom generation created the need for a statewide expansion of school facilities, resulting in the corresponding growth in the firm with the addition of Richard B. Shive and Martin J. Spinelli, Jr., as associates.

In 1972 Shive and Spinelli became partners, and in later years Scrimenti retired from practice. In 1985 Jay F. Perantoni was named as an additional partner to the firm, and recently three new associates have been named, including Michael Marconi, Jeanne Perantoni, and Brian Rogaski. Today the firm practices as Shive/Spinelli/ Perantoni & Associates, Architects & Planners.

The firm's three principal partners and its three associates are all registered architects. Their efforts are supported by four project architects, seven nonregistered graduate architects, four architectural drafters, three construction superintendents, and an administrative office staff of seven people. In addition, director of educational services Dominick V. Chianese performs educational reviews and assists in the preparation of educational specifications for school projects.

All of the firm's partners participate in both individual projects and the firm's general administration. This nondepartmental organization allows for total participation of each partner. Each client has a single principal contact with the firm throughout the project's duration to assure strict control of authority and responsibility over the project by the partner in charge. For both professional and business management functions, responsibility is spread among all the partners and yet allows a broad voice for each in the overall policy-making.

The end result is that clients receive personal service and conscientious leadership by an individual partner, and the staff supports his efforts with specialized expertise and the ability to handle large complicated projects.

The firm's philosophy states, "We are strongly committed to the belief that architecture is capable of enriching the daily experience, but only when the owner's functional needs are met and satisfied. We believe that the variety of our firm's commissions and our long heritage has been an asset in our favor, especially in teaching us how to listen, analyze, formulate, and respond to the needs of each client."

The firm is noted for its ability to complete projects on time and within budget. Shive/Spinelli/Perantoni offers its clients the ability to design, bid, and complete projects within a given time parameter using critical path scheduling of design work and fast-track coordination. Its in-house computer system efficiently organizes and monitors the project management, design planning, and construction administration process throughout every project's duration. The firm's record of designing to meet construction budgets has proven excellent on projects as large as multimillion-dollar lab facilities to relatively small roof replacement or maintenance projects.

The firm's commissions have ranged in scope from the state's first solar-heated college dormitory, located at Ramapo State College, to a chemical/biological weapons antidote research laboratory for the Salk Institute. While Shive/Spinelli/Perantoni provides a broad range of professional services, the vast majority

The Shive/Spinelli/Perantoni & Associates office building in Somerville was converted by the firm from an old residence into 5,000 square feet of design space.

of its architectural services are performed for public school districts and colleges within New Jersey by a specialized design team.

The scope of the firm's practice includes commissions at numerous colleges and universities including Princeton, Rutgers, Kean College, Trenton State College, and Somerset County College. True to its heritage, the firm continues to serve more than 60 public school districts statewide.

"Special expertise in school design requires understanding the educational process. It also calls for understanding the State of New Jersey approach to school design and meeting its strict standards. As a firm, our most valuable asset is our strong reputation in school design," states Richard Shive.

Highly specialized research labs, such as a recent addition to the Connaught Lab in Swiftwater, Pennsylvania, continue to be an area of expertise within the firm. Municipal projects range from the new police headquarters facility in Branchburg to ongoing maintenance and upgrading projects in Somerville. The firm also does residential commissions and office interior design and space planning.

The firm's recent client list includes more than 80 public-sector owners, including

state agencies, county governments, municipalities, and boards of education. The list of private business clients includes such *Fortune* 500 firms as AT&T, Bell Labs, CIBA-GEIGY, and Squibb as well as numerous local business establishments.

Within the past five years, Shive/Spinelli/Perantoni & Associates has been responsible for the construction of public and private facilities within New Jersey whose total construction value exceeds $200 million.

The design and technical ability of the firm has been recognized through numerous state and architectural chapter design awards on a wide range of projects from model teaching schools to senior-citizen housing projects. In addition, the firm's critical and analytical ability has been recognized by the numerous state agencies that have engaged it for consultation, investigative, and corrective repair services relative to existing structures.

Shive/Spinelli/Perantoni & Associates, Architects & Planners, is committed to maintaining its long history of offering exemplary architectural services. According to Richard Shive, "We hope this firm or its successors will still be a healthy, viable firm for another 100 years from now. We expect it to continue."

Seated (left to right) are partners Richard B. Shive, Martin J. Spinelli, Jr., and Jay F. Perantoni. Standing (left to right) are associates Michael A. Marconi, Jeanne K. Perantoni, and Brian K. Rogaski.

THE OLD MILL INN

Somerset County abounds in famous landmarks boasting that "George Washington slept here." While The Old Mill Inn makes no such claim, it is safe to assume that the original structure played an important part in General Washington's campaign when his troops were quartered at nearby Jockey Hollow.

The inn, which predates the Revolution, was once a large barn in which grain was stored to be ground into meal for Washington's men. The old gristmill, built in 1768, still stands directly across Route 202.

In 1930 the old barn was renovated by William Childs, the famous restaurateur. Not a single change was made in the roofline or exte-

The Old Mill Inn in Bernardsville features elegant accommodations in a historic setting.

rior walls. The interior subdivisions themselves suggested what to do architecturally during the renovation. The Wagon Room became the large dining room; the horse stable became the grill. The living room, entrance hall, and passageway from front to rear were created from the original partitions in the old barn. In the great haymow on the second floor, seven small bedrooms have been updated with baths.

Throughout the building, the great beams, hand hewn from massive oaks, untouched by saw or ax, were left exposed. Thus was born The Old Mill Inn. Old prints and antique furnishings help create the atmosphere of another day. In later years the luxurious Fox and Hounds

room was added, along with an ultramodern, all-electric kitchen.

Unlike the majestic old gristmill across the way, the inn continues to serve the area in restoring dining to its rightful mission, as a time for relaxation and good conversation in charming surroundings. Guests today dine among the original fireplaces, old prints, and antique furnishings. The restaurant of The Old Mill Inn was the recipient of gold and silver medals from the Geneva Culinary Association in recent years.

Today The Old Mill Inn is owned and operated by Milhil Corporation, a member of the W.G.A. family of exceptional hotels and restaurants. Company owners William and Joan

Graulich are dedicated to providing guests the epitome of service and comfort. Whether a business traveler or vacationing family, the management and staff of The Old Mill Inn are dedicated to serving the special needs of their guests.

The Old Mill Inn is conveniently located on the border of Morris and Somerset counties, just minutes away from Morristown and Somerville. All major routes, including routes 287, 202, 80, 46, and 10, are easily accessible from its central location. Newark International Airport is 45 minutes away.

The Old Mill Inn accommodations include 104 beautifully appointed guest rooms available in king-size or double beds. Special nonsmoking rooms are available.

Every guest receives a complimentary country breakfast and a complimentary cocktail in the eighteenth-century-style Coppertop Lounge. Guests also receive free parking, newspaper, valet service, and cable television, and low-cost airport shuttle service. Corporate, relocation, and weekend rates are available.

According to company owner William Graulich, "Somerset County has much to offer our guests—beautiful countryside, many historic sites to explore, and great retail shopping. Businesses who have conferences or special events here appreciate our centralized location that enables them to take advantage of the area's amenities while having easy access to both New York and Philadelphia."

Recreation facilities of The Old Mill Inn include an outdoor courtyard pool surrounded by elegant gardens, an exercise room equipped with Universal equipment, and jogging trails mapped out for guests. Guests may also use the golf and tennis facilities of the nearby Pennbrook Country Club.

The Old Mill Inn Conference Center consists of nine meeting rooms and three banquet rooms. Modern and well equipped, these rooms can accommodate up to 300 people. The Old Mill Inn's professional sales staff sees to it that every detail of business and social functions is attended to.

Charming is the word used to most describe The Old Mill Inn. Guests may choose to stay in one of seven guest rooms restored back to the period style of this historic site or in a modern guest room available in the new hotel.

Whichever one chooses, excellent contemporary service and fine amenities help to make every guest's stay most memorable.

"We are dedicated to serving our guests' needs. We have not only preserved the inn's historic beauty—we have maintained a long tradition of service," says Joan Graulich.

THE COURIER-NEWS

The Courier-News is owned by the Gannett Co., Inc. The newspaper covers portions of five counties in central New Jersey. It is an afternoon newspaper Monday through Friday and a morning newspaper Saturday and Sunday, with more than 52,000 readers.

The newspaper has grown dramatically since its birth as a four-page collection of news and gossip in 1884, but has never strayed from founding publisher Thomas W. Morrison's promise to his readers: "All the local news possible to obtain shall be collected and printed. It will be the people's newspaper—or nothing."

The Courier-News is a consolidation of *The Evening News,* the *Plainfield Daily Press,* and the *Plainfield Courier.* Thomas W. Morrison gave birth to the *Plainfield Evening News,* the city's only daily newspaper. The *News* was a crusading newspaper, staunchly Republican. Unlike newspapers of today, it made no claims of neutrality in politics or objectivity in reporting.

Plainfield already had two weeklies, but Morrison believed that the growing area would support a daily newspaper. For two cents readers got scores of stories telling of births and deaths, weddings and anniversaries, political meetings and social gatherings.

Morrison had the daily newspaper field to himself for three years. But in 1887, two brothers who published weekly newspapers started *The Daily Press.* Fierce competition lasted until Morrison sold *The Evening News* in 1894 to the owner of *The Courier;* and the combined *Courier-News* began publication. After the merger *The Daily Press* slipped in the battle for circulation, and in 1916 it was sold to *The Courier-News.*

The newspaper became part of the Gannett newspaper chain in 1927. Frank Gannett later bought full ownership in 1940, making *The Courier-News* the fifth newspaper in the Gannett group.

One aspect of *The Courier-News* remains remarkably similar after more than a century. Editorial decisions continue to be made by the people who work and live in the area. Gannett's policy calls for local autonomy in all of Gannett's 85 newspapers.

While central Jersey grew into an industrial base, *The Courier-News* gave birth to a professional maturity of its own. Gradually, the advertisements and obituaries dropped off the front page. The news headlines grew bigger and bolder, the society meeting stories got trimmed, and the editorials cut deeper. Local news remained top priority, but often what happened halfway around the world, where World War I was in progress, had the highest interest.

As the population masses moved westward, so did the paper's advertisers and subscribers. Suburban coverage was reorganized in 1938 and the territory expanded to more than 40 communities in five counties. By the end of 1940, circulation had reached 16,300 and *The Courier-News* had taken over all of its Park Avenue building. Ground was broken for a new building at Church and East Second streets.

What happened to central Jersey in the 1950s set the framework for the central Jersey of today. As the area progressed into the 1960s, stability in housing, shopping, and business patterns defined the counties and gave their residents a comfortable standard of living. True to its roots as a crusading newspaper, *The Courier-News* took an active role in influencing the community, including a campaign to have school boards throughout the area release the salaries of teachers, as well as one to extend the Route 22 concrete barrier, construct additional overpasses, and reduce the speed limit for trucks to 45 miles per hour.

Over the years The Courier-News *has continually expanded and modernized. Yet founding publisher Thomas W. Morrison's promise to make it the "people's" local newspaper has always been fulfilled.*

The Courier-News already had expanded several times in its Church Street building, yet more room was needed. The problem was that Plainfield did not have the space for the modern, expansive facility envisioned. The newspaper decided to move out of its lifelong home city to a point halfway between Plainfield and Flemington in prosperous Somerset County, where central Jersey's major highways converged.

The $4.5-million Bridgewater plant was the home of the largest evening offset daily newspaper in the country at the time, and offered a sharper, brighter, full-color newspaper. It converted the paper from the old-fashioned hot metal and letterpress printing to photo composition and offset printing.

After the move The Courier-News was on top of a long period of expansion and circulation growth. More improvements were made in 1982, when the newspaper became a printing site for Gannett Co.'s new national newspaper, USA Today. The company upgraded its presses, and The Courier-News reassessed its own operations.

As part of that process, new managers were hired at a higher level and higher salaries. The reassessment has led to significant expansion and upgrading of The Courier-News in technology, reporting, and ad staffing.

The Courier-News has won numerous awards in recent years from national organizations, the state press association, Society of Professional Journalists, and the Best of Gannett competition.

The Courier-News sponsors a charity fund called "Lend a Hand" and is a main sponsor in the regional Festival of Ballooning, which is a major community event each summer. The newspaper participates in many other community activities, including educational programs in conjunction with area schools.

The news emphasis now—as it was a century ago—is local news, says managing editor Carol A. Hunter. "Residents have a right to know when their taxes will be raised or when a new building will go up next door. But 'local news' has a much broader meaning today than traditional town-hall coverage. There is nothing more local than the television set in the living room, so we provide extensive coverage of what's coming up on TV. The New York sports teams and Broadway plays are considered local events for us, since so many people here travel in to see them. Every day, we hope to provide the information people need to live and work in central Jersey."

NATIONAL STARCH AND CHEMICAL COMPANY

variety of common and exotic products, from hair sprays to microprocessors, gravy to airplanes, houses to surgical powders.

Its story begins in 1895, when company founder Alexander Alexander purchased New York City based-National Gum Mica Company for $1,200. The firm produced glue sizings (used to prepare paper and textiles for printing) and related materials, such as paste for boxes.

National's destiny would be linked to its development of adhesives. The advent of packaged goods created a new industry, and National's adhesives business evolved with this new field. Specialized fast-drying starch-based adhesives were developed. In the 1940s the company developed polyvinyl acetate adhesives that are not only moisture resistant but also have properties favorable to high-speed packaging.

National's adhesive business grew quickly. Adhesives sales in 1920 were only $300,000, but within six years volume jumped to one million dollars. During the early 1930s National built a new starch refinery in Plainfield and bolstered research activities to create an expanded line of starch-based adhesives.

In 1928 National merged with two smaller adhesive companies—Glucol Manufacturing Company of Cleveland and Dextro Products Company of Buffalo. The corporate name became National Adhesives Corporation. A San Francisco plant was acquired in the merger, and National became one of the first adhesives companies on the West Coast.

With cornstarch as a basis of National's liquid adhesives, the firm sought its own cornstarch supply. In 1939 National purchased the Piel Brothers Starch Company in Indianapolis and obtained its own cornstarch plant. That same year National changed its name to National

ABOVE: Research and development at National includes operating pilot plant equipment, such as this cooker/extruder, to emulate customers' processing environments.

RIGHT: Saturating and coating nonwoven fabrics with resins from National provides water resistance, durability, texture, and a host of other desirable properties.

Founded in 1895, the history of the National Starch and Chemical Company and its predecessors has spanned radical changes in society and incredible progress in science and technology. National has both anticipated and responded to the world's industrial, social, and economic demands. The firm began as a small compounder of adhesives that were based on corn, potato, tapioca, and other vegetable starches. The needs of the United States during World War II led the company to develop synthetic adhesives and other chemical products and expanded its activities around the globe.

The firm became a developer of unique products—an expert in both basic technology and the technological requirements of the industries it serves, and it grew by giving the customer compounds that would speed production, control costs, and improve operations and sales.

Today National makes thousands of products that are crucial components of a dizzying

Starch Products Inc. to reflect its diversified product line.

National greatly expanded its research efforts, a tradition that continues to this day. Employing both chemical and genetic modification techniques, the company became the leader in developing and marketing specialty starches for use by the food, pharmaceutical, paper, corrugated board, and textile industries.

With this expanded technology came enormous growth. Sales grew from $16 million in 1949 to $65 million by 1961. With the development of synthetic adhesives, chemistry became a large part of the business, and so in 1959 the company changed its name to National Starch and Chemical Corporation.

By 1960 National had subsidiaries in Canada, England, and Mexico. In 1967 it acquired glue and furniture finish manufacturer LePage's Ltd. of Canada, and International Adhesives and Resins Pty. Ltd. of Australia. National forged overseas joint ventures in England, France, and the Netherlands while also expanding its domestic operations. In the 1970s National further expanded by purchasing California-based electronic-industry adhesive maker Ablestik Laboratories, and high-tech adhesive manufacturer Permabond International Corporation. In the 1980s the acquisition focus turned to electronics, adhesives, specialty polymers, and international operations.

Today, with more than 100 manufacturing and customer service centers in 23 countries, National serves many industries with basic product categories, including adhesives and sealants for packaging, publishing, disposables, furniture, construction, transportation equipment, appliances, and electronics; resins and chemicals for cosmetics and toiletries, paper, nonwovens, textiles, building products, industrial coatings, photography, water treatment, oil field services,

and other specialties; industrial starches for paper, textiles, corrugating, building products, gummed products and adhesives, cosmetics, and oil-field services; and food products for baby foods, bakery goods and desserts, confections, sauces and dressings, and pharmaceuticals.

Paramount in National's approach to meeting its customers' needs are the company's wide-ranging research and development programs. The company has developed technology and products that have become the standards in the industries that it serves. Bolstered by a worldwide research and development staff of more than 700, National holds more than 1,000 worldwide patents, and many of its products are industry standards. Today more than half of the company's sales come from products developed within the past 10 years, an indication of the firm's research and development strength.

Today National continues to provide its customers with innovative products that will become tomorrow's standards. National's growth has continued, and it has increased sales annually. The main force behind its growth is its technological know-how.

Although its headquarters in Bridgewater continues to be the focal point for new product and process developments, there is an increasing degree of technical exchange among National's worldwide affiliates—an indication of its maturity, strength, and international cohesiveness.

National's New Jersey roots began in 1920 when it opened an operating plant in Dunellen. The original plant in Dunellen eventually expanded into Plainfield, so today its buildings straddle between these two towns' borders. In 1973 National purchased the former Johns-Manville Research Center at Bridgewater, a 97-acre complex with 550,000 square feet of floor space, combining administrative, research, and marketing operations.

Today at National Starch and Chemical Company, a close-knit atmosphere remains despite the years of tremendous growth. Many employees have worked there for more than 40 years. Teamwork and cooperation are the hallmark of its operation.

"Two qualities of our company stand out most sharply in my mind. One is our ability to anticipate and respond to the technological demands of the marketplace; our skill at providing service to our customers goes hand in hand with this. And the second is our concern with people and the remarkable talent, devotion, and energy of the men and women who work for National," says Nicholas G. Marotta, National president and chief executive officer.

National is the worldwide leader in specialty food and industrial starches—adding texture, good appearance, and stability to food and providing strength and processing improvements in the production of paper, packaging, and textiles.

Products in development are thoroughly tested at National's corporate research center in Bridgewater. This scientist is gauging the strength of the hot melt adhesive used to attach a base cap to a plastic soft-drink bottle.

WBRW 1170 AM

At noon on December 23, 1971, radio station WBRW signed on the AM airwaves blanketing the central New Jersey area with a 500-watt signal capable of reaching 500,000 people.

For the past 20 years, "Community Voice" WBRW-AM has been broadcasting at 1170 on the dial, targeting Somerset and Hunterdon counties with a blend of news, features, and adult contemporary music.

Although the signal extends to Allentown, Pennsylvania, in the west, Morristown to the north, and Mercer County in the south, WBRW focuses primarily on local events.

The radio station is noted for its active involvement with such community groups as the Boy Scouts, United Way, Greater Somerset County Chamber of Commerce, Mothers Against Drunk Driving, and the American Heart Association. The station sponsors baskets for the needy at Thanksgiving and a Toys for Tots program during the Christmas season.

RIGHT: WBRW's studio and radio towers are located in the middle of a farm in Bridgewater.

BELOW: Longtime WBRW personality Glenn Allison entertains central Jersey with comedy, music, information, and audience participation games such as Trivia, Name that Tune, and What's My Line.

Annual events for which the station is noted are its live remote broadcasts of the three-day 4-H fair held each August at the Somerset County fairgrounds, Grand Prix Days in Bound Brook, and the Somerville Downtown Street Fair. Other special programs have included appearances by comedian Uncle Floyd and a piano concert sponsored by Hoescht-Celanese.

The main objective of the station's news coverage is to keep listeners in touch with the Somerset-Hunterdon area. The WBRW news team covers municipal meetings and area events. During local elections the station has a network of staffers who conduct interviews and broadcast results as quickly as possible to the community.

To gauge the local political climate, the station also broadcasts what the freeholders and local mayors have to say about their communities. To provide a forum for community residents and local politicians, the station sponsored a debate about a controversial $28-million education referendum in Bridgewater.

As a means to focus attention on the day-to-day demands of running a city, a WBRW disc jockey switched places with Bound Brook Mayor Ron Fasonello with the mayor acting as a broadcaster while his counterpart served as mayor for a day.

In addition to live coverage of local news and events, WBRW announces local school sports results and does live coverage of high school football games. During inclement weather, cancellations of area schools and businesses are announced throughout the day. The station also features "Shadow Traffic" and weather reports to keep listeners up to date on rush-hour road conditions and weather forecasts.

The station is committed by FCC regulations to present a certain number of hours of public-affairs programs regularly weekly and weekends. These include a weekly forum on Sundays, interviews with public officials, and other community information shows.

Besides news, WBRW features many special interest programs. Over the years these have included "Consumer Watch," helpful hints to shoppers and "do-it-yourself" people; "Eye on TV," which gives a daily preview of what is on network and cable television channels; "The Mini People," a weekday-morning comedy show that appeals to the whole family; "On Stage," which reviews and updates listeners on local theater performances; "A Closer Look," which focuses on pressing local issues; "The Sound of 4-H," and "Star Date," which highlights astronomical phenomena.

The station also broadcasts various church services every Sunday morning and gears special programs to the holiday season such as "Snow Country Ski Reports" and "'Tis the Season," a collection of carols and holiday trivia. In addition, WBRW features the "Community Datebook," where disc jockeys announce the events and activities to be held by area nonprofit organizations.

One local favorite is on-air personality Glenn Allison, who has worked for WBRW for 10 years. His "Allison Wonderland Show" features popular trivia contests such as Name that Tune.

Because WBRW is designated as a day station by the FCC, it may broadcast only between sunrise and sunset. The station is on the air longest during June and July, from 6 a.m. to 8:30 p.m. By December the hours are down to sign on at 7:15 a.m. and sign off by 5 p.m.

As a source for advertising, one of WBRW's biggest advantages over other stations broadcasting in the area is its ability to target small retail businesses in the Somerset/ Hunterdon region. WBRW works closely with its advertisers to determine the image they want to project. The staff writes and produces commercials or may suggest special promotions advertisers can offer customers.

The station's longtime advertisers include Hoescht-Celanese, which presents community trivia during the news; Effinger's Sporting Goods, sole sponsor of the high school football game of the week; Angelone's Florist; and the Somerville Circle Cinema, who sponsor free movie tickets for listeners who win the station's trivia contest.

Between 1989 and 1990 the station changed ownership. Initally its former owners thought the station would have to be closed. Media attention from the local newspapers, the *Courier News* and the *Somerset Messenger-Gazette,* as well as the television news program "NJ Network," focused attention on the possible threat of shutting down. An outcry of community support led to more than 30 offers to purchase WBRW 1170 AM.

Station manager Glenn Allison says, "This is a great place for a community-based radio station. Somerset County is one of the richest and fastest-growing areas in the country. Local residents take a more active role in the community than other areas—such as 30 to 40 people attending community meetings. People here care about community issues. As a radio station our purpose is to serve the community."

When previous ownership no longer wanted to own a radio station, employees Al Gambino, Nancy Carmody, and Glenn Allison (left to right) held the station together until new ownership was found.

CARRIER FOUNDATION

A view of the main hospital building in the early 1900s.

Russell N. Carrier, owner of Carrier Clinic, proudly points out his new sign to Robert S. Garber, newly appointed medical director, in the late 1950s.

In its 80 years of treating emotional illnesses and substance abuse, Carrier Foundation has experienced many changes. Today there are different people, more services, more beds, and a different name. But the dedication to the patients has remained. The philosophy of the facility is dedication to people who have been forgotten and who deserve the best treatment available.

Belle Mead, Montgomery Township in New Jersey in 1910 was an ideal time and place for a farm colony. The land was fertile and Dr. John Joseph Kindred's certificate of incorporation stated the purpose of the Belle Mead Farm Colony and Sanitorium was "to produce, purchase, sell, and deal in milk, butter, eggs, vegetables, hay, grain, and other food, farm, and dairy products." Only after that paragraph is a clause "to establish and maintain a colony for the care and treatment of sick persons, particularly for the care and treatment of nervous and mental diseases and all allied diseases."

Much has changed, however. The animals have been sold; the land is no longer tilled. But with 321 beds, Carrier Foundation is now the largest private nonprofit psychiatric hospital in New Jersey. Some of the specialized inpatient programs are the Adolescent Program, Anxiety Disorders Program, Addiction Recovery Service, Eating Disorders Program, Mood Disorders Program, Women's Program, and the Senior Treatment and Evaluation (STEP) Program. Carrier has also established a day school that provides emotionally troubled adolescents with a special program that combines academic study with therapeutic care. Carrier's outpatient services include an Outpatient Department for individual and group psychotherapy; a Family Therapy Institute for family and marital counseling; and Outpatient Addiction Treatment Service, includ-

ing intensive six-week addiction treatment, aftercare, and various family programs.

The Industrial Referral Program at Carrier is designed to maximize the benefits of outpatient treatment or hospitalization for employees of the business community and their family members. The clinical treatment teams have specialized training in the program, thus assuring the employer of the highest quality of care and personalized service available. The referring companies receive comprehensive treatment for their staff, employee educational programs, consultation services, and back-to-work conferences.

In 1952 Dr. Russell Carrier became owner and medical director of the Belle Mead facility. At that time the farm colony consisted of old buildings with chronic, elderly people. Within one year Dr. Russell Carrier was moving the Belle Mead Farm Colony and Sanatorium on the path to the present. The search for better psychiatric treatment intensified soon after. Dr. Carrier hired a staff of experts. They pushed for new testing and research. As a result, Carrier became one of 20 hospitals nationwide to test manic patients with lithium, which is now the standard treatment for manic/depressive patients.

Dr. Robert Garber, who was hired and became medical director in 1958 and president in 1973, was mostly responsible for Carrier becoming nationally known in the field of psychiatry. The staff under Dr. Carrier and Dr. Garber consisted of four other doctors, along with several nurses.

Now the medical staff has expanded to include more than 30 psychiatrists and the hospital employs almost 1,000 people. The hospital also offers health promotion programs for industry and the community. After considerable research regarding the needs of employers, employees, and members of the community, the hospital has created the Center for Learning

A current view of the entrance to Carrier Foundation's admissions area.

to enhance productivity and job satisfaction and to improve the quality of life. The Center for Learning programs were created and initiated after a thorough needs assessment and evaluation completed by Carrier staff.

Two of the center's programs are Smoking Management Clinics and "Stress: Signals and Solutions." The stress program is a seven-hour program that provides an overview of stress and its management. The Smoking Management Clinic is a smoking cessation program using a philosophy of addiction treatment dedicated to providing straightforward, practical information about what individuals can expect from the process of quitting smoking.

The Purolator Company, of oil filter and overnight delivery fame, purchased the Carrier Clinic from Dr. Carrier in 1971. At the same time, the Addiction Recovery Unit at the hospital began treating addicted patients. Carrier's multidisciplinary approach to specialized programs began and came into its own.

Today the treatment approach to drug and alcohol abuse is based upon the Alcoholics Anonymous (AA) and Narcotics Anonymous (NA) philosophy in combination with a broadly based individualized clinical approach. The Addiction Recovery Service includes an Addiction Recovery Unit for the chemically dependent person who may suffer from a coexisting psychiatric illness. The service also has a residential treatment program housed in a free-standing building for adult patients with a primary diagnosis of substance abuse. Patients in this program do not have a concurrent psychiatric illness or a medical complication.

Carrier Foundation believes the family of the patient plays an important role in the recovery of the addicted person. Carrier's Weekend Codependency Program, which is free of charge, is open to the families of a chemically dependent patient and to the public. It consists of six differ-

ent sessions geared to helping individuals understand the disease of substance abuse and dealing with their feelings.

Carrier serves as a major teaching facility for a number of medical schools, universities, and hospitals in the Northeast. Seven symposia are also planned each year by the education division dealing with a variety of mental health subjects. In addition, Carrier offers free evening educational programs for the public on topics ranging from depression to divorce.

Located in a rural setting at the foot of the Sourland Mountains, Carrier's spacious campus with its tree-lined walks provides a serene and therapeutic atmosphere for patients, families, and visitors. Carrier Foundation is committed to a philosophy of short-term, intensive, individualized treatment designed to return the recovered patient to his or her family, job, and community in the shortest possible time and at the least possible expense.

One of Carrier Foundation's 400 scenic acres, located at the foot of the Sourland Mountains.

LEDERLE/AMERICAN CYANAMID COMPANY

The first three Calco buildings were erected in 1915 at a cost of $8,400. The Bound Brook location eventually grew to house 3,000 employees working in 150 buildings.

Using new technology from Germany, in 1907, Frank Washburn built a plant on the shores of the Niagara River in Canada to bring the world's first synthetic fertilizer to the developing farmlands in North America.

From that first product, calcium cyanamide, came a company name and a company mission. Cyanamid would bring products based on science to a world eager for solutions—more plentiful food, better health care, higher industrial productivity, and enhanced care for the individual and the home.

Through the 1920s and 1930s Cyanamid grew from being a small chemical company into a major industrial corporation. This growth stemmed from relying principally on growth from within through research and product development, and horizontal expansion through acquisition of new product lines.

Cyanamid expanded at a fairly conservative pace during the early 1920s and 1930s by broadening its line of fertilizers, adding a line of mining chemicals, and honing its research abilities. In 1929 Cyanamid acquired the Calco Chemical Company and its Bound Brook plant. Founded in 1915, the Calco Chemical Company produced dyes and the building-block chemicals, beta naphthol and aniline. As a result of the national needs during World War II, the plant expanded its operations and achieved tremendous growth in a short time.

The Bound Brook plant was among the earliest chemical facilities in Somerset County and in the state. Its leadership under Cyanamid set the stage for other chemical companies to establish themselves in the area, providing jobs for area residents, a strong tax base for local government, and a model for other chemical companies throughout the United States to follow.

From the original complement of scientists needed to start Calco's production in the first three buildings, all erected at a total cost of $8,400, the Bound Brook location eventually grew to house 3,000 employees working in 150 buildings. Where once plant property was enclosed in 15 acres, it expanded to 600 acres. From a handful of products, the plant grew to more than 800 products produced by highly skilled personnel.

In 1937 Cyanamid established its first central research lab in a former silk factory in Stamford, Connecticut, and began to produce sulfanilamide, the first sulfa drug in the United States, at the Bound Brook plant. Millions of pounds of sulfa drugs were produced at Bound Brook for the war effort. Cyanamid also developed other products to support the armed forces, including acrylonitrile, a chemical compound used to produce synthetic.rubber, fibers and plastics, and polyester resins, used extensively in aircraft construction.

At its most productive stage the plant was so vast it used 20 million gallons of river water daily, burned 700 tons of coal per day, manufac-

A still tower is raised onto its foundation in the Naphthalene Department in 1940.

An aerial view of the Bound Brook plant in 1978.

tured ice for its own use at the rate of 140 tons per day, and purchased, among other things, 35 tons of salt per day. Its tools ranged in size and ease of dexterity from a small delicate lab scale to a crane with a 100-foot boom.

The plant held 300,000 gallons of water suspended high in the air in three towers, used hundreds of miles of piping, and 2,500 pumps protected by 20,000 fire sprinkler heads.

To build its effluent treatment plant, one-quarter of a million cubic yards of earth were removed (equivalent to the excavation of 1,500 house cellars), 1,450 tons of steel were used (equivalent to about 10 miles of single-line railroad track), and 20,000 cubic yards of concrete were poured (equivalent to a two-lane highway from Bound Brook to Plainfield).

Its employees produced one patentable idea per week and a profusion of products as diverse as a resin to protect silk and a pharmaceutical to aid ulcer victims.

Cyanamid's Bound Brook plant was one of the largest producers of sulfa drugs and catalytic aniline in the United States. It produced the most beta naphthol of any source in the nation, operated one of the largest biological waste treatment plants in the world, and had the largest lab extractor of its kind in the world.

Based on its strategy of growth through expansion, Cyanamid acquired the Brooklyn firm of David & Geck, manufacturers of a growing line of surgical sutures, and Lederle Laboratories in Pearl River, New York, producers and marketers of ethical pharmaceuticals and biologicals. The Lederle acquisition in 1930 attracted top scientists and doctors and helped intensify research and development efforts throughout the company.

In 1942 Lederle undertook the largest blood plasma processing program in history for the American Red Cross and other divisions undertook a host of defense projects.

The era following the war was one of rapid growth for Cyanamid as it was for the country. A Lederle research team, headed by

the late Dr. Benjamin Duggar, discovered Aureomycin® chlortetracycline, and in 1948 it became the first broad-spectrum antibiotic made available to physicians, thus introducing the age of "wonder drugs."

The Bound Brook facility grew with the other divisions of the company. By the 1970s the Bound Brook plant was producing 1,000 products, including fine chemicals for agricultural and pharmaceutical products, elastomers, rubber chemicals, dyes, chemical intermediates, organic pigments, and plastic additives.

Cyanamid's diverse activities in Bridgewater provided employment for 2,400 people and annually contributed some $42 million in wages and salaries and $94 million for materials, supplies, utilities, and taxes to the economy of the area and New Jersey.

In addition to being a center of chemical manufacturing, the location also was the administrative and sales headquarters for Cyanamid's Organic Chemicals Division, which is known as the Chemical Products Division, headquartered

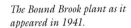

The Bound Brook plant as it appeared in 1941.

ABOVE: A view of the Bound Brook plant manufacturing buildings, looking east, in the mid-1930s.

RIGHT: A section of the dye manufacturing shop in 1941.

in Wayne, New Jersey. It also was the site of major research and development labs of the company's Chemical Research Division.

Late in the 1970s, growth in the United States chemical industry began to be negatively impacted by a lack of new products and technology and severe cost/price constraints from the higher cost of energy and increased foreign imports. Cyanamid began withdrawing from chemical product lines that offered little opportunity for profitable growth over the long term. As a result, operations at the Bound Brook plant were reduced.

Today Cyanamid's Bound Brook manufacturing facility is part of Cyanamid's Lederle Laboratories Division and manufactures fine chemicals for the agricultural and pharmaceutical industries and elastomers—elastic rubber-like materials—for the automotive industry.

The plant employs about 400 people, has an annual payroll of more than $4 million and paid more than one million dollars in taxes in 1986. In 1990 the Bound Brook plant will celebrate its 75th anniversary.

From its modest beginnings in 1907, Cyanamid today operates 17 research laboratories and nearly 100 manufacturing facilities throughout the world. Its products are sold by its divisions and subsidiaries in more than 135 countries. Cyanamid employs more than 34,000 people in 38 countries worldwide. In New Jersey Cyanamid employs more than 4,000 people at various locations, including Bridgewater, Clifton, Linden, Princeton, Woodbridge, and the company's world headquarters in Wayne.

Cyanamid's medical business includes Lederle prescription pharmaceutical products, adult and pediatric vaccines, vitamin and multivitamin/mineral products; Davis & Geck surgical sutures and mechanical wound closure devices; Acufex Microsurgical Inc., a prominent supplier of arthroscopic surgical devices; and Storz Instrument Company, a leading supplier of ophthalmic and ear, nose, and throat surgical devices.

Lederle produces vitamin and multivitamin products such as Centrum® multivitamins and Caltrate® calcium supplement. Lederle also manufactures Novantrone® mitoxantrone, an an-

ticancer agent approved in 30 countries for the treatment of advanced breast cancer, leukemias, lymphomas and hepatomas; Pipracil® piperacillin, a semisynthetic penicillin used to treat life-threatening infections; Minocin® minocycline, which is used for the treatment of acne, sexually transmitted diseases, and respiratory infections; and various pharmaceuticals and antibiotics to treat a wide variety of human diseases and conditions.

Cyanamid's chemicals business consists of more than 5,000 chemicals and related products serving major global industries ranging

from paper, textiles and water treating to mining, aerospace, and petroleum production and refining. The business provides plastics and resins to the automotive and aerospace industries to help achieve higher efficiency and environmental safety. Cyanamid's chemicals business also serves the electronics and computer industries by providing metal-coated fibers that effectively shield computers from outside interference.

Cyanamid's agricultural business consists of animal feed and health products and crop protection chemicals, including herbicides and insecticides. The agricultural research division discovered a unique new chemical class that should put Cyanamid in the top ranks of the global herbicide industry. Products already on the market from this chemical class include Scepter® soybean herbicide; Assert® herbicide for wheat, barley and sunflower crops; Arsenal® herbicide, used to kill weeds along highways and railroad rights of way; and Pursuit® herbicide, used in soybeans.

Other agricultural products include Counter® soil insecticide, used in corn and banana crops and Cygro® coccidiostat, a new drug used by poultry producers.

Today Cyanamid's products are sold in every part of the world. American Cyanamid Company is optimistic about its continued success as its employees put science to work serving people's needs and solving the problems and challenges of the twenty-first century.

THE SOMERSET HILTON HOTEL, THE SOMERSET HILTON AND CONFERENCE CENTER

Set on 100 park-like acres, the acclaimed Atrium Corporate Park in the Somerset section of Franklin Township is home to such corporate giants as Merrill Lynch, AT&T, Merck and Company, and the Garden State Convention and Exhibit Center. Widely recognized as an architectural masterpiece and one of the Northeast's premier corporate centers, the Atrium complex provides the best in *Fortune* 500 facilities in a superb setting.

Anchoring the complex on 19 lush acres is the acclaimed Somerset Hilton and Conference Center, offering a unique blend of big-city service and country charm, less than an hour's drive from Manhattan and convenient to all New Jersey interstate and state highways.

With 361 spacious, designer-decorated guest rooms and suites, the Somerset Hilton is central New Jersey's largest and most complete meeting and convention center, providing 27,000 square feet of dedicated meeting, conference, and private dining facilities. When used in conjunction with the adjacent Garden State Convention and Exhibit Center, the Hilton can provide meeting facilities for as many as 5,000 guests or 450 exhibit booths.

The Somerset Hilton's recreational amenities abound. Two outdoor tennis courts, indoor and outdoor swimming pools, fitness center, sauna baths, whirlpool, outdoor children's play center and game room, and a 19-station, three-quarter mile par fitness circuit provide the best in recreational features.

Dining is a special event at the Somerset Hilton. Whether guests select the casual country atmosphere of the Garden Café or the more ambient Greenfields, Somerset Hilton cuisine is a delight to both the eye and the palate. The Garden Café, overlooking the landscaped atrium lobby and reflecting pool serves breakfast, lunch, and dinner daily, plus lavish specialty buffets. The Somerset Hilton's award-winning chefs present an American menu with a continental flair in Greenfields. Hearty American beef, delicate seafoods from around the globe, and specialty entrées are served daily for lunch and dinner. During the spring and summer seasons, Greenfields' terrace offers al fresco dining overlooking the outdoor pool and gardens. Greenfields' Sunday brunch is an experience not soon forgotten.

For the discriminating traveler, the Somerset Hilton offers the Towers at Somerset, a hotel within a hotel. Nestled on the Hilton's top floor, the Towers provides the ultimate in luxury accommodations and service. The concierge is always available to see to the smallest of details, and the private Towers lounge provides an intimate club-like setting where guests enjoy a complimentary continental breakfast, afternoon hors d'oeuvres and cocktails.

Since opening in 1983, the Somerset Hilton has earned a reputation for quality service. The Hilton's highly trained and well-motivated service staff takes pride in making the extra effort, taking the next step, and anticipating the need. The business traveler and weekend vacationer alike have grown to expect the best from the Somerset Hilton. After all, at the Somerset Hilton, it is all in the name and in the reputation.

ABOVE: The elegant lobby of the Somerset Hilton.

LEFT: The Somerset Hilton Atrium office complex.

PATRONS

The following individuals, companies, and organizations have made a valuable commitment to the quality of this publication. Windsor Publications and the Greater Somerset County Chamber of Commerce gratefully acknowledge their participation in *Somerset County: Three Centuries of Progress.*

Adidas*
Beneficial Corporation*
Carrier Foundation*
Celgene Corporation*
Central Jersey Industrial Park*
The Chubb Corporation*
The Claremont Companies*
The Courier-News*
Egan Machinery Division/John Brown Inc.*
Elizabethtown Water Company*

Forbes Newspapers*
Haines Lundberg Waehler (HLW)*
Highland Packaging Labs, Inc.*
Hockenbury Electrical Company, Inc.*
Johnson & Johnson*
Lederle/American Cyanamid Company*
Lowenstein, Sandler, Kohl, Fisher & Boylan*
National Starch and Chemical Company*
New Jersey Savings Bank*
The Old Mill Inn*
Ozzard, Wharton, Rizzolo, Klein, Mauro, Savo & Hogan*
Philips Lighting Company*
PyMaH Corporation*
Rebtex, Inc.*
Ronson Corporation*
Seal-Spout Corporation*
Shive/Spinelli/Perantoni & Associates/ Architects*

Somerset Hilton Hotel, The Somerset Hilton and Conference Center*
Somerset Medical Center*
Somerset Trust Company*
Somerset Wood Products Co.*
Suburban National Bank*
Taylor Oil Company*
Thomas & Betts Corporation*
3M*
Union Carbide*
WBRW 1170 AM*
Woodglen Graphics*
Zeus Scientific Inc.*

*Partners in Progress of *Somerset County: Three Centuries of Progress.* The histories of these companies and organizations appear in Chapter IX, beginning on page 116.

BIBLIOGRAPHY

Agricultural Investment Opportunities in Somerset County. Somerville: Somerset County Agriculture Development Board, 1986.

Among the Blue Hills: Bernardsville, a history. Bernardsville: Bernardsville History Book Committee, 1973.

Bebout, John E., and Ronald J. Grele. *Where Cities Meet: The Urbanization of New Jersey.* Princeton: D. Van Nostrand Co., 1964.

Bill, Alfred Hoyt. *New Jersey and the Revolutionary War.* Princeton: D. Van Nostrand Co., 1964.

Brecknell, Ursula. *Montgomery Township: An Historic Community 1702—1972.* Montgomery Township Bicentennial Committee, 1972.

The Brick Academy. Basking Ridge: Basking Ridge Historical Society, 1978.

Cawley, James and Margaret Cawley. *Along the Old York Road.* New Brunswick: Rutgers University Press, 1965.

Clark, Grace, Jessie Havens, and Stewart Hoagland. *Somerset County, 1688—1938.* Somerville: Somerset Press, 1976.

Craven, Wesley Frank. *New Jersey and the English Colonization of North America.* Princeton: D. Van Nostrand Co., 1964.

Compendium of Censuses 1726—1905. Trenton: NJ Department of State, 1906.

Cunningham, John T. *Railroading in New Jersey.* N.P.: Associated Railroads of New Jersey, n.d.

————. *New Jersey, America's Main Road.* Garden City: Doubleday & Co., 1966.

Dec, Mrs. Joseph, ed. *Somerset County, New Jersey, 1961.* N.P.: The League of Women Voters, 1961.

Dillisten, William H. *Directory of New Jersey Banks 1804— 1942.* N.P.: New Jersey Bankers Association, 1942.

Dunbar, Holly Jean, Joann Kohler, Bruce Ryno, and Norma Schneider. *Looking Back, A History of North Plainfield.* North Plainfield: Blue Hills Historical Society, 1985.

English, Jack, Richard Doyle, and Robert S. Grumet. *Hillsborough Township, Somerset County, NJ: Aspects of Its History.* Neshanic: The Hillsborough Historical Commission, 1978.

Feldkirchner, Irene E., and Louise Langdon. *Our Town: A History of the Township of Green Brook.* Green Brook: n.p. 1976.

Franklin Township, Know Your Township, Handbook and Map. Franklin Township: The League of Women Voters of Franklin Township, 1969.

Haussaman, Brock. *The Iron Horse in Somerset County.* North Branch: Somerset County College, 1984.

Hillsborough Township: The First Years 1746—1825, Earmarks and Town Meetings. N.P.: Hillsborough Historical Commission, 1975.

Historical Booklet of Bernards Township, NJ: Published to Commemorate the Bicentennial 1760—1960. Basking Ridge: Historical Booklet Committee, 1960.

Honeyman, A. Van Doren, ed. *Somerset County Historical Quarterly, Volumes I to VIII.* Plainfield: Somerset County Historical Society, 1912—1919.

Hyer, Richard, and John Zec. *Railroads of New Jersey.* N.P. n.p. 1975.

Inside Bernards Township: a community handbook. Bernards Township: League of Women Voters of Bernards Area, 1977.

Jamison, Wallace N. *Religion in New Jersey: A Brief History.* Princeton: D. Van Nostrand Co., 1964.

Kobbe, Gustav. *The Central Railroad of New Jersey.* New York: n.p. 1890.

Kraft, Herbert C. *The Lenape.* Newark: NJ Historical Society, 1986.

Know Your Township, Bridgewater. N.P.: The League of Women Voters of Bridgewater Township, 1959.

Lane, Wheaton, J. *From Indian Trail to Iron Horse.* Princeton: Princeton University Press, 1939.

Landsman, Ned C. *Scotland and Its First American Colony 1683—1765.* Princeton: Princeton University Press, 1985.

Leaming, Aaron, and Jacob Spicer. *Grants, Concessions and Original Constitutions of the Province of New Jersey.* Philadelphia: W. Bradford, 1758.

Low, George C. *The Industrial Directory of New Jersey.* Camden: Bureau of Industrial Statistics of New Jersey, 1915.

Lundin, Charles Leonard. *Cockpit of the Revolution: The War for Independence.* Princeton: Princeton University Press, 1940.

Maas, Edward J., ed. *North of the Rariton Lotts: a history of the Martinsville, New Jersey area.* Neshanic: Martinsville Community Center Historical Committee, 1975.

McCormick, Richard P. *New Jersey From Colony to State 1609—1789.* New Brunswick: Rutgers University Press, 1964.

McGuinness, John. *The Catholic Church in Bernardsville and Vicinity 1766—1939.* Bernardsville: n.p. 1939.

Messler, Abraham. *Centennial History of Somerset County.* Somerville: C. M. Jamison, 1878.

————. *Memorial Sermons and Historical Notes.* Somerville: n.p. 1872.

Minutes of the Justices and Chosen Freeholders of Somerset County 1772—1822. Somerville: Somerset County, 1977.

Minutes of Votes and Proceedings: NJ Assembly Journal. n.p. 1843.

Murphy, John, Leslie Jones, and Cynthia Goldsmith. *Rocky Hill, NJ; Preserving a 19th Century Village.* N.P.: Rocky Hill Community Group, 1981.

Mustin, M. *Somerset County, NJ 1688—1930.* Camden: Somerset County Board of Freeholders, 1930.

New Jersey Golf Courses. Trenton: NJ Department of Community Affairs, 1989.

Post, Allison Wright. *Recollections of Bernardsville, NJ, 1874—1941.* New York: J.J. Little & Ives Co., 1941.

A Place Named Carrier. Belle Mead: Carrier Foundation, 1984.

Pomfret, John E. *Colonial New Jersey—A History.* New York: Charles Scribner's Sons, 1973.

————. *The New Jersey Proprietors and Their Lands.* Princeton: D. Van Nostrand, 1964.

Prince, Carl J. *Middlebrook—The American Eagles Nest.* Somerville: Somerset Press, 1958.

Rosenthal, Alan, and John Blydenburgh. *Politics in New Jersey.* New Brunswick: Rutgers University, Eagleton Institute, 1975.

Ryan, Dennis. *New Jersey in the American Revolution 1763— 1783: A Chronology.* Trenton: NJ Historical Commission, 1975.

Salsbury, Miriam, ed. *This is Watchung: A Know Your Town Government Survey.* Watchung: The League of Women Voters of Watchung, NJ, 1957.

Schmidt, Hubert G. *Agriculture in New Jersey: a three hundred year history.* New Brunswick: Rutgers University Press, 1973.

Simcoe, Lieutenant Colonel J. G. *A History of the Operations of the Queens Rangers.* New York: Bartlett & Welford, 1844.

Sliney, Diane, ed. *Portrait of a Village: A History of Millstone, NJ.* Millstone: Historical District Commission, Borough of Millstone, NJ, 1976.

Smiley, F.T. *History of Plainfield and North Plainfield.* Plainfield: Plainfield Courier News, 1901.

Smout, T.C. *A History of the Scottish People 1560— 1830.* New York: Charles Scribner's Sons, 1969.

Snell, James P. *History of Hunterdon and Somerset Counties, NJ.* Philadelphia: Everts & Peck, 1881.

Snyder, John P. *The Story of New Jersey's Civil Boundaries 1609—1968.* Trenton: Bureau of Geology and Topography, 1969.

Somerset County Comprehensive Master Plan. Somerville, NJ: Somerset County Planning Board, 1985.

Somerset County Data Book. Somerville: Somerset County Planning Board, 1989.

Somerset County Master Plan Update: Draft Discussion Paper on Land Use Patterns. Somerville: Somerset County Planning Board, 1986.

Somerset County 1989 Office Guide. N.P.: Black's Guide, Division of McGraw-Hill Information Services Co., 1989.

Spangler, Jane H. *Somerset County, New Jersey, Economic Resource Profile.* N.P.: US Impressions Inc., 1990.

————. *Windows of the Past: A Tercentennial History of the Presbyterian Church of Bound Brook, NJ, 1688—1988.* Bound Brook: n.p. 1988.

Stryker, Elsie B. *Where the Trees Grow Tall.* Franklin Township: Franklin Township Historical Society, 1963.

Studley, Miriam V. *Historic New Jersey Through Visitors Eyes.* Princeton: D. Van Nostrand Co., 1964.

Swan, H. Kels. *Borough of South Bound Brook, Somerset County, NJ: A History.* South Bound Brook: South Bound Brook Tercentenary Committee, 1964.

Taber, Thomas T., III. *The Rock-A-Bye: A History of the Rockaway Valley Railroad.* Muncie, Pa.: n.p. 1972.

Terhune, Laura P. *Episodes in the History of Griggstown.* Griggstown: n.p. 1976.

Tomblin, Barbara. *Villages at the Crossroads: a History of Warren Township 1806—1976.* Warren: n.p. 1976.

Vecoli, Rudolph J. *The People of New Jersey.* Princeton: D. Van Nostrand Co., 1965.

Veit, Richard. *The Old Canals of New Jersey.* Little Falls: NJ Geographical Press, 1963.

Walter, Frederick. *The Township of Bedminster.* N.P. n.p. 1964.

Weiss, Harry B., and Grace H. Weiss. *Old Copper Mines of New Jersey.*

Trenton: Past Times Press, 1963.

West, Roscoe. *Elementary Education in New Jersey: A History.* Princeton: D. Van Nostrand Co., 1964.

Wheelock, Keith. *New Jersey Growth Management.* Skillman: Managing Growth in New Jersey, 1989.

Whiston, Jean L., and G. Wallace Conover. *Somerville in Picture and Story.* Somerville: Somerset Press, 1959.

Whyte, William H. *Cluster Development.* New York: American Conservation Association, 1964.

INDEX